Mountain Time

Kenneth S. Norris

Photo courtesy of the Norris Collection

Mountain Time

Reflections on the Wild World and Our Place in It

Kenneth S. Norris

Copyright © 1998 by Kenneth S. Norris

First printing 2010
Published by University of California Natural Reserve System
Produced and distributed by lulu.com
All rights reserved.

Cover photographs:
(front) The Palisades, Sierra Nevada, viewed from
the White Mountains of California, by Kenneth S. Norris
(back) Ken Norris at Laguna Creek below the Norris house
in July 1996, courtesy of Dick and Teresa Norris

Cover and book design by Susan Gee Rumsey
Index by Michael Brackney

ISBN: 978-0-557-62175-0

Contents

Foreword ... ix
Editor's Preface ... xiii
Acknowledgements ... xxi

To Begin With ... 1

Part I • Field Quarter

Chapter 1: The Granite Mountains ... 17
We journey to the lonely Mojave Desert mountain range that will be our outdoor classroom.

Chapter 2: What a Lousy Bird! ... 33
Among the desert boulders, we begin the long process of learning to see how the wild world works.

Chapter 3: The Wind and the Sky ... 43
With our gaze so often directed over the landscape or down at the earth, we naturalists and naturalists-in-training sometimes need to look upward and explore the world of the air—and the desert affords us an excellent opportunity.

Chapter 4: The Most Elegant Thing on Earth ... 55
Floating on a North Coast river, we learn to understand it as part of a dynamic system that carves down a mountain and carries it to the sea.

Chapter 5: The Canyon ... 71
We dig deeper into the space-time fabric of Mountain Time as we become intimate with the life in a wild Big Sur canyon.

PART II • FROM DESERT TO OCEAN

Chapter 6: The Two-Legged Lizard — 89
The sliding and colliding plates of the earth's surface brought one of the planet's more unusual creatures to its present-day outpost on Mexico's Baja Peninsula.

Chapter 7: Adaptation — 101
On the uniform sand of a desert dune system, the coloration of the Mojave fringe-toed lizard has evolved in response to two opposing selective pressures.

Chapter 8: Desert Iguana — 113
This lizard's ability to withstand body temperatures that would kill most animals allows it to feed with impunity in a world temporarily free of predators.

Chapter 9: Girella — 125
The behavior of a little tidepool fish suggests that our consciousness has very ancient roots.

Chapter 10: The Blessed Frogs of Hidden Spring — 139
The arrangements of sex, birth, and death are all part of the directive to spread the life force.

Chapter 11: Mabel, Myrtle, Frank, and Floyd — 149
Dolphins possess a culture that in some ways may be as complex as ours, and it is certainly far older.

Chapter 12: Dolphin Jazz — 167
In the leaderless society of spinner dolphins, the group makes up its collective "mind" through musical improvisation.

Chapter 13:
Of Fighter Pilots, Chorus Lines, and Shark Attacks — 183
Dolphin schools frustrate the fearsome predators of the sea with a coordinated response borne of their intense sociality.

Part III • Windows to the World

Chapter 14: Creation Myth — 199
We can better understand our relationship with Mountain Time by contemplating its origins billions of years ago.

Chapter 15: Yin and Yang — 211
In all the many manifestations of the male–female duality, there's a profound need for the opposing elements to clasp in oscillatory union.

Chapter 16: Uncharted Territory — 223
Human culture disconnects us from the usual cause-and-effect of natural selection—but only partially and temporarily.

Chapter 17: The Salmon's Run — 231
Unlike salmon, humans can postpone death well beyond the time when an individual has any biological purpose —but are we expending our very substance to fight an unconquerable windmill?

Chapter 18: A Natural History of Gods — 247
Our sense of the ineffable—its roots older than our species— defines us as humans and may serve us well in the coming ecological crises.

Chapter 19: A Bowl Full of Earth — 263
During a few moments of insight I sense the Earth whole and realize how small and fragile it is.

Chapter 20: Embracing the Mountain — 269
On my final Field Quarter trip, high on a majestic fin of a mountain, I send the students off into the wide world with a little speech inspired by the trace of an ancient worm in Cambrian rock.

Afterwords by Phyllis Norris and Richard D. Norris — 291
Notes — 301
Index — 311

Ken Norris at the University of California, Santa Cruz campus, 1975.

Foreword

To understand how Dr. Norris's final work, *Mountain Time*, can keep a significant readership awaiting its publication nearly ten years after the author's passing, it is necessary to recall the life and stature of this unusual man. As a scientist, teacher, author, and champion of the natural world, Dr. Norris left a rich and varied legacy.

For eighteen years, he was a professor of natural history at UC Santa Cruz, where he became legendary for his ability to inspire students. He taught the highly popular Field Quarter class in UCSC's Environmental Studies Department, a wide-ranging and rigorous course in the natural history of California. Each spring, Dr. Norris led two dozen Field Quarter students into California's mountains, forests, and deserts to learn firsthand from nature. As a teacher and mentor, Dr. Norris influenced both undergraduate and graduate students, helping to launch many careers. In *Mountain Time*, Dr. Norris imaginatively recreates the experience of "going on Field Quarter" and, once again, emphasizes how critically important direct observation of nature is in both the sciences and the arts.

As a researcher, Dr. Norris divided his time and attention between the desert and the ocean. His early research focused on desert reptiles, and it was as a desert ecologist at UCLA that Norris discovered circadian rhythms in snakes and the function of color changes in reptiles and amphibians. By 1959, however, when Dr. Norris began teaching herpetology at UCLA, he had already spent a number of years as the founding curator at Marineland of the Pacific, the country's second oceanarium. Eventually, his interest in marine life led him to Hawaii, where he served, from 1968 to 1971, as founding scientific director of the Oceanic Institute. His research in Hawaii included studies of spinner dolphins and fish culture, and much of what is now known about whales and dolphins, particularly their social patterns and echolocation skills, is due to groundbreaking investigations by Dr. Norris and his various research teams. In *Mountain Time*, Dr. Norris describes his desert experiences, in the Mojave Desert and in Baja California, and his marine experiences, in California and Hawaii, that led to some of his most remarkable discoveries.

Dr. Norris authored several books on whales, dolphins, and porpoises, and coauthored or acted as editor for several more. In 1992, he was awarded the prestigious John Burroughs Medal for his distinguished book of natural history, *Dolphin Days: The Life and Times of the Spinner Dolphins*, published by W. W. Norton and Company. His stature as a scientist enabled Dr. Norris to influence public policy in significant, long-lasting ways. As a scientific adviser to the U.S. Marine Mammal Commission, he helped write the Marine Mammal Protection Act of 1972. He also led a national campaign to reduce the numbers of dolphins killed in tuna-fishing nets.

Among Dr. Norris's many life accomplishments, he was especially proud of having conceived of and played a crucial role in founding the UC Natural Reserve System (NRS). Even as an assistant professor at UCLA in the late fifties and early sixties, he possessed the foresight to recognize the need to set aside undisturbed natural areas for teaching and research. Through his efforts and those of other UC faculty and administrators, the NRS was established in 1965 with seven original UC properties; today the NRS manages a reserve system of 36 sites. In June 1998, 33 years after the start of the UC reserve system and only weeks before Dr. Norris's death, the NRS received a $4-million endowment from the David and Lucile Packard Foundation, which was named the Kenneth S. Norris Endowment Fund for the California Environment as an enduring tribute to his leadership.

Mountain Time will naturally please long-time devotees of Dr. Norris who are eager for new stories told in that idiosyncratic narrative voice they still remember so well. Readers of natural history will appreciate the insights Dr. Norris offers into our natural world.

For *Mountain Time* is also a work of considerable didactic power, in which Dr. Norris raises issues regarding the environment, and our understanding of it, that are even more relevant and more critical to the well-being of the Earth and our survival as a species than when he completed the book.

— *Susan Gee Rumsey*
Tim Stephens
NRS Publications Program
Natural Reserve System
University of California

Ken Norris and his field assistant Larry Ford kneel beneath a tree for a reverential moment during the 1979 UC Santa Cruz Natural History Field Quarter.

Editor's Preface

Mountain Time has taken a long and somewhat unusual route from Ken Norris's keyboard to these pages. Those of us involved in getting the book into print recognize that readers—many of whom were acquainted with Ken—deserve to know what transpired between its composition and its publication. This preface tells some of that story and offers other information that may enhance your reading of the book.

Ken Norris began working on *Mountain Time* shortly after he retired from active teaching in 1990, seeing the book as an opportunity to write about his diverse passions free from the formal constraints of academic publishing. He wanted to recount his scientific epiphanies, describe how he inspired students in the field, warn about our ongoing destruction of the environment, explain how it was possible to meld the objectivity of a scientist and the emotional engagement of a poet—and not be terribly concerned about how it all fit together.

On the several occasions when I saw Ken post-retirement, he talked of his progress on *Mountain Time* with obvious enthusiasm. I understood that the book was to be much more than a memoir—Ken wanted it to be a vehicle for passing on his insights about teaching and the way the world works, a soapbox for airing his views on what really mattered. And I gathered that he was spending considerable time writing and rewriting, honing each piece and changing it to reflect his evolving ideas on each subject.

When a malfunctioning heart began necessitating doctor visits and tests, Ken was still writing. There were more stories to tell, better ways to say what had already been put into words, and new ideas to explore. Soon, operations and hospital stays intervened. But Ken made *Mountain Time* a priority. By the time he was admitted to the hospital for the last time, Ken's final work was essentially complete—in the sense that drafts of all the planned chapters were written—but not, in his view, truly finished.

After Ken's death in August 1998, the manuscript for *Mountain Time* languished on his ancient computer at his home near Santa Cruz, California. After six years, two of Ken's former students—Larry Ford, a consultant in rangeland management, and David Hart, director of the Senator George J. Mitchell Center for Environmental and Watershed Research at the University of Maine—received permission from Ken's widow, Phylly, to begin shepherding the work towards publication. Ken's son Dick had copied the files to a floppy disk before Ken's computer was discarded, but those files were in what had become a nearly inaccessible format (and neither Larry nor Dave had a computer with a floppy disk drive). Fortunately, Dick's 15-year-old son, Tom Norris, knew how to read the files and copy them to a CD. After they received the CD from Tom in early 2005, Larry and Dave set about reassembling the manuscript, which involved much reformatting, restoration of footnotes, removal of in-text page numbers, and the like. Larry and Dave were subsequently joined in their editorial planning by Steve Gliessman, professor of agroecology at UC Santa Cruz (and Ken's teaching colleague), and Susan Gee Rumsey, principal publications coordinator for the UC Natural Reserve System, a program that Ken conceived of and founded.

Larry, David, Steve, and Susan ("the publishing committee") carefully reviewed and critically analyzed the *Mountain Time* manuscript. They noted that it was overly long and in need of editorial attention. They identified chapters that should perhaps be left out of a published volume because they were incompletely developed or on topics peripheral to Ken's central themes. In time, they also realized they lacked the time and expertise to carry out the editing that seemed necessary if the manuscript was to be published. That's when they contacted me and asked if I would be interested in editing *Mountain Time*.

Just skimming through the manuscript, I could see that it had many needs. There were four distinct pieces that might qualify as an "Introduction." Several chapters were in such a rough form that they seemed more like expanded outlines. One chapter existed in two alternative versions. Halfway through a long chapter about religion, after a "postscript" notation, Ken had interrupted himself with a paragraph about plans to go to the hospital the very next day for open-heart surgery. The table of contents, which divided the chapters into three sections, called for placing the final chapter in the third section all by itself. In a few chapters, there were short passages that seemed out of place, possibly former footnotes now floating in the running text.

Reading the manuscript in depth, I discovered much else that required my attention: present-tense narrative shifted suddenly to past tense, long sections seemed to repeat much of what had been said in other sections, stories and arguments had noticeable gaps, chapters opened with vague big-picture ideas, reflections on the narrative appeared suddenly and without warning. Everywhere were the results of Ken's tendency to digress, to forget the point he was making and begin exploring some new thread of an idea that his writing had just revealed to him. To the extent that Ken was aware of these problems, he had probably thought of them as extraneous to the real thrust of his writing, yet they most certainly stood in the way of readers navigating the text and gleaning the intended meaning.

Despite the manuscript's faults, Ken's writing enchanted me from the very beginning. Along with the hard-to-follow tangents, he had created evocative images, invented apt and lovely metaphors, used juicy verbs, and set down crisp detail. At his best, he had made his points with an elegant, poetic economy of words. The passion he felt for his topics was vibrating just below the surface of his prose, emerging at just the right times to send a tingle down my spine or a tear down my cheek.

The challenge I faced was clear: allow the poet, the wise sage, the perceptive scientist, the inspiring teacher to emerge from the tangle of the manuscript. I had to force Ken, *ex post facto*, to be a more disciplined writer than his nature had allowed. It was one thing to hear Ken expound on some subject in person—you could follow him even if the path was crooked—and another to be reading his words without the benefit of dialogue and context.

I suspect that many readers want to know in some detail how this book, in its finished form, differs from Ken's manuscript. Therefore, I will deviate from standard editorial practice (which is to be quiet about such matters) and tell you. The first thing to know—which you may already have inferred—is that the level of editing I applied is what's known in publishing as "heavy" or "developmental." I excised long passages of mostly redundant manuscript, moved paragraphs, re-ordered sentences, wrote new sentences and paragraphs, even moved passages from one chapter to another. I changed all the Field Quarter chapters from mostly past tense to consistent present tense. I combined short paragraphs into longer ones, restructured dialogue, resolved contradictions, and fashioned new chapter openings. Through it all, however, my utmost goal was to preserve Ken's lucid and distinct voice and be true to his intentions. When the need for continuity called for inserting a new sentence or paragraph, for example, I constructed it, as much as was possible, with Ken's words, phrases, and sentences—taken from the considerable store of deleted material.

This published version of *Mountain Time* has five fewer chapters than Ken's original (four of the five were earlier recommended for deletion by the publishing committee). Unfortunately, you won't be reading the chapters Ken titled "Patent Application," "Microbes in the Mist," "Of Dolphin's Ears and Violins," "Lamb Chompksy," and "Mountain Time in Brooklyn." In addition, "What Can Eyes See?" no longer exists as a separate chapter, though its core has been preserved in "The Canyon." These chapters contained worthy material, but each was either too roughly written, too speculative, or too far outside what the publishing committee and I considered to be the core of Ken's philosophical universe. The manuscript had to be shortened if it was going to be published, and we deemed these chapters the most expendable.

Editor's Preface

Three chapters now bear titles different from Ken's. "The Granite Mountains" was formerly called "Field Quarter"; we changed it because we wanted "Field Quarter" to be the title of the first section. We changed the fifth chapter's title from "Mountain Time" to "The Canyon" because we didn't want to imply that this chapter had more to say about the Mountain Time concept than any other. Finally, we replaced Chapter 13's former title of "7±2" with "Of Chorus Lines, Fighter Pilots, and Shark Attacks" because "7±2" has acquired some unfortunate baggage over the years.

The book's chapters are still divided into three sections, as Ken had it, but they are allocated somewhat differently. Ken had placed all the chapters that weren't about Field Quarter into one long middle section he called "Windows to the World." Now, chapters about events in Ken's research career make up a shortened Section II titled "From Desert to Ocean," and the set of six philosophical, essaylike chapters (along with a final Field Quarter chapter formerly placed in its own section) comprise Section III, which retains its original title: "Windows to the World."

The table of contents includes a one-sentence description of each chapter. Although many of the phrases that make them up are Ken's, the summaries are my inventions. I decided to add them because they reflect one of Ken's intentions. He filled up considerable space in the introductory pieces of his manuscript with previews of the chapters, and since I deleted virtually all of these I wanted their function to live on in some form. In any case, they seem a good counterbalance to the cryptic nature of most of the chapter titles.

The current introduction is really a composite, made up of four introductory pieces included in the original manuscript: "To Begin With" (which contributes the title), "Who is This Author of Yours?" "An Autobiographical Note," and "What Do I Mean by Mountain Time?" The current introduction is much shorter than these four pieces together; what's been excised is mostly redundant material and summaries of the chapters. The chapter entitled "Uncharted Territory" is also an amalgam of two manuscript parts: the chapter by the same name and a free-floating essay (not in Ken's original table of contents) called "Humans and the Environmental Crisis."

Throughout much of *Mountain Time,* Ken tells stories about his life and experiences. He recounts his childhood and college career in "To Begin With," trips with Field Quarter classes in Section I, and his work with lizards, fish, and dolphins in Section II. You may be tempted, therefore, to think of *Mountain Time* as a memoir or autobiography. But Ken never intended for it to be that kind of work. The narrative in the book exists mainly as a means of communicating ideas and demonstrating points.

If you read *Mountain Time* expecting it to chronicle Ken's life accurately and comprehensively, you will be disappointed on both counts. Whether it came from faulty memory, a perceived need for pedagogical efficacy, or his impish nature, Ken sometimes did get facts wrong, leave out critical details, order events differently from the way they actually occurred, and narrate in a way that might create mistaken impressions. How often this occurs no single person can say. I became aware of a few such embellishments; there are probably others.

The important thing with regard to the editing is that I did not attempt, for the most part, to find and correct narrative "errors." Not only would this have been virtually impossible, but it would also have meant being too fussy about something Ken thought unimportant. Leaving in some facts of questionable veracity is a way, I think, of honoring one of Ken's signature traits—he was a masterful teller of tall tales who oscillated freely between seriousness and whimsy.

I mention the issue of biographical comprehensiveness in part because of how it may concern those family members, colleagues, friends, and former students who took part in important parts of Ken's life but don't find their names mentioned here. For you, I cite again the fact that this book is not an autobiography. It is necessarily selective. Many people play major and minor roles in these chapters, but their inclusion has more to do with their connection to particular trips, events, or work that Ken picked out as exemplifying certain concepts or principles than with their significance in Ken's life or career. If you are not among these folks, you should not feel slighted.

Editor's Preface

Although I did all the actual wordsmithing, I must acknowledge the active assistance and support of Larry Ford, Steve Gliessman, Dave Hart, and Susan Gee Rumsey. They reviewed the edited chapters, helped clarify details, answered questions, provided guidance when I asked for it, and relinquished control of the details of the process. When larger decisions had to be made—which chapters to leave out, what order to put them in, how to divide them into sections—we put our heads together and came up with a consensus view. And of course it was these four people who rescued Ken's manuscript in the first place, did the editorial groundwork, and committed themselves to the goal of getting the book published. If they hadn't taken the initiative and contributed many hours of their time, this book would not exist. I know they share my sincerest wish that you experience this volume as the living voice of our beloved "professor of wonderment."

— *Eric W. Engles, PhD*
EditCraft Editorial Services
Grass Valley, California

Ken Norris at the Granite Cabin, Granite Mountains.

Acknowledgements

Thanks to Phylly Norris—"Far and away my best critic"

And thanks also to—

Jim André
Al Allanson
Bruce Bridgeman
Chris Browne
Shannon Brownlee
Fred and Sus Carlson
Philippe Cohen and
 Cynthia Stead
Ev Evans
Mary Flodin
Dave Ford
Larry Ford
Steve Gliessman
Dawn Goley
David Hart

Ann Harvey
Joe Jordan
Anne Lamott
David Lee and
 Charlotte Anderson
J. Paul Loomis
Tim Loomis
Claudia Luke
Bill MacFarland
Ray Mireles
Betsy Norris
Kathleen Norris
Phil Pister
Paul Rich

As well as—

Miss Preen and Dr. V.

Finally, the Mountain Time *publishing committee wishes to thank Alexander N. Glazer, director of the University of California Natural Reserve System, 1997-2009, for "spinning the wheel" to support the development and production of this book.*

Ken Norris's original field vehicle, as it was in the desert at the Granite Mountains around 1949 (below, with Ken far left) and as he later remembered it (above).

To Begin With

I'll admit it: this book skips all over the map. It might not seem to be about anything in particular except the wild world and our place in it. That's because I wrote it, and that's the way I am. Bear with me and the pieces may begin to fit together for you. They have fit together for me in a way that locks me to the earth and its life with the impassioned embrace of lovers.

To say what I want to say, I seem to need to talk about all sorts of seemingly unrelated things. I need to write about the shifting plates of the earth and who has hitch-hiked on them, the airy world of spores and floating spiders and those birds that slice by up among the clouds, and the myriad tiny spheres of quartz and feldspar that make up the dunes of the desert. I have to see if mere words can say why there is absolute elegance in a watershed, and in so doing I must describe the journey of water molecules after they slam as cold drops of rain into the soil skim of high crags and gather into a filigree of channels where trout flash, and then flow downward in close to a single precise arc while they wiggle like snakes in a graceful dance until they meet the sea. I must take you to a crystal cold sweet seep out among jumbled monoliths of pale peach granite and tell you what it was like to live by a song, sung by Chemehuevi elders, that knitted the austere-appearing world of the desert together into a place of plenty, where food could be had by sweeping the nodding heads of grass or chia with baskets, or in fall by sending young lads up scaly piñons oozing with sticky amber sap to gather cones.

You could simply skip ahead and read about these things, but I suspect you may want to know a little about the person who put them on these pages. That's the way it works for me, anyway—when I pick up a book such as this, I want to know something about the author. Who is this guy preaching to me?

The book you hold is an old scientist's book, the product of a reasonably gentle, social man who cares a great deal about those who travel the earth with him, would rather tell a joke than start a fight, and spent his life following the threads of his excitements. I began writing it when I entered the province of old age and realized I should no longer hold back because my perceptions might differ from those of friends. (I hope they will excuse me, even dismiss me, if I prove too troublesome. That is easy enough to do with old guys. You just prop them in a corner with some pillows and let them prattle on.)

So, I'll mention a few of the experiences that set me on my way, made me who I am, and determined the shape of this book. My childhood and early career were most formative—I imagine it is like that with most people—so it is mostly those times that I will describe here.

As a child, I was a clear amalgam of my mother and father. My artist mother, Jessie, was a resolute and remarkably energetic woman who dragged our family through the Great Depression by the scruff of its collar. She would shoo my brother, Bob, and I into the 1928 Chevrolet and head for Senegram's Used Clothing Warehouse down in the depths of skid row in Los Angeles, where the three of us winnowed through pungent piles of old clothing looking for wool items—old polo coats, pants, and the like—that she'd buy for a nickel a pound. At home she washed her treasures, cut them into strips, dyed them two dozen colors, rolled them into balls and then created the loveliest rugs you ever saw. These found favor with interior designers who catered to some of Hollywood's top stars. So, the Senegram's forays were matched with ones in which we drove the little Chevy, a lovely new hooked carpet poking out a window, up the arcing driveways of such personages as Lily Pons, the famous opera singer-actress. (As we approached Lily's home, Mom leaned over and told us, "Kids, she's a famous star, but remember, you're as good as anybody.")

My engineer father, Robert, kept his 4H pencils sharp for his elegant draftings of hospitals, check dams, and airports, but his heart was mostly in the mountains, flicking his fly line across the water. I remember him as a dreamer and a sponge for the wild world. He knew much less about how to survive in the hurly-burly of the commercial world than my mother.

With such parents, it seems only natural to me now that I should grow up thinking in patterns, like my mother the artist, but also loving to thread my way through the analysis of natural puzzles, piece by piece, like my father. Exhibiting these tendencies early on, it was clear that I was a naturalist down to my toes and fingertips—teetering between art and science, seeking synthesis. Even when I was very small, the fascinations of the wild world gripped me. My little room was full of dried bats; the odorous tails of road-kill animals were tacked to the wall; stones with fossils protruding were piled around; and live lizards scurried in a sand-filled dresser drawer. (I can't recall where I put my socks and shirts, but I did understand my priorities.)

I grew up in the welcomed shade of a talented and very forgiving older brother, who became a well-known geologist and a magnificent teacher, and who seemed to know just how to do things. Bob and his pals took long trips across the wild lands of the West in the old cars he had salvaged, and he graciously invited me along. Those trips nurtured my love of nature and became the very foundation of most of what I would later do.

My unfolding as someone who could write this book started, of course, with childhood, but I was shaped and prodded into something close to a professional scientist as I explored my way through the University of California at Los Angeles (UCLA). When I came back from World War II, a grateful country paid most of my educational expenses, and the University didn't seem wholly rigid about how I spent the money I was given.

So, at UCLA I began a search through my loves. I started with the oldest one—chemistry—lured by romantic tales, such as the Curies starting with a ton of pitchblende and somehow reducing it to a tiny pinch of radium. But the reality of chemistry was pipe runs, foul air, and dark benches down deep inside a building.

I fled upstairs toward the light, to geology where people dealt with the entire earth. The concept of isostasy—the notion that mountains of "light" rock actually float in the denser rock beneath, like apples in a tub—was undergoing its first tests in those halls, and it was an exciting time. But for me, there seemed to be an invisible line drawn by many geologists. It separated life from non-life. Few seemed to notice the lizards that skittered across the sand or the cawing ravens, rolling and diving in the air above the dune slopes. I wandered on, seeking my center.

My hiking buddy, Bob Lindberg, suggested I come along on a class trip with a naturalist whose class he was taking. I signed up. The instructor, Dr. Ray Cowles, had been raised among the Zulus of South Africa, and he spoke that curious clacking language and still slept with a pistol under his pillow for protection from the many dangers of his youth.

Cowles seemed to miss nothing. As we drove along, a dove flew next to us. Cowles adjusted his speed until he could hold the bird at the edge of his rear-view mirror. Then, looking at the speedometer, he said, "Twenty three miles per hour, slower than most people would guess."

Near dusk, we made the night's camp amid the Joshua trees. Cowles heard a rattle, as from pebbles being shaken in a bowl. He stepped quickly back, peering into a bush. There was a two-and-a-half-foot rattlesnake, backed into a sinuous striking coil, its head and upper body wavering back and forth at ankle height. Swiftly, Cowles pinned the snake to the ground with the snake stick he routinely carried—another holdover from his days as a young boy in South Africa, where cobras, boomslangs, and vipers were common facts of life. He bent down and slipped his thumb and forefinger tight behind the snake's jaws, while with his other hand he grasped the snake's tail as its body looped and twisted, seeking purchase. Then he stretched the snake out, until it was held nearly immobile.

Under the pressure of Cowles' fingers, the snake's mouth opened, revealing erect needlelike fangs, drops of honey-colored venom welling from their tips. "It's a Mojave Green; see the broad scales between its eyes. This is the most dangerous rattlesnake in the United States. Those venom drops are neurotoxic; you slowly stop breathing. The venom is about three times as potent as that of any other rattlesnake."

"Look at its upper lip," he said, turning the snake's head toward me. A chill passed over me to be so close. "That pair of pits are its heat sensors. This snake can hit a jumping mouse in the dark. It uses those pits to sense the mouse's body warmth and to triangulate its strike."

"I'll put him down now," he said. "Stand back." He bent close to the ground and lightly tossed the snake next to a bush. It quickly slid away among the branches. I was deep in a chaos of emotions—of fear at being so close to this deadly snake, of fascination about its remarkable attributes, and of awe at the insouciance of the Doc in handling it for us. (Later, I was to repeat this demonstration once a year for my own classes, always knowing that sometime I must slip and perhaps be bitten. Then toward the end of my teaching career, I quit the demonstration for different reasons. I'll tell you about them later on.)

After our sparse dinner was complete, Cowles called me over. Already he had seen how keen I was in that class of twenty. "I thought you might be interested in this," he said, digging into a deep pocket of his canvas field jacket. "It's the seed pod of the Joshua tree." He opened it, showing me the black seeds stacked like poker chips.

"Notice," he said, handing me a pod, "that many of these seeds have holes in them, while others don't. The holes are made by the larva of the moth that pollinates only the Joshua tree." He told me that the tree is entirely dependent upon these little moths if it is to reproduce successfully, and that the moths take their tithe by laying eggs that hatch into caterpillars that ultimately eat many of the seeds—but not all. Perhaps 30 percent survive uneaten. Cowles told me of the moths that might flutter near our camp at dusk, and then we saw them. He speculated that the big ivory-white Joshua flowers are beacons for the moths in the twilight.

Moths and Joshua trees! A tithe of seeds paying one for the service of another, and the other way around, too! Moths that must emerge and find Joshua trees at the right time for their species to continue. Precise interlocking life plans had somehow stitched together two very different species. I walked through the dusk filled with wonder.

In a week, even though I was a senior geology student and all my requirements for graduation were complete, I switched to biology. It was total, instant commitment. My companions were Charlie Lowe, the teaching assistant for Cowles' class, and intent, humorous Dick Zweifel. We three virtually lived in the lab next to Cowles' office where all the lizards and snakes were kept, and where the big zinc cabinets of bird and mammal skins sat. Charlie cooked hot dogs in a beaker while we steeped ourselves in desert biology. (All three of us would go on to careers in field biology: Charlie to a distinguished professorship at the University of Arizona, where only a few called him "Charlie," and Dick to the curatorship of reptiles and amphibians at the American Museum of Natural History in New York, where he became a world authority on amphibian evolution.)

Ray Cowles proved to be much more than a desert biologist to me. He was also a seer, a man of deep concern for and knowledge about the earth, writ large. His gentle accessibility and patience let us ask him anything at all that was coursing through our restless young minds.

One day, a sheaf of yellow typewritten paper in my hand, I approached Cowles' office door and looked inside to see him working at a pile of correspondence. He motioned me to the chair beside his desk and turned toward me. "What is it, Ken?" I can't remember how I broached it, but the gist of my question was this: Nature's rules seem so concrete, so ultimately definable (even though many remained only partially understood), yet in our society we often seemed to disregard these rules altogether in favor things we make up about ourselves. For instance, we seemed to regard ourselves as above Nature. In some ways, it seemed to me, we lived in a self-constructed dream world.

"Wouldn't it be better," I asked, "if we learned to run our affairs in terms of who we really are, and how the natural world actually works, than to live by imagined rules?" I placed my little treatise on Cowles' desk, its title—*The Naturalistic Ethic*—plainly visible. "I've put some of my ideas down here; could you take a look at it when you have the time?"

The Doc nodded and swiveled around. "That's a handful, Ken. Do you have time to talk a little?" That was the Doc for you—he so graciously pushed aside his own affairs that I quite forgot my intrusion. "You know, Ken, I've thought about those questions a lot. Our understanding of ourselves is way out of kilter with how we behave in the world." He talked of our exploding population, which even then was eroding the world. He talked of our agriculture, which traded tractor fuel for food, without concern for where the fuel was coming from, its effects, or how long it would last.

"And what sense do wars make, Ken?" he added. Pulling a volume from the shelves alongside his desk, he said, "Here's a book you might find interesting. It's about us and the great apes and aggression." He pushed the volume toward me. I rose, and took it.

"Thanks, Doc," I said, and walked, bemused, out into the laboratory. Those yellow, badly typed pages (which I still have) and that conversation mark the beginning of this book. Though many of my formulations seem now to miss the point, and my views of human society have evolved, the questions I grappled with then are alive in the chapters that follow.

Later, as a new-minted zoology graduate student, I found myself immersed, with a kind of timid awe, in profound debates about the nature of inheritance and how species are formed. Remember, this was the late 1940s, before the DNA molecule was revealed as the road map of inheritance, before we understood that continents were rafted on the earth's mantle to rift apart, swirl, and grind, or to dive under each other, taking their skim of life with them.

Charlie Lowe had acquired a remarkably subtle understanding of how evolution was then thought to work. He located an almost clandestine epicenter of the debate up high in the botany building, in the laboratory of a gentle old botanist, Carl Epling. I trooped along after Charlie, taking it all in. It surprises me even now that such centers of ferment can exist on a big university campus without ruffling the surface of most of what goes on. Most of the staff of UCLA in those days had no idea that the very conception of how life had evolved was being tested on their own campus. The old conceptions flowed placidly along in the minds of most scholars, while the basic underpinnings of their world were being nudged and prodded.

A few from campus were regulars at our seminars. Usually it was Professor Dan Axelrod from Geology, who even then was a major student of ancient floras, Professor Harlan Lewis, another botanist who was soon to become an important figure in studies of plant evolution, Mildred Mathias, Epling's totally encyclopedic assistant, and we zoology students who gathered up in Epling's lab to experience the ferment.

The great outside protagonists of evolutionary theory came through as well, and we graduate students listened and argued interminably about the doctrines they espoused. Better still, we went into the field with these almost mythic figures and ate each other's cooking. The greatest evolutionary geneticist of that day, Theodosius Dobzhansky, had set up a massive experiment with Epling to test whether or not they could actually document evolution as it took place in nature. The idea was that if a long series of stations where wild fruit flies could be collected was established across the top of Mount San Jacinto and down the desert slope toward Palm Springs, the scientists should be able to test the effects of the changing seasons and climates upon the genetic structure of the flies, who reproduced more than once a year. Some of the fly's gene frequencies should change over time.

Nobody cared if you squashed flies, so Dobzhansky and Epling attempted to detect such change under their microscopes by raising thousands upon thousands of flies, derived from ones caught in nature, smearing out their chromosomes, and matching up the banding patterns, the loops and inversions of the chromosomes they found there. This test, begun out across the mountain, had the potential of detecting evolution as it occurred.

Along with the two scientists, several students and I combed the mountain pass for fly populations (though I spent much of my time catching reptiles). Finally we did show that these little animals were "genetically polymorphic." In one season, one genetic arrangement predominated over another, and then as the season changed, the frequency of the arrangement shifted back again. This was not quite evolution, but it was very close. Should the climate of the pass have changed permanently, it seemed certain that the populations of flies and their genetic structure would have responded, adjusting to the new climatic regime. And that would be evolution.

Another thing the test showed, and almost as important, was that such evolutionary changes could be expected to occur rapidly—even from one generation of fruit flies to the next—using stored-up variation. That, I later came to understand, was how multicellular creatures managed to keep up with the simpler forms, who simply played out evolution through their almost incalculable numbers, chance change in their genic arrangements, and the ubiquity and statistics of cell division and death.

Epling tried another brave test, and we students—his enlisted, unpaid research army—followed after him. We crept the desert floor, attempting to make exact maps of a tiny inch-high "belly plant," *Linanthus parryi*, that flowered in dense profusion in two color morphs, one white and one royal blue, all scattered together like pepper and salt across the desert gravel. Epling hoped that he could show changing patterns of the two colors, which he knew were lodged in the plant's basic genetic structure, and thus show gene exchange in a wild population of a living species, something that must happen in the course of evolution, but which remained untested. This quite staggering effort didn't bear any fruit—foundering on the sheer difficulty of making exact maps, year after year, of where each flower type had been sprouted from its tiny seed and where it had shouldered aside the gravel grains. But for we students, on our hands and knees amid the cactus spines, what mattered more was that we were savoring actual contact with a frontier in human understanding.

We were down there, sitting on the desert sand with brown bags and sandwiches, eating lunch with the greats in the field. What we participated in was not a new understanding about the world, but a demonstration of the integrity of our leaders. To them, it mattered only that we all get it right and that the results be interpreted without any human bias at all. Their willingness to cast off disproven ideas, and the sheer difficulty of the task they undertook, told me how the naturalist must work. Nature didn't always give up easily; that was obvious.

After these experiences, my search progressed from the desert to the sea, from reptiles and amphibians to fish. I moved on to Scripps Institution of Oceanography, where I studied a little piscine inhabitant of the local tidepools. In the course of this research, however, I became enamored of the open ocean, and it turned out that this new fascination would steer my course for the next two decades and beyond.

All Scripps students were expected to go to sea, so I took part in an expedition trawling for deep-sea fishes. I marveled at these otherworldly creatures, with their rows of living lights, and then succumbed to malaise as I tried to sort our catch on the afterdeck, the fishes sluicing back and forth in their tray as the ship rolled. But I was transfixed when a great blue whale coursed alongside our inadequate 85-foot seiner, and I sucked in a breath as the whale swung under us, producing a false bottom on our fathometer seventy feet down. I watched enthralled when, on a black night, Pacific white-sided dolphins crowded to our bow, sleeves of phosphorescence sliding over their bodies and roiling behind their fins as they cut and dove. In time, I came to understand that, out there in the open sea, different imperatives rule than in the intertidal fringe or on land. For a terrestrial naturalist like me, the open sea was a world that needed much rethinking.

Even before I finished my PhD, I landed a job as director of the brand-new Marineland of the Pacific. Soon, dolphins and other cetaceans became a major focus of my efforts to build up the collections and exhibits at the oceanarium. With the dolphins, I found myself immersed in the study of mammals that, in the total isolation of a long evolution at sea, had evolved brains to rival our own in size. Of what use was this obviously powerful possession? I wondered. What hidden purposes had it come to serve? As I spent more time with these remarkable creatures, many other questions arose. Why did dolphins always swim together? What did I mean when I talked so blandly about "schools"? What lay hidden in their internal communication?

Then followed a twenty-five-year-long natural history effort, the most difficult I ever undertook, to learn about the lives of these graceful, elusive animals at sea. My colleagues and I came part way, but most still remains out there, masked from our present understanding by the sheer difficulty of our being in one world—the air—and they in another—almost always beneath the water.

While still embroiled in dolphin work, I took a position at the relatively new University of California, Santa Cruz, where I would finish out my career. It was here that I resolved more than three decades of confusion about what to call myself, finally settling on "Natural Historian." So, for years the little card on my door in the Department of Environmental Studies said "Kenneth S. Norris, Professor of Natural History" and listed courses in both the traditional discipline of Biology and the new interdisciplinary field of Environmental Studies.

Beginning in 1973, my first full year at Santa Cruz, the spring quarter slot on this list was almost always filled by what would become a three-course, 15-unit composite called "Natural History Field Quarter." For this class, a teaching colleague and I, together with a teaching assistant, explored wild California with twenty-three eager students, camping, teaching each other, and beginning to unravel the fundamental patterns of nature. We left campus in a patient old blue bus, prepared our camp meals on student budgets, and reported our ideas to each other while sitting around a campfire, smoke swirling around, considering such things as the behavior of trees in high mountain winds, why rivers twist and turn, how the Forest Service protects our National Forests, and the source of our deep emotional attachment to the things of life. In between trips, the students invaded libraries, called officials, consulted authorities, and composed their presentations.

We leaders recognized that there are many windows to the world and so we selected our students broadly. We traveled with emerging biologists, musicians, economists, grade-school teachers, outdoor educators, agriculturalists, geologists, poets, and more. I think there were a few more women than men out of the 400 who ultimately traveled with me in my fourteen years in the bus.

In such intimate company, we found our way deep into each other's lives. One day, two of the students came to me and asked: "Ken, would you marry us?" I dismissed the idea with a wave of the hand, citing my lack of credentials to do such a thing. "No problem, Ken, we'll fix that." And so, accepting that I was something like a ship captain, I became a lay minister, and later, certificate at the ready, six more couples were joined by me in the most intensely human rituals I was to experience. Our theatre, as you might expect, was in each case the majesty of Nature.

I learned much from the students, who were in that formative, often painful time of life when a new-minted adult breaks loose from family to seek his or her place in the swirling chaotic world, all the while listening to the powerful imperatives of growing up. They were searchers themselves—the world spread out before them, theirs to interpret, theirs to change, theirs to lead. Thus I found myself in an exploration of our world much broader than I had planned. Together we held a slice of time, a little longer than either of us could have held alone. Sometimes we could see where things had come from; sometimes we could sense where they were going. And in this way we came to form little incomplete windows of wisdom that most others seemed unable to see.

I carried a long string of insights and observations with me in these fervent explorations with our 400 students. As I learned and pondered with them, I reflected over and over about the questions I posed so many years ago on those yellow sheets of paper that I had given to Doc Cowles.

This book is organized in a way that reflects—in a nonlinear way, of course—the wandering trajectory of the life I've just described. I think of the chapters as beads on a string, which together form a single, complete necklace. In the first five chapters (Section 1: Field Quarter), I describe some of the ventures during which the Field Quarter students and my colleagues and I found our place with each other, how we learned to see in Nature, how we grasped that the scientific viewpoint is just one way to see the world.

Then, because every teacher like me is the sum of his or her experiences, I go back in time to describe, in the next eight chapters (Section II: From Desert to Ocean), some of the moments when I saw deeper than before into some aspect of life, the times when I formed my personal understanding of natural process. These times of insight sketched out what I could teach and shaped the philosophical core that I could bring to that endeavor. These chapters more or less follow the unfolding of my scientific career, which led from the desert to the edge of the sea, and then to the *terra incognita* of the open sea. Through them run several themes, the most inclusive of which is the antiquity of the arrangements of life.

In the last section of the book (Section III: Windows to the World), I take this theme further to reflect on how the unbroken sweep of life takes human history deep into the past—far, far beyond what we usually think of as our origins, revealing our species as a simple twig on a very large, ramifying tree of life, a tree that has taken at least three quarters of Earth history to grow. It's in this section that I present my sometimes-iconoclastic ideas about human society, our systems of faith, and our clouded future as a species.

At the very end, I take you back to the Field Quarter class on our last trip high on a majestic fin of a mountain, where we share an intense last time together, emotions held in check just below the surface—the students poised to leave the safe capsule of the blue bus and each other, to scatter throughout society, and me looking at the end of my teaching career.

I hope, when you are finished reading, that all these times of seeing and of insight seem strung together into that necklace I mentioned, painting in the pieces of my larger view of Mountain Time and beyond.

If you've followed me this far, I expect you want one more question answered before you launch into the chapters: "What the heck does he mean by 'Mountain Time'?" Mountain Time is simply my metaphor for natural process. At its basic level, it expresses something akin to what ecologists mean when they use the concept of niche. By making *Mountain Time* the book's title and central metaphor, I hope to impart the idea that Nature is not just a here-and-now thing, but a thing-through-time, built of nesting, connected layers of organization that allow the many faces of life to be expressed.

Life, of course, exists in space as well as in time. Plants and animals occupy a patchwork quilt of space out on the wild mountain. Think about redwood trees. They don't grow everywhere, especially down where their occurrence is patchy, as on the southern edge of their range. They are down in river canyons and on north-facing slopes, out of the hottest sun. That's mountain space, and you can go and actually see it. What you can't see is that the distribution of redwood trees has changed profoundly through time. They were once much more widespread than they are today, and then before that they had a beginning somewhere. That time dimension has been just as complex as the space dimension is now.

By using a term that doesn't refer directly to the space part of the equation, I know that I irritate some people and sow a little confusion. But I don't want to call the book *Mountain Space-Time*, because that would throw my poetry out the window. So, trusting that most readers will infer the spatial aspect of Nature lurking within my title, I stick with *Mountain Time*. Anyway, *Mountain Time* has a nice ring to it, and I like it.

— *Kenneth S. Norris*
Santa Cruz, California
1998

Part I • Field Quarter

Students visiting Kelso Dunes during the travels of UC Santa Cruz Natural History Field Quarter 1984 rest in the shade of the Blue Bus.

Photo by Steve Gliessman

UC Santa Cruz Natural History Field Quarter at the Granite Cabin, Granite Mountains Reserve: (top) the cabin nestled among the boulders, 1984, (middle) students setting up camp, 1989, and (bottom) students on deck, 1981.

Chapter 1:
The Granite Mountains

A slight, almost forlorn figure stands under a parking lot floodlight, surrounded by a mound of her field gear. A zippered field notebook hangs like a tether around her neck.

"You're Kathy, aren't you?" I ask as I drive up.

"Yes," she replies tentatively, peering into my pickup window in the fading darkness.

"It's me, Ken, your fearless professor. You're in the right place. The others will be coming soon."

As dawn begins to streak the eastern sky, students pour into the Barn Theatre parking lot at the University of California, Santa Cruz, and then the big blue bus rumbles up. We are beginning an odyssey during which we will quit our campus in favor of living, camping, and traveling in the outside world. We will stay out most of the spring and wander wild California from top to bottom, from the starkest desert to the glaciated crest of the Sierra Nevada. We will become explorers together. The rigid separations between student and teacher will quickly soften until we become a tiny society built, as it should be, of elders who carry the dimension of time and of new questers, looking ahead to see how the world must be changed. We will learn from each other, and in the end many will never want to go back.

Steve Gliessman, my teaching colleague, and Larry Ford, our teaching assistant, jump out and begin to organize the packing of the bus for the long trip ahead. A massive mound lies on the ground: crated vegetables; cardboard boxes bulging with bagels, loaves of bread, fresh tomatoes, a sack of potatoes, peppers, onions, and garlic; the first aid kit; and the "Parnassus," a portable library with carefully selected books arranged in two long wooden boxes.

I will soon tell everybody that we carry a dehydrated librarian, Miss Preen, in a separate box and that, when we get to camp, all we will have to do is add water and she will sit up and rap anyone's knuckles who doesn't get his book back on time.

But, alas, she is imaginary.

Soon everything is passed into the bus, bucket-brigade style, and strapped in place. Larry and Steve take extra pains to see that the rear door of the bus remains unobstructed by this huge pile, so that we can all escape out the back in case of an emergency on the road.

A pair of sweethearts drives up in a battered old car, the engine revving in neutral. A young woman decked in field gear steps out, embraces her friend, and slings her bags on the pile. The two reach toward each other, lock hands for a moment, kiss, and then he drives off. I must warn her, I think, that when she returns from this trip, she cannot hope to share her new world fully with him. He will want her back in his reality, and she will be partly in another.

We three teachers have learned that none of us can guide this little society alone; not one of us is to be a leader for everybody. Some students will gather around Steve, he the quiet deep seeker, sometimes on a buffeting ride of his own. He will prove a magnet to those who share similar paths. Buses and engines love Steve, telling him where it hurts and letting him get them going again with pieces of wire or paper clips. I, older and no longer so challenged by the present, can dispense my hopeful vision, and so another group will hew to me. Alas, mechanical things fall apart in my hands, and I can name you ten places on our travels where we would still be calling for help were it not for Steve.

Larry, our teaching assistant and just recently a student himself, never met a list or a schedule he didn't like, and he understands the crosscurrents flowing among the students better than either of us. He will tell us: "Laura needs assurance from one of you; she wonders if she fits here."

Each of us, in his own way, deals with the constant social battering we take as leaders in this questing, intense society. As a first line of defense, I protect my private space with jokes, and then sometimes I sign out and wander alone near camp, to lie down under a pine and watch the clouds sweep by. Steve's refuge is sometimes his tent, but more he often walks to some mountain ledge to watch the sunset as the cold wind begins to grip and the owls to call.

Our invited visitors this trip are "Cosmic" Joe Jordan, a scientist from the space laboratory of NASA Ames, over the hill in Silicon Valley, and his estimable lady, Mary Flodin. When he can find time from work, Joe handles the cosmos for us. He visibly vibrates at the chance to show students the things of the physical universe, such as double or pulsating stars, 46-degree haloes and sun dogs, the Moire patterns formed by rows of grapes as the bus glides by, or the curious behavior of raindrops falling in tire ruts. He is a treasure. Mary, a very experienced outdoor education teacher, will gather around her our half dozen fledgling outdoor teachers and quietly show them the way.

We climb aboard Old Blue, Steve at the wheel. Larry sits behind him, while I stand in the front door well. Steve starts up our familiar old bus for another year's adventure; the air brakes are checked with a hiss. I pull down the microphone hanging from the door stanchion above me. "Welcome to Field Quarter '82. Check your triads."

Throughout the spring, this little triad routine will save us hours of counting heads. Each student had previously been assigned to a private group of three. They didn't even have to like each other. Whenever we ask, they have but to look around to see if the other two triad members are present. It gives us an almost instant answer to whether or not everybody is down off the mountain.

Steve inches the bus forward, crunching over the gravel.

"Robert is not here," comes a voice from the back of the bus.

We look back at the now-vacant parking lot and, sure enough, here comes Robert, trotting hurriedly out of the big California Bay thicket, pulling at his fly. The three of us look at each other and wordlessly file Robert in the "to be watched" category.

On this first trip, we are heading south, down between the Coast Range mountains, across the southern toe of the great Valley of the San Joaquin, up the tilted granite slab of the Sierra Nevada, out through a gap in its crest, Walker Pass, down onto the limitless desert, and 150 miles later we will stop at a tiny shack, a redoubt set among the rocks of a lonely mountain in the wildest Mojave Desert. There we will stay for seven days, learning to know each other, dispelling fears, and beginning the long process of learning to see how the wild world works.

For we three leaders, mother-henning it over our diverse and largely unknown brood, the spring will be an almost constant exercise in vigilance. Thus Larry, Steve, and I learn about motherhood. We silently wish for a safe spring, as fervently as any parents.

I have come to understand that these trips mean much more than teaching in any formal classroom setting. I am not up there behind a lectern, proper and remote, handing down the holy writ. Instead I am a sharer in the quest as much as they. They will draw that sense of time's dimension from me, and from them I will come to partake of the present shape of their changing world, its fears and vibrance. Rednecks, I had come to understand, were people who had stopped their growth and become frozen in time and place. These students were to keep us from that, and were to keep alive my wonder at this world of ours.

There is, indeed, much ahead for these students, and we will work them hard. Each will keep a daily personal journal, which we leaders will share with each student after each trip, all twenty-three volumes of them. We write our comments in pencil in page margins, should they want to erase them. Many will pour out hopes and fears in those pages, and thus we will come to know them better than most friends. We, older, have little trouble imagining ourselves back at their age, to that time of earliest adulthood when families, lovers, futures were often a trembling muddle, yet to be sorted out.

Each student will prepare and give oral presentations, often their first, on matters as diverse as the state of forestry practice, the habits of coyotes, or how mountains are formed. Sometimes, in past years, these have been given as little playlets, a practice we came to accept as a good and reasonable way of getting across the gist of, say, how continents collide. They will form their own thoughts more silently about larger, deeper puzzles.

Between trips, the students use libraries to prepare their reports, then contact officials, if need be, and compose their remedies. The results are delivered to the group after dinner in some cabin or around a windy campfire with the smoke swinging in to sting the eyes of listeners. On the trips, each will practice the arts of observation and record the results in special journal entries called "Observation Series." The subject might be how a three-foot waterfall shaped the rock onto which it fell, the curious clumping behavior of brine flies, or the vigilant behavior of hummingbirds, who continuously swivel their heads in a search for rivals and predators.

We will clean up camps until every last shred of trash has disappeared from the pine needle blanket. Frequently the students will jog us with some new wrinkle of care for the wild world, just when we thought we were leading them. New replaces old, and they are from a more-concerned generation than we had been at their age.

The students settle back as Steve noses us out onto the nearly vacant street. Most of them know from student word-of-mouth that they are beginning an adventure that will change many, that lifetime bonds will be cast, and that the spring will be one long epic of as-yet-almost-unfathomable form. Most are still alone, sitting quietly in their seats, watching the streets of Santa Cruz go by, waiting for it to happen.

The bus skirts by the little harbor at Moss Landing, on deepest Monterey Bay. I take the microphone. "Out there under that flat ocean, lies one of the deepest submarine canyons in North America," I say, pointing to the calm sea. "Beginning right here at Moss Landing, the canyon drops below the sea surface, following a zigzag channel down to about 6,000 feet below sea level, deeper than almost any other canyon in North America. After that, it winds its way down to the 12,000-foot deep abyssal sea floor. In its black waters live some of the most exotic life-forms on earth, and they are just now being seen for the first time, transmitted up a long fiber-optic tether from the underwater television cameras of the Monterey Bay Aquarium Research Institute's remote-operated vehicle. The institute's headquarters is that big gray building over there. It's somehow hard for me to grasp that one has to go just half a dozen miles offshore to reach one of the least-known parts of the earth and to see living creatures that almost no one has ever seen before."

On south we drive. Steve takes the mike and begins identifying the native trees of the nearby hills as he drives along. "Those ones with the bluish caste to their leaves are blue oaks. Look down in the river valley and you will see one of California's most magnificent trees, the valley oak. You can tell it because its leaves are greener than the blue oak. It can be huge, and it has long dangly branches and leaves that hang down like a skirt. The valley oak is in trouble, since grazing animals apparently eat every young tree before it can grow up." He pauses. "Who knows what its Latin name is?"

"*Quercus lobata*" comes a voice from the seats. Steve looks in the rear view mirror to see who his new botanical confrere is.

A few miles later, I take the mike again. "Here it comes, everybody. We're about to go across the San Andreas Fault. That's where many of the earthquakes in California come from. Think of it as a long, deep crack in the earth that runs all the way up from Mexico and goes out to sea way north of San Francisco. The San Andreas is the boundary between two tectonic plates that ride on the earth's surface. We'll be leaving the Pacific Plate, which is to the west, and we'll drive right onto the North American Plate to the east, if all goes well. The fault's just up ahead in that broad valley there." I point to a jagged fault trace running up the hills to the south. "I hope we make it. If that baby goes off while we're on it, we'll spin like a top."

"Aww, Dr. Norris, you wouldn't josh a naïve young student, would you?" comes another voice from the seats. The student telegraph had been at work again. They are already onto me. On across the south end of the Great Valley we drive. I explain that in Miocene time there had been a deep, almost enclosed arm of the sea in this valley. Then we climb up the south end of the Sierra Nevada mountains amid the wildflowers of early spring.

"A dime for the first Joshua tree," I announce.

I can faintly see a forest of them in the east-west valley we were traversing. It is a westward salient of this typically desert tree that

The Granite Mountains

at a somewhat warmer time had made it over the mountain pass ahead of us.

"There," says Rebecca, pointing. "Where's my dime?"

Steve soon pulls to a stop just off the pavement. Among the blocks of tumbled granite he has sighted the gaudy blaze of a Sierra redbud in full bloom and, up the hill behind, the sticky golden cups of the flannel bush, newly unfurled.

"Two new plant families for you to learn," says Steve.

The old blue bus groans its way over the pinyon-clad crest of Walker Pass and onto the east-sloping margin of the Mojave Desert. Ahead of us is a vast vista of buttes protruding from sloping aprons of alluvium called bajadas, while deep in the valleys between lie pale, dry lake beds.

"We didn't even have to use granny gear," says Steve. "Old Blue is running good, so far." He cruises to a stop. "You take over, Larry, after we look around; I need a snooze."

We know we have hit a "flower year." Every sixth or seventh spring, the western desert lights up with flowers. Apparently, when the fall rains come at the right time and in sufficient quantity, they prepare the seeds, which are then incubated in moist soil to burst forth into one vast garden. Yellow *Lasthenia* tints the dun hills; lower down, amid the dark Joshua forest, the pale orange mounds of desert apricot are in bloom; and the gravel between is washed with purple *Gilia* and tiny yellow poppies.

In moments, Steve has a dozen students down on the ground, learning to identify plants. "Key them out" is the phrase he uses for learning to fly our plant bible, *A California Flora and Supplement* by Philip Munz.[1] "A half dozen well-prepared students carry this big red volume in special zipped shoulder bags, just as Steve does. We know that, before the spring is over, these six and probably several more will be arguing about the newest plant taxonomy and spitting out Latin names at a remarkable rate.

I kick over the rotted trunk of a downed Joshua branch and see movement amid the fibrous duff. I call the nearest students to me and soon hold a tiny wriggling brown lizard, *Xantusia vigilis*, by one hind foot. This creature, I tell them, violates what zoology textbooks tell you about the difference between reptiles and mammals. This lizard nourishes its unborn young internally through a placenta-like structure and then gives birth to one to three minute brown young, each wrapped inside an enveloping membranous sheath. At birth, the little mother bends around to bite and tear away the restraining membranes, freeing her young, which at once wriggle deep into fallen Joshua tree debris. After that, they're on their own.

We rumble our way down past the east rampart of the Sierra Nevada, its crests hidden in clouds, on down the sweeping bajada. Inch-high flowers grow so thickly between the clumps of saltbush that melted butter seems to have been poured there.

On we drive in the afternoon warmth. All, except Larry the driver, begin to succumb to the somnolence of the afternoon, and the buzz of voices subsides. Feet go up on seat backs and heads nod. Finally, three hours later, Larry swings the big bus off the pavement and onto a two-rut dirt road, banked on each side by a colonnade of big creosote bushes, almost touching the bus as it passes. He picks our way along delicately, if one can be called "delicate" driving a bus. The ruts lead toward a thousand-foot wall of huge granite slabs and pinnacles looming just ahead of us. Larry expertly bridges ruts that I expect to hang up the bus at any moment, but rocking and creaking we wind through an arid scrubland, which becomes ever more dense with bushes of several kinds as we near the mountain. Some flower yellow, and the spiky-leaved yuccas are in full bloom, topped by thick opulent spires of waxy white. Everybody is up in their seats, looking for some evidence of the cabin. There is no habitation to be seen, only that rampart of granite, notching the sky.

"Look up the mountain a little," I instruct. "It's colored like the rock. I can see the chimney now, and the roof." I point. "That's it. What did you expect, the Sheraton Mojave?"

Larry pulls the bus to a stop atop a gravelly hill across a deep sandy wash from the granite outliers of the mountain. We cannot drive further, so everything will have to be portaged down the hill, across the wash, and up the rock stairs to the cabin, which is built in amongst the huge boulders—two inner walls are faces of the rocks themselves. The portage takes a remarkably short time. A long winding line of students, each bearing a box, a sleeping bag, or a tent threads its way from the bus and up to the cabin. Soon an enormous pile of dunnage is heaped on the cabin's spacious wooden deck, with things rodents would like to eat stowed in cabinets and drawers inside.

I gather everyone around me on the deck. "I'll tell you how we found this place. It was in the late 1950s. We had decided to build a desert retreat. So we began exploring. I knew about these mountains from my earlier work on dune animals, and so we came here. The others were making lunch out there on the bajada as I climbed along this rock face. I came up over that boulder there," I said, pointing south past a gnarled old pinyon pine. "I saw that crack in the rock, with a film of water running over its face. Goldfinches were clinging to the rock, drinking. Even a little seep of water like that is precious in the desert so I immediately wanted to explore its source."

"The others shouted from below, saying the sandwiches were ready. I told them to hold on, that I'd found water. I made my way toward the cleft, entered it, and there in the semi-darkness I saw a clear pool of water gleaming in the shadows. I knelt and tasted it. It was sweet and cool, a priceless find on this arid desert, where most water is heavy with salts."

"'I've found it, I've found it!' I shouted to the lunch makers. The upshot was that we looked up who owned the land—it was the railroad—and we obtained a lease on one acre, including the spring, and built our cabin. It was built mostly out of discarded materials from abandoned mines or from old railroad ties that had been pulled out from under the rails by maintenance crews and thrown aside as new ones were put in place. Today the railroad saves all those old ties and sells them to gardeners for building walkways and retaining walls, but not then. They just tossed them out. The desert was littered with them. Every rancher had built his corrals out of them and sometimes his headquarters buildings, too. The roof beams of the cabin were built of telephone poles that had been struck by lightning and likewise thrown aside."

"One could never do things now the way we did back then. It was all John Wayne and the Wild West out here. It's much better now. This desert is not being torn up the way it once was. I have hope for the wildlife and the plants now the way I never did then."

Today the cabin site is far inside the fenced and protected boundaries of a huge university teaching and research reserve. When the reserve was formed, the cabin was given to the University of California and sometimes used for classes like ours.

I know that some of the students, not yet in tune with the exotic and austere landscapes of the desert, view our surroundings with fear, but experience tells me that it won't take long for such concerns to dissipate as we introduce them to the flowers now blooming, the gaudy cactus and succulents cupped in dozens of hidden rock gardens, the singing toads that emerge at dusk to crouch in rocky pools, trilling, the flitting canyon bats who crawl alone from crevices in the afternoon while it is still light, and the canyon wrens whose fluted calls ring like liquid silver in every little draw. Tonight the cacomistle may even come out, though it seems impossible that this lovely ring-tailed cat, a wild animal that lives under the cabin, will stand such traffic as we have brought with us. (Amazingly, the beautiful animal will later appear right among the students and lay down on the highest bunk.)

Steve instructs the students about the flight log. "Before going on any hike out of earshot of the cabin, everyone must—I repeat, *must*—fill out the flight log. It's that black-covered, bound notebook marked 'Flight Log.' Take your topographic maps with you (we had provided copies for everybody). Write exactly where you plan to go, and, above all, stick to your plan. Do not change it in the middle of a hike."

A special urgency fills his voice as he emphasizes the flight log, but we three know that we will have to keep after these new companions for a while until the urgency of the matter strikes home—probably after some group is a bit late coming down off the mountain. Then the looks of concern on everyone's faces will show that Steve's serious words had finally been taken to heart.

"Look around you. This place is a wilderness. Someone could fall off a rock and not be found until the stink attracted vultures." He pauses for emphasis. "We have saved three groups of hikers with that flight log. Because the hikers had done what we'd asked them to—filled out exactly where they planned to go and then stuck to it. In every case, we were able to walk right to them."

I feel a little private grip of fear, a fear that will not wholly go away until we deposit everyone at the barn parking lot after the last trip of the spring. Such restrictions of freedom as we try to extract are the price of coming here, I think. Nature could care less. (Looking back, though, in all my seventeen years we never had an injury we couldn't care for, and though sometimes people wandered, in the end they were all safe, all 400 of them.)

The food group begins preparing our first meal together amid much chatter, as others shift and store supplies in the lockers. A huge pot for spaghetti goes on the propane stove, long loaves of bread are fished out of the chaotic pile of gear, sliced and buttered and put to warm by the now-crackling fire. Over on the drain board, three other members of the food group begin assembling a giant salad.

Good, good, we leaders think. It seems like a wonderful, willing group, full of good spirits. We already know from the interviews that there are many talents among them. Such folks will, in time, be our extra teachers.

By this time, more than a decade after my first trip, a great many lessons have been impressed upon us, most having to do with the social equation presented by traipsing off across wild California with twenty-three young people deep in finding themselves, each at that stress-filled fulcrum point of life where they know they must break free of families, loved or not, to find their own way. Fears in these adults-in-formation are often deep, their need for love deeper still, and the necessity of forming a new world from the old a commandment.

My natural reticence and a perhaps subliminal sense of my role carried me through the early years before I began to understand what must guide the leaders of such a class. We must be guides and adjudicators, sharers of discoveries, salvers of sorrows, and givers of the hope and excitement of life just ahead, but we must remain outside the intimate tug and haul of the student dynamic. Otherwise our presence will polarize rather than weld the group together. "We leaders must become sexless uncles," I finally verbalized to myself.

My first intimation of this came on my first class in 1973, on a trip to Santa Cruz Island, a few miles off the coast of California. We had hiked hard that day, climbing the highest peak of the island and had then skirted down the long dry slopes to a tiny pond impounded in a rocky draw near the center of the island. The water was deep and bone-chillingly cold. A single stream, like the water from a farm pump, arced in from ten feet up, drawing a veil of bubbles down into the black water.

In a trice, with no word from me, clothes were cast aside and sleek young people were diving off rocky perches and into the water, their laughter ringing from the cliffs. I, too shy and uncertain to join them, clambered around the rocky shore to a secluded place where I too, shed my clothes and slipped into the water for a refreshing moment before coming quickly out to sit shivering on a pool-side rock.

I hadn't been there long when I heard loud, garbled, echoing voices from around the bend. Five young women in gay conversation appeared and paddled toward me. They saw me and, with a cheery welcome, swam over, slid out of the water like penguins onto the ice, and took places on both sides of me, dabbling their toes in the water.

"Hi," I said, reeling off their names, but feeling alone and wholly exposed. They continued their previous conversation as if I had not been sitting there between their dripping bodies. The discussion turned to menstruation, and to the problems of taking long hikes when one's period came, and then, for Heaven's sake, one of them began discussing the state of her clitoris. No one had ever discussed the state of her clitoris in my presence before.

For all my discomfort, something vital was revealed in those moments. I had been accepted as a sexless uncle. I was above the fray, which was exactly where I strove to be. Yet, like the monk taking the vows of celibacy, I knew that I remained just as I had been, a sexual being. The monk could speak of the Lord testing his will. I simply knew that sexuality is an intrusion that can shatter and divide. It wasn't so hard, really; our trips were interludes, and it was wonderful to sing old show tunes up in the front of the bus with my new young woman friends, with none of the usual electricity or tension between us. Miraculously, we could ask the questions that came to mind, exchange ideas, fears, and hopes, once our different sexes were out of the equation.

Other dimensions of this odyssey of ours have slowly come clear to me. I know that we leaders have three major roles. First, we define the journey and lead the way across the mountains and down the rivers. We describe the world through which we travel in all those dimensions I have mentioned. That is a pretty straightforward assignment. Not simple—but straightforward.

Second and not so obvious, we try to release in each of the twenty-three, shy and bold, the feeling that they are free to explore with us, that their eyes are as good as ours. I know instinctively that we leaders must not overwhelm these young people with our own attitudes; many are so tentative, so uncertain of their personal worth. We must make clear that, while we are repositories of knowledge who can provide much of what has been learned about this wild world, they are the ones who will take these materials and reshape the present, and they will take different paths than ours. They are the ones to begin the redefinition of the future. We are, student and leader alike, integral parts of the process of social change, neither better nor worse than the other.

Finally, the key to releasing this feeling of belonging, of freedom to take part, is to make our blue time-capsule a moving island of trust where everyone inside feels safe, where everyone feels listened to. I know it will take much of the quarter for some in this year's group to emerge from their layers of reticence, and that it will only happen because we provide different ways, different levels of expression to them.

On this trip, I've noticed that some already feel free to express themselves—to borrow the bus mike from us, for example, and tell everyone what it was like to grow up on a farm like the one we are passing. I know that others, a little less bold, will feel released a few days hence when they get a chance to demonstrate their knowledge—

identifying a phainopepla, being the first to key out a bladderpod, giving a report under the glowing lantern about the elements of bird migration. Others, more private still, will speak at first through their journals.

This first night, some of them write on the kitchen tables until long after midnight, late enough that I finally shoo them out to their sleeping bags so the lanterns can be doused and others can sleep. "Time to quit now. You can't see Orion very well with the lamp turned on."

The brilliant white of the mantles fades, turns to pale wavering blue, and pinches off into darkness. Tomorrow I will show them how to see.

Resident ringtail at the Granite Cabin, Granite Mountains.

Ken Norris and UC Santa Cruz Natural History Field Quarter 1980 students imitating reptiles warming in the sun at Snake Springs, Granite Mountains.

Photo by Lawrence D. Ford

Chapter 2:
What a Lousy Bird!

The night was crowded with stars for those of us who had spread our sleeping bags outside on the deck of the Granite Cabin. Now and then a breeze came breathing through the piñons, the wind a presence, a wraith. It went on its way down the slope and strummed the big juniper in the wash below. Pulling my bag close over my shoulders, I lay there in contentment, watching the pinpricks of light wheel by. Polaris, just over the black rim rock to the north, was the hub. No wonder there were astronomers among the Arabs, who tracked and named these stars. They must have watched them most of their nights, bedded down in the open much as I was.

I closed my eyes, pulled my head under the warm down, and drifted off again, to awaken as dawn paled the eastern sky. Ultramarine evolved from black, resolved to rose, and then distant cloud tendrils lit up with vermillion and gold.

We're up, and the spring routine begins. The food group soon has tea water steaming, and a huge aluminum pot of hot oatmeal and raisins, ladle sunk deep, is ready for serving. Once breakfast is completed, Steve will wander the canyons till noon with six students, sketching in the plant life of the mountain. I will lead another such group to learn how to see in Nature. In two days, we will explore with all twenty-three students.

I consult my list of names. My first six are Ann, Jenny, John, Caitlin, Ken, and Dave. Bearing our notebooks and binoculars, we wander off down the circumferential wash that bounds most of the mountain. No footprints yet mar the immaculate gravel.

We walk by a kettlehole where the intermittent stream has crossed granite to set stones swirling in the current, grinding the rock down to produce a smooth-walled pit three feet deep. The rock crystals inside are beaten almost as smooth as glass. The kettle is half full of greenish water and teeming with tiny insects, most in the water, but some skating the surface. Because the kettle walls are so smooth and in places overhanging, toads cannot escape, and two hang flaccid and dead in the water. Imagine that! You can drown a toad! Down on our hands and knees, we watch mosquito larvae hanging upside-down, held by minute hooks through the water's surface film.

I ask Jenny if she can see the jewel at the end of the mosquito larva's tail. She looks questioningly at me. I tell her to get closer and look at the very tip of the tube from which it hangs. "That's its breathing tube, and the jewel is the air bubble inside it."

I hear Caitlin exclaim as she locates the jewel.

We set off crunching down the curving watercourse again. From my years here, I know every turn, every tree, where I can find the liverworts back deep in a dark crevice under a granite shelf. I instruct Ken and Dave to crawl ten feet in and feel the damp cold face at the back of the cave to which these primitive plants clasp. It seems incomprehensible that any plant dependent upon a tiny swimming reproductive stage could persist in this desert. But they do, and they are not rare at all.

At the mouth of Xanadu Canyon, a choked and jumbled wilderness of huge boulders, I spy a dark rock amid the peach-colored gravel of the arroyo and hand it to Ann. It is an Indian mano of volcanic rock, one side worn smooth during the grinding of innumerable seeds. We muse together that the mano was probably once held by a Chemehuevi Indian woman, and that it must have been carried here from volcanic Van Winkle Mountain, three miles to the southeast. Ann runs her fingers over the ground-down surface, in touch with that ancient woman.

The canyon tightens and a streamlet appears in the gravel, which then trickles into a dark, echoing passage between boulders the size of houses. By summer, this water will have disappeared deep into the gravel, and the stream course will bake with heat, leaves and flowers will dry and blow, parched and brittle, across the sand. But now the stream bottom is a lush garden. Water monkeyflowers, *Mimulus guttatus*, paint a border yellow and orange, and near the water the creosote is abuzz with flowers and insects. A clump of deepest blue Canterbury bells nods on the bank, anthers bright gold, and behind, scarlet Indian paintbrush heads rise from amid mounds of buckwheat.

I choose a sunny place on a granite slab and gather my friends around me. I begin to tell them how a naturalist can hope to unravel the stories of the wild things that live here. To many scientists, what the naturalist does seems like guesswork. Yet truths keep emerging from the naturalist's hands anyhow, because he begins by taking in the natural world on its own terms.

I say that at first there is no real difference between what I do and what a little child playing in the same stream bottom would do. The child and I take in the scene the same way—wordlessly—and before long we both know what is right about this bit of Nature. Little of this is committed to language. Both child and naturalist come to know the actors in the scene, we know how a brief rain will wake up the black patches of desert moss that cling to the granite surfaces, making them dark green and lush like velvet. We come to know that cholla spines will shine in the afternoon sun as if lit inside. Like carefully aged wine, our understanding, the child's and mine, becomes more complete with time.

What we learn are the true things of the stream bottom, what makes up the entire warp and woof of life in any such canyon as this. This gestalt of a wild world provides what I rather irreverently call my "baloney filter." After a time, it's hard to fool a naturalist or a country kid about a stream bottom like this.

I'd noticed that near the margins of a tiny pond were a dozen drowned bees, wings outstretched, floating on the water surface. Was the water somehow a trap for them?

So I pose a tiny hypothesis: "All those drowned bees got too close to the water and fell in."

Nature replies: "Not bad for a youngster, but there's more." I look closer. The bees seldom drink from the pond edge, I find, and they don't appear to drink while flying. Instead most of the drinking bees probe the sand inches back from the water's edge. Hmm. Why? The bees act as if the still pond is dangerous.

Then I see a bee flying over the water catch a wing and cartwheel in, to lie with wings beating on the surface film of the pond, spiraling here and there in a pool of aimless vibration. Finally its curving paths take it toward the bank; it touches bottom and pulls itself free of the water.

I pose a modified question and make up a new hypothesis: "Maybe the way a bee flies can trap it." I look again. Sure enough, the bee's wing beat is a dangerous one for any insect flying close over water. The wings go about as far below its body as above. Any miscalculation, flying too close, a wind gust, and a wing will dip in and pull the bee in, too.

In this process, I must throw away failed ideas as quickly as I pose my new questions. My "throwing-away muscles" must be just as good as my "asking muscles." I call this whole process "spinning the wheel." For some questions, such as why these bees drink back from the water's edge, you can spin the wheel over and over again in a morning, asking and refining. But for other questions, it may take years to get a few iterations. Or you may get none at all.

For instance, up Cottonwood Gap, that V in the mountain ridge to the north, I have turned boulders while trail building and twice found the exceedingly rare black-headed snake, *Tantilla hobartsmithi*. I'll bet they're common, but simply live their lives mostly below ground. Maybe they stick that little black head of theirs out from under the rocks to soak up heat, but we'd never see them do it.

I pose a new question for my student friends: "That tent caterpillar's nest, up on the desert almond bush, let's try to tease out its design. Ann, what do you see?"

She inspects it and replies that the nest appears to be made of silk, that it hangs from several small branchlets, with a bigger branch running up the middle, and there are at least three layers of silk, one inside the other.

"Are there single-layered nests?" Ann finds one and reports that it is much smaller than the three-layered nest. They must build one around the other, we guess.

"Can the caterpillars go between the layers? Are they stuck inside?" John peers closely at a nest and tells me that there are holes between the layers. The caterpillars can move throughout the nest.

The wheel spins on.

"Are those droppings inside the nest?" I ask. John checks them, and they are droppings, thousands of them inside the silken web. So the caterpillars must be feeding.

"Where?" asks John. "Where's any food?" The leaves inside the nest are either tiny or all gone.

"Yes, indeed," I reply. The caterpillars seem to keep the leaves inside the nest grazed down until they're just green nubbins. I wonder to myself if the caterpillars feed on leaves around the nest.

"Can the caterpillars get out of the nest?" I ask. Jenny soon finds a dozen crawling along the branch just beyond the nest.

On and on the questions go, each a tiny hypothesis waiting for Nature's answer. Over a career, I tell my young friends, you will come to ask better and better questions, deeper ones, as your experience grows.

"But you can also be blinded by what you think you know," I tell them. "Not infrequently the child's wide-open eyes will see what no one else sees." Science—or good poetry, for that matter—involves people struggling with their preconceptions, while the child may have none.

"The times when your eyes are really open are priceless. Unfortunately, though, these times are fleeting. We seem to see the world and then turn away." Then, I tell them, all concourse with Nature ceases. A troubled mind looks inward. Even your body can intrude until seeing stops.

"The phenocrysts protruding from this boulder I'm sitting on will get me in time, and it won't be long off." I explain that my dented rear will soon transmit anguish and will soon sweep away all my attempts to see. So, I go in for a comfortable blind, a folding chair, a thermos full of cold lemonade.

"I trust my eyes first and foremost." I explain that, while I use cameras and telescopes and various measuring devices freely, even avidly at times—because they can counteract my human emotionality and correct my inability to count or to measure very well—they do intrude. "Machines make me nervous," I say. Have I messed up Nature by putting all those wires down the rodent's burrow? Is it going to work if I remove a petal from the evening primrose so I can look inside to see how pollination takes place? "Careful, careful," I say. "Will what I learn be real?"

I go on to talk about time. I explain that we humans live and see within our own limited time frame, while other creatures live in time-worlds nearly separate from ours. I give examples. Mouse courtship and mating is one. I explain that it occurs in such a blur that it's very hard to resolve what's happening. At the opposite end, I talk of an acquaintance of mine who photographed a tidepool in freeze-frame slow motion, one frame every minute or so. In his film, the starfish, which we thought just lay still on the bottom, danced around each other, touching arms in apparent recognition of one another.

"The scientist will want to put numbers on everything," I tell them. "How big? How far? How fast? But poetry's different. The poet will search for just the right word. Would Longfellow have written: 'This is the forest primeval—the murmuring pines and the forty-meter hemlocks'? Never!"

"Choose your words with care. Make them fit. That's both science and poetry."

"Well, there's more to say, but we're all tired of sitting, so let's find ourselves a subject to watch. Afterward, let's read our results to each other. I think you will be surprised at how differently each of us sees things. Each of us will see things that the others didn't see at all." As we walk up out of the wash, I begin to look hard for a suitable bit of Nature's business to observe. We make our way down into a draw where a little pond has collected behind an old check dam. I see the subject right away. Two ruby-crowned kinglets are repeatedly flying up into midair and returning to sit in a small catclaw bush. Over and over, they make the same maneuver.

"Quietly now, lets see if we can get close enough to the two birds to find out what they are doing. Once we find a place to sit, fill out the journal heading and then write down what you see. Describe the whole event. Then we'll compare our notes."

We find a smooth rock not more than fifteen feet from the two birds, and they seem totally undisturbed by us. Quietly, we fill out our pages and begin our descriptions. I write a little note to Caitlin, sitting nearest me.

"What are they doing?" I write.

"Flying up, catching insect, back in bush," she whispers.

I had been looking ahead, and I can see that something beyond Caitlin's simple description is going on at the moment of capture.

"Look, top of flight." I whisper back.

We look hard at several forays.

"Wow, look at that," comes a hushed voice from our group. The birds are pursuing small fluttery insects that seemed to drift down from the head of the pond. Each foray is a gymnastic event, beyond anything we imagined the birds capable of doing. A bird flies up from its perch in the bush, climbing in a steepening arc. At the highest point, when only an inch or so from an insect, the little bird brakes with outspread wings and ever-so-delicately plucks the prey from the air, while lying almost on its back. Then it tumbles over, catches itself with its wings, and swoops into the protective bush so fast we cannot resolve it.

I look ahead again and whisper: "Even those little birds weigh something. How do they stop? Shouldn't we be able to see those little branches move?"

The catclaw bush is a fairly open affair, about six feet high, made up of an array of branches, each equipped with a formidable armament of cruel hooked claws, like those of a cat. The birds pay no evident attention to these weapons as they fly into the bush—right into its middle—so fast we can hardly follow them. When they settle, none of us can see any movement of the branchlets at all.

"How can they do that?" comes an awed voice from our group. It is a feat we would never come to understand. Spinning the wheel always generates more questions than get answered.

At that moment, across the pond a California towhee lumbers by, its wing beats slow and obvious compared to those of the kinglets. "What a lousy bird," says someone in our group.

"Look again, " I suggest. "Watch the towhee as it flies under those bushes."

The bigger bird spreads and flicks its broad wings, maneuvering with bewildering ease beneath the spreading bushes. "To each his own," I say. "Every species here has its own way of fitting in." As we turn back toward the cabin, I think: no wonder our national parks are just scenery to most people. Not many people "spin the wheel."

When it comes time for we leaders to read the journals from this trip, I am, as always, overwhelmed by the unseen emotional crosscurrents that flow not far down, and by the power and beauty of our students' growing connection with these wild scenes. Leslie writes:

> *I still haven't found my niche in this group of people. I must try to be a part of situations, instead of standing off as a discerning observer... . It seems that insecurities are running rampant with this group, and I am one of the few admitting and trying to understand why.*

(Not long afterward Leslie would find her place, and before the end of spring, her penetrating insights and her wit will have made her quite central to blue time-capsule culture.)

Helen writes:

> *The Granite Mountains! They have become home. I wish we could stay a month! The way the morning light tinged them rose, the cold feel of head, hair, and shoulders in the water trough before you were quite awake, the wide expanse of alluvial flats, the gentle ecosystem—birds, rodents, reptiles, plants. The cabin tucked up under the towering masses of ancient granite, rounded and bouldered, majestic and strong.*

I am moved by the beauty and loving grace of her words, but a grip of fear goes through me when I read the next part:

> *The exhilaration of jumping a little further, climbing or scrambling down a rock face a little steeper, doing things just a little scarier than I'd ever done before.*

Doing things a little scarier is part of the learning process, I tell myself and read on:

> *Sitting way up near the tiptops of the mountains, whispering, as if in reverence, while watching hawks, eagles, falcons glide in the sunset sky. Watching shadows grow long until they claim the lava mountains and the horizon to the east. Clambering down the mountains, trusting friends who lead, two great horned owls seen because we took, by no intent of ours, the "scenic" route. And gaining the cabin just in time, by moonless nightfall, and flying high with sweet dry desert air, the breath and sweat of the climb, the new friends already made and further friend potentials. Great, jointed, vertical-with-a-slant-to-the-northeast shoulders of granite, my ever most favorite rock—what beautiful mountains—I wish I had drawn their picture!*

I am reassured that all is well when I get to the end of Helen's entry:

> *Back-to-cabin thoughts: the sitting and singing so freely and not caring in particular what you'd sound like. Some lonely moments, silent moments, shy and hoping I can live up to the caliber and expectations of these fine people. And the little "answers," deeds and laughter that let you know acceptance and warmth is the rule here, and not the exception, and you must give your share and it will come back to you as much more. What a rush! There is something magical that is going on here. Treat it gently and with care and warmth—no telling what good things it could grow into!*

UC Santa Cruz Natural History Field Quarter class 1993, overlooking the Hole-in-the-Wall, eastern Mojave Desert, just west of Woods Mountain.

Photo courtesy of the Norris Collection

Chapter 3: The Wind and the Sky

There is a fairly easy way up hunchbacked Woods Mountain, over layered lava extrusions long since cooled and stilled. Once on top, we take seats on a slim bench of lava, right next to an ancient rhyolite vent from which molten pinkish rock, banded like taffy, once flowed. The rhyolite was a favorite of the Chemehuevi people for fashioning arrowheads because it spalled off predictably when struck with a pointed stone, and because it flaked cleanly when pressed hard with the tip of a deer's antler. Many evidences remain of the ancient peoples of Woods Mountain.

From our high, windy perch, we look down at the desert floor spread out below. The biggest creosotes and yuccas define the filigree of watercourses that wander down the bajadas, playing over the contours of the land toward distant lowland sinks. Just to the north, we can see sacred Table Mountain, once the home of the Indian's trickster, Coyote. Above it all is the big blue dome of the sky, demanding our attention. In our lives down below, we so seldom seem to look up, fixed as our eyes are on things within a few degrees of the horizon.

From Woods Mountain in the summer, one can often see anvil clouds, castle-shaped, that touch the stratosphere and can generate awesome shows of local thunder and lightning. Such clouds make late summer on the Mojave one of its most magnificent seasons. If we were on Woods Mountain in August, we might be watching a parade of such cloud-castles sweep over the land. Beneath them would be the trailing veils of falling rain—the dark gray virga—and if we were lucky, we would smell the spicy odor of newly wetted creosote bush.

The bench on the mountaintop is just wide enough for a row of my companions to sit in a line, with spaces in between where rocks have fallen away. Taking in the scene seated thus, we notice birds volplaning around us. "White-throated swifts," pronounces Kent.

One at a time, the little birds beat up the side of the peak, catch the wind blast, and rocket up into it. Some pass right between us, only four or five feet away, flying through the mountain notches. With scythe-like wings, they slice away from us in a twinkling flicker, in moments becoming dark dots high over Table Mountain, far, far out into the vast freedom of the blue sky. Above the swifts, we can see mare's tails—clouds made of ice crystals that tell of high-altitude winds, the upper boundary of the swift's domain.

It seems as if the Woods Mountain peak is a guide-on for their play. I suspect there is no better word than *play* for what they are doing. A swift flashes between Caitlin and me. "Did you see that, Dr. Ken? I thought I could see the pilot. He had goggles and a leather helmet."

"Did he have a scarf on? Hot pilots should have scarves, shouldn't they?" I ask.

We climb back down the brushy defile, stopping in a warm nook to talk a little of swifts. "They're among the most aerial of birds," I explain. I tell the class that they catch their insect food in the air, swoop in over ponds for a drink, all on the wing. Their legs are tiny. Mostly they're good for clinging to the walls of crevices into which the birds fly at frightening speed. "At Big Creek, we'll probably see black swifts, and maybe see them fly behind a big waterfall to their nests stuck on the rock behind." I explain that the swifts' nearest relatives are the hummingbirds. That seems to fit, the way both birds zoom around.

"Do they mate on the wing?" asks Sheila.

"Yes, I've seen them mate over the pond south of the cabin. The bird pair spirals together—upside-down, right-side up."

When we reach the bottom of the mountain, I announce: "On our way back to the cabin, we will stop near the Kelso Sand Dunes, where Big Jim and I will show you one of the most important wind rules." I have alerted Jim about all this, and he remains conspiratorially mum.

Just east of the huge heaped dunes, light peach against the olive-dun desert, Steve turns the bus onto the washboarded road that slices

The Wind and the Sky

between the dunes and the north side of the Granite Mountains. The wind seems to be just right. Often, cool air from the heights of the north slope of the Granites drains down into this low, heated valley. As it makes its way down the bajada, it begins to hurry and swirl. It may speed fast enough to pick up flotsam from the desert floor, and then you see it as a "dust devil." Up close, you can hear dust devils: they rattle and swish. Get closer still and they pelt you with sticks and gravel, tear pages out of your journals, whip your glasses off. Other local winds, the thermals, sometimes move upslope and boil off into the air above, like bubbles in a pot of boiling water. Today the prevailing northwest wind, a product of larger atmospheric dynamics, is in control.

We stop at a dry watercourse—a "wash" they're called on the Mojave. The breeze is blowing at a steady pace, not fast enough to pick up sand, but if I throw a handful into the air, it blows away in a cloud.

"Stand here, will you, Jim?" I ask. Jim faces away from the breeze. "Put your feet about a foot apart." I scoop out a handful of bone-dry clay from the bank of the wash and roll it into loose dust with my fingers. Then I walk in back of Jim, perhaps three feet behind him. "What I want you all to see is this: when I throw this dust into the wind, watch its speed as it approaches Jim, and then as it passes between his ankles, and again as it emerges in front of him."

I stoop and gently throw my handful of dust into the air, a foot above the ground. It blows toward Jim's ankles at the speed of the breeze coursing along the wash. Just as the cloud begins to converge near Jim's ankles, it speeds up, then suddenly races between them in a flash. When it emerges in front of his ankles and spreads, it slows again to desert-breeze speed.

"Do it again, Ken. Pam couldn't see it," a student asks. Jim and I repeat the demonstration.

"What you are seeing is Bernoulli's theorem in action. Daniel Bernoulli, one of those unfathomable geniuses that come along now and then, a Swiss scientist of the 1700s, discovered it. It's what holds airplanes up. I think it makes sand dunes pile up at certain places.

Beyond that, it regulates where spiders build their webs and how desert plants conserve their water."

I explain: "What's going on is this: when the wind blows, it becomes squeezed between Jim's ankles, pushing through very fast. The air gets going so fast between his ankles that it actually becomes rarefied—the molecules move farther apart, creating a partial vacuum, an area of lower pressure. That's what holds airplanes up, when air passes over the top of an airplane's wings—the difference in air pressure between the top of the wing and the bottom."

These relationships are fairly slippery for most of us—I didn't get it right away myself. "Shall I do that once again?" I ask.

"Yes," comes a voice. And so we go over the profound relationship another time. Then we move on.

The Kelso Dunes seem to me to have been piled up, in large part by a gigantic Bernoulli effect. I point out two little outlier mountains, one on either side of the stretch of flat desert a mile or so upwind of the westernmost edge of the dunes.

"Think of those mountains as a giant version of Jim's ankles."

"The prevailing northwest winds sweep down the broad Mojave River valley," I say, pointing beyond the dunes. "They pick up sand and speed up between the two little mountains, sweeping the desert between them all but clean. Then they move upslope and dump their load, right here—and voila! the Kelso Sand Dunes."

"That theory, I should tell you, is my own notion, and you mustn't simply accept it as is. File it, think about it."

Steve sits on the bank of the arroyo, watching the demonstration, and then tells his own story to the students gathered around. "Wind and water. For the plants, no two things are more important out here," Steve says. He explains that the two dictate the form of bushes, the time a grass plant sprouts from the soil, the shape of leaves, the kind of roots. He holds up a branch from a wild heliotrope, a hairy-stemmed desert shrub.

"The hairiness of this desert plant," he explains, "slows air movement right at the surface of the leaves and stem and reduces the wind's ability to suck out moisture. And the plant doesn't stop there—the breathing pores open inside deep pits where the wind can't blow away moisture." We can barely see the pits as little dots of dark, but it is no problem to see and feel the hairiness that cloaks the plant's leaves.

As we walk the wash, Steve points out the great cable-like roots of the Mormon tea and catclaw bushes that have been exposed by flash floods. "These roots are what tap the deep water table. Other plants, such as the barrel cactus, do it differently. They have shallow roots all around them. It's amazing how little rain is needed for them draw it in and store it in those heavy stems of theirs."

Steve leads us down onto the wash where the still-damp sand supports a cluster of bright green wild rhubarb plants, a species I've dubbed "the refrigerator plant." An anachronism on the desert, this plant of broad green leaves, a foot and a half high, stands out from the gray-green foliage of the other desert vegetation.

"Feel its leaves," Steve suggests. They are downright cold from evaporative cooling. Such a plant can live just as long as moisture from winter and spring rains remains in the sand and can be used without limit.

The rhubarb, he explains, produces flowers and goes to seed very rapidly. Then, when the sand dries at the end of spring, the plants wither into fragile brown remnants, which break and scatter. "As the plants dry up, their seeds are cast by the hundreds. Look at their seeds. They are built like little pinwheels."

I strip some seeds from a drying rhubarb stem and toss them into the air. They catch the wind and dance away across the sand at wind speed. Wind and water! I think.

As we drive up the desert road leading to the Granite Cabin, Steve stops the bus, and points to a bright green patch among huge house-sized boulders, close to the base of the mountain. "That's Cove Spring," he says. "The green is a grove of Fremont cottonwoods. When we hike there, you'll see that the trees live on the banks of a little desert stream that, after only a few hundred yards, sinks into the sand. Those cottonwoods are what we botanists call 'phreatophytes'—plants that send their roots into permanent water. You'll also see that their leaves are as thin as paper and bright green, much different than the thick, furry leaves you've already seen on desert plants. That's because the cottonwood leaves don't have to resist water loss when the wind blows, and don't heat much in the sun because evaporation cools them. There's always more water down in the sand."

Wind and water—the phrase runs through my mind again.

Back at the cabin, we sit at the edge of the deck, legs swinging in relaxation, looking east into the darkening sky. The sun has just set at our backs and a broad, hazy, blue band stretches across the eastern skyline.

"That's the shadow of the earth on its own atmosphere," says Joe. "That band will grow deeper because the earth is spinning away from the sun." I sit there in silence, trying to soak up this cosmic view of the world. It turns my mind outward, away from the smaller things of the day.

"I can think of a few things the wind does, global things, that we didn't come close to today," I say. I talk of collecting insects from barren little San Nicolas Island, far off the coast of Southern California. "To an insect, San Nicolas is an oceanic island. Very few fluttery insects have been found living there. I didn't find any." I note that the fluttery kind are simply blown out to sea to drown, and that's why such islands end up with mostly ground-dwelling species.

"Don't tell my story," says Paul, anxiousness in his voice. He has asked to present a talk on the MacArthur-Wilson theory of why little islands have far fewer species than big ones. I put my hand over my mouth at my near-gaffe.[1]

My compadres seem lulled by the delicious warm air and the closing of the day. They let me ramble on.

"I remember another wind thing. It was late spring, and I was out on an oceanographic cruise, about 20 miles off the Southern California coast. A Santa Ana wind was blowing. Those winds are the hot ones, the ones that blow from inland. They heat up by compression when their air slides down the mountains toward the sea. The air over the sea turns brown, and the sunsets are spectacular."

"What really struck me, though," I say, "were the birds."

I tell of little warblers fluttering to our rigging and of an exhausted flicker that tried to reach us, but pinwheeled into the ocean instead. A little wake wave curled over the bird and it was gone.

"I figured that what we were seeing were birds just off the nest, being blown offshore." Normally such birds would have made their first flights and settled into the chaparral or forest in search of a vacant place to live. I concluded that their fates, once they settled onto the wild land, must have remained only a little better than those of the hapless birds flying out over the ocean. There's only so much space in the Mountain Time matrix. Ever since that time, I've carried a clear sense of the harsh imperatives that animals and plants face on every wild mountain, the wind only one factor of the equation.

Talk turns to high-altitude winds and how high up living things go. I mention a scientist who fastened little traps to the wingtips on his small plane. He flew as high as he could, and still he caught spiders, rafting on their own silk. I mention the reports of mountaineers telling of geese flying over the Himalayas, at perhaps 27,000 feet of elevation. They even honk up here. Imagine honking at 27,000 feet!

Someone mentions hearing that spores had been found in the stratosphere and that they might even be shed off into space.

Joe, bringing us up short again, says, "Did you know it's very, very hot in the layers above the stratosphere—the ionosphere?"

Could a spore, we wonder, make it into outer space through such a barrier? It seems unlikely.

Walking on the earth, as we did that day on Woods Mountain and down the washes leading to the Kelso Dunes, allows one to watch the sky, but not to know it. One must somehow be up there with the birds and the spiders, the clouds and the wind. I decide that I need to begin a natural history of the sky, to somehow fly with the birds and soak up the gestalt of the atmosphere. For a nonfeathered, 190-pound man, the best approach seems to go aloft in a glider. I think immediately of my nephew Jim Norris, whose personalized automobile license plate announces: "Eye Soar," and resolve to give Jim a call upon our return.

My flight with Jim is out of Minden, Nevada, in a valley noted for its soaring weather. The precipitous Sierra Nevada mountains define the valley's west boundary, and the 9,000-foot Pine Nut Mountains rise to the east. When we arrive, the air over the valley is clear and dust devils churn the desert floor. A day later, the weather has begun to change.

My turn comes just as a low-lying stratus deck has begun to slip over the valley, an apron in advance of a Pacific storm. Vertical air movement is about to go tame, and it is probably just as well. For me, there are enough first-time things to sense and put in their places without real adventure.

We hurry. Soon the clouds will cool the desert and damp down the rising, bubbling columns of warm air. Already gone are the largest castles of thermal air, the great, roiling, cumulus clouds.

The obvious dawns on me: neither pilots nor birds see the air. They both learn to read the clouds and the land below; and, from such experience, they know where the air will lift them or where it will be so rough they can be tumbled willy-nilly.

As we stride toward the glider, off the runway a quarter of a mile over the Sarcobatus Flats, turkey vultures circle and bank, spiraling upward. I can see them tip their wings, rocking, turning, correcting. They have found a column of updrafting warm air.

The towrope is stretched to us and snapped into the nose of the glider where Jim can release it at will. We are strapped into our seats, the glider still tilted onto one of its long albatross wings, a remarkably slim, 54-foot span of precise carbon fiber and resin. The tow plane revs forward and, in a very few yards, the dancing glider rights and lifts off. It seems almost animate, waiting its chance to spring into the air where it belongs.

Once in the air, we circle upward under tow, westward toward the Sierra scarp, and then around to the east. The tow plane ahead of us rises and dips fifty feet or more relative to us. It moves in slow, heaving leaps, a dynamic you can never sense fully from a single plane. The air is revealed as a churning, invisible surround.

When we are so high above the observers on the ground that we have faded to distant glints of reflected sun, Jim lets us go. The cable whips and snakes away. We buck and turn sharply, one wing pointed steeply downward over the flank of the Pine Nut Range. Jim locates a jitter in the air. Then bigger bumps begin heaving us up and, just as quickly, drop us. He circles tightly. We watch the variometer, which records vertical velocity. We rise a respectable 500 feet per minute—the roily air of a little thermal is pushing us up.

I wish for an eagle to come alongside and share the air with us, but none does. I have been told they are imperious, going on their way, looking you over. Red-tailed hawks and white pelicans, on the other hand, can be feisty, Jim tells me. They sometimes contest a glider's right to be up there.

Gliders always fly with their noses angling downward in a glide, and I suppose gliding hawks do, too. I've never thought of that. The only way gliders go up is on rising air, and all they can do is glide toward earth; the hawk, in contrast, can always avoid disaster by flapping its wings or by settling onto earth without benefit of an airfield.

I crack a little vent on the side of the canopy to cool the warm air around us. I think I can smell the desert vegetation. Jim says, yes, he's smelled the land many times. Once, when he flew over an orange grove, the sweet perfume was cloying and powerful.

Chip Garner, a competitive soaring pilot, put it this way: "Smell a feedlot thermal, smoke thermal, decomposing dump-stuff thermals. Uvalde thermals have cornhusks in them. Fall thermals with leaves. Plastic-bag thermals, trash thermals. A good thermal has a solid feel when you crash into it. Smell the hot dust when you are low."[2]

I think of vultures. They circle upward in a thermal and then fly to the next and the next. When the odor of decay or death is sensed, they swoop and tip away to locate the dead animal upon which they will feed. Their ability to smell the faintest of odors wafted on the air seems to provide a compass of almost incomprehensible sensitivity.

I recall a time when I stood in our sheep pasture deep under a canopy of oaks. Below me on the grass lay a dying sheep, fluids from her stomach welling out through her mouth. At that moment, two turkey vultures circled low over our meadow and settled like kites at the edge of the oaks, folding their wings with a shimmy. Seeing me, they hesitated in surprise, then turned to lift off and circle away. Before she was even dead! What almost infinitesimal cues the vultures must have picked from the air. At first, they surely couldn't see her. Or me. It had to be the odor of impending death they had sensed. How little we humans sense of the things that must be common concourse in the sky!

The Pacific Ocean storm continues to sweep in, sliding up the sloping Sierra block to the west and pouring over the mountain scarp above Minden, like invisible water over a dam. In rebound from the valley beneath, a longitudinal ridge of air forms parallel to the Sierra face, one that I cannot see, but Jim knows is there. A good pilot can soar for a hundred miles down such a ridge.

Above the Sierra crest is a line of lenticular clouds, produced by high-velocity winds. There's great lift for gliders over both ridges and lenticular clouds. Pilots and birds know the signs. Hawks, eagles, and white pelicans are common passengers up there. I look a thousand feet above the Sierra to its row of lenticular clouds, each shaped a bit like the cross-section of a flattened airplane wing, planed smooth by the storm's winds.

Jim talks of his experience of soaring a lenticular cloud. At 15,000, feet he had topped one and slipped just over its upwind margin, crabbing across at an angle, heading into the wind blast, but being blown over the cloud. He glided down very close. Fifty feet below him, the cloud top was planed clean, pure white, and gleaming, wind-sculpted smooth. Then he soared down a seemingly limitless, curved plain of purest white, each detail defined sharply in the brilliant, high-altitude light. A gleaming aura glowed around his glider.

I want Jim to find a lenticular cloud for us, but it is not to be. Our time in the glider is already at an end. I know I have only just begun a naturalist's penetration of the world of the sky. I will be back.

The Wind and the Sky 53

This sky we've entered for just a moment moves as an invisible sheet over the land, swirling against the mountains, and from its clouds, the rains and snow fall to begin the rivers. One such river would be the Field Quarter's next exploration.

Lenticular clouds over the Providence Mountains, Mojave Desert.

UC Santa Cruz Natural History Field Quarter 1988 students preparing to launch at the Mattole River, Humboldt County, California.

Chapter 4:
The Most Elegant Thing on Earth

It is near dusk as we pull into the Albert W. Way Campground on the Mattole River in rainy, forested northwestern California. We are here specifically to learn how rivers work. We peer nervously at the sky. Dark clouds roil over the ridge, and there is the feel of rain in the air. We are always worried about rain when heading for this coast. The entire class has to sleep in tents for eight days and cook outdoors. Storms sweep in up here as if on a conveyor belt.

We've barely braked to a stop when a roly-poly figure, with a face like Santa Claus and a great, flowing, white beard, jumps into the bus unbidden and announces, "I'm Hawkeye. Welcome to the Mattole."

Class members peer at him like frightened rabbits as he strides up and down the aisle within inches of them. Thanks to an earlier briefing, they know exactly who he is: Dr. Vandenburg, the patron saint of field trips.

Dr. Vandenburg was first discovered by my field companion Dick Zweifel, back when we were fellow graduate students. Vandenburg would appear as a scruffy old man with a white beard, proclaimed Dick, and if we saw him, it meant we would have a good trip. We usually managed to see him.

As our lore had it, our imaginary Dr. Vandenburg had once stalked the halls of the California Academy of Sciences in San Francisco. Then, in 1922, he disappeared, to be found days later, his bowler hat and umbrella propped by the door of the basement where the Galapagos tortoise shells are kept. He, in striped pants, braces, and arm garters, was curled up inside the carapace of a Hood Island tortoise. When Vandenburg was removed from the shell, Dick told me, he weighed only twelve pounds. He had been "etherealized" into a spirit whose sole function was taking care of field naturalists. Never mind that a very real scientist, Dr. John Van Denburgh, the authority on western United States reptiles and amphibia, worked in the same institution. As you can see, he spelled his name differently.

I had discovered that Dr. Vandenburg was watching over Field Quarter trips, too, and that there was much more to interpreting his visitations than Dick or I had ever imagined. By many subtle signs he would indicate what the trip would be like. Blue pants and prepare for rain; a trimmed accountant's beard and bureaucratic difficulties were coming; red somewhere and it was going to be hot. If he was really scruffy, with a flowing white beard, we could bank a fine carefree time together, with lots of good songs. Thus Hawkeye's appearance here, within seconds of our arrival, bodes well.

"Can I sing you a song?" he asks. Someone assents, and Dr. V. bursts into a quite beautiful version of "Toora Loora Loora," in a fine Irish tenor.

"Aren't you afraid of the rain?" he asks.

"Yes," I reply, quite seriously.

"Don't worry," says Hawkeye. "I have special connections. I'll be back." And with that he steps off the bus and walks off into the trees. Honest.

Next morning, we inflate our rafts and slide the big aluminum canoes into the river. Steve and I check the students into their boats to be sure there are experienced river runners in each, and we make sure everyone is wearing a life vest. The other half of the class goes with Larry to set up camp near the river mouth.

The Mattole is generally gentle, classed as a 0.5 to 1.5 river. Even so, for the uninitiated almost any flowing water holds unseen hazards. A canoe can upset, go crossways on a rock, and, even in such a small river as the Mattole, refuse to budge. Or the river can sluice a boat into the overhanging willows to pinion it among the branches. It can be a devilish, dangerous job to pull it loose.

"Can you row, David?" I ask.

"Yes, I've had lots of experience," he replies.

So David goes in raft No. 1, and, boat by boat, the students slide into the river, bowling off downstream. Gales of excited voices fade into the hiss of water over stones, and the boats disappear around the first bend.

Not long afterward, my canoe begins to close on the raft ahead, which is spinning rapidly in the current, totally out of control, laughter rising from the oarsmen collected in a mass of arms and legs in the bottom. It is David's boat. Acting like traffic cops, we pull them onto a gravel bar.

"David, I thought you said you could row!" I bark in asperity.

"I can, only I didn't know you had to use two oars!" comes David's reply. David had been a member of a rowing club where he rowed in a shell, from only one side.

"I know how to row with two oars," says Melanie quietly, so she takes David's place.

We glide on, swept into a sensation that is the unique property of river runners, of sliding downward as if the canyon itself is greased, of moving through a slow-moving motion picture. We look into a copse of cottonwoods and see a deer standing there. In moments we are by, before the deer decides to bolt. The scene changes to a lonely cabin with smoke swirling from its chimney, then that, too, is gone, and a huge, beetling rock looms at the edge of deep water. We slide through a swirling pool flecked with foam and into the open again. There we pass a family of ducks, paddling in a line at the edge of reeds. It never grows dull on a river, even such a gentle one as the Mattole.

We enter a steep-walled canyon and grind to a halt at a little pocket beach, all shingled at the water's edge with flat stones—the kind that are good for skipping. We walk to a sunny spot on the warm sand.

I begin my first sermon on rivers: "There are two ways a mountain can thrust upward above the surrounding earth." The first way, I tell them, is when the core of a mountain is built from below, deep in the plastic mantle of the earth itself. Such mountains are made of "light" rocks, such as granite—the skim from atop the plastic magma—and so they rise upward like corks.

"On the Mattole, we have begun to float through another kind of mountain. Our mountain has been squeezed up between deep faults—like a melon seed between fingers."

I tell my young voyager friends to imagine a perfect mountain, its peak faceted with sheer faces of rock, nearly vertical cliffs reaching into the sky. At the bases of these cliffs, I tell them, lay perfect cones of fractured stones that have leapt from the high rock faces. There are chutes where avalanches have swept everything before them at express train speed. Further downslope, my imaginary mountain curves outward, less and less steep, until outside of the mountain's lowest hills, it runs almost flat, and then its rivers empty into the sea.

I draw my mountain in the sand with a stick. "I envision a single, simple, mathematical curve that describes the shape of the slope from the mountain's peak to the sea." Only two factors, I tell them, form my magic curve—gravity and the movement of water. At the highest crags, gravity alone propels rocks and gravel in long arcs through the air, after being cracked loose by ice or etched free by water-borne acids. I tell them how, lower down my mountain, where streams begin to gather, the power of water increasingly takes over, to roll, fly, and creep boulders, stones, gravel, mud, and sand toward the sea. Remarkably, if you average out the river's speed, everywhere on that curved face of the mountain the water would run at much the same speed, the high rills about the same as the main river.

I describe how the highest water is caught by the crags from the racing clouds to flow in sheets over rock faces and gather into rills, which then join to form streams. "The streams merge again and again until a river appears. As the river reaches the flood plain beyond the base of the mountain, it becomes a single river wandering back and forth." It runs, I say, across a sloping, bouldery plain and finally slides into the ocean itself.

"There are other such watersheds on all faces of every mountain and all carve inward together, according to the dictates of their magic curves. It is the tending of this curve that is every river's business."

I let them think for a moment before going on. Then I describe how rivers tend to respond to keep the shape of their magic curves intact. A river will carve, if need be, or fill in to reestablish its magic curve. It seems as if the river is thinking, but it isn't.

With my stick, I draw two curves moving into the mountain from two sides, meeting and toppling the high crags, cutting into the substance of the mountain until all that is left are low hills.

"The river's time is not our time," I say. "It can be almost unimaginably longer. It may take thousands of years, or three times that, for a boulder from the crest of a mountain to move the length of a mountain's curve."

The treelike pattern of rills, streams, and rivers, I tell them, planes back the mountain everywhere, changing its height, but keeping the magic curve roughly intact. The whole process, I explain, is a little like sharpening a pencil. Pencil shavings or river rock, both are cuttings to be carried away and dumped; both the mountain and the pencil are consumed in the process.

"Here on the Mattole, this planing down of a mountain does not happen smoothly. The earth we sit on is fissured with earth faults and grinds between deep moving sheets of rock, the earth's tectonic plates. Earthquakes are common up here."

I take them again through time. With the jolting thrust of each new quake, the magic curve is disrupted again and again. The river automatically responds, cutting in a new pulse until the curve is restored. Then the mountain lies fallow again, to be cut anew after the next quake, leaving the mountain's face stair-stepped.

I describe how rare, great storms sometimes roll in to overwhelm the mountain's equilibrium and send countless tons of rock and soil sluicing down the slopes. Such debris, I say, moves in heedless landslides that tear deep into the rock of the mountain, carrying the skim of life with them, jumbled trees and shrubs twisted this way and that.

I explain that, focused as we are on the work of mountain building and flowing water, we must know that most of the carving of our curved mountain slope is done in a simpler way. More than 90 percent of the mountain surface is simply dirt and rock, not rill and river. So the first prime movers are raindrops, or hail and ice, working on the crystals of rock that have been loosened by chemical weathering. The simple impact of raindrops may be the most powerful force of all. The splats of water into mud, which send brown droplets flying downslope, I explain, are what carve a mountain.

"We're on just a middlin'-sized mountain. The King Range is only a little over 4,000 feet high, and it is split into several slices by faults and scarred by foresters who have cut away the protective cover of trees. Even so, we should be able to piece together this mountain's story."

I stand up, stretch, and add: "As we continue down the river, I want to show you some of the finer details of the ways rivers work. I call them 'rules for rivers.' They aren't rules, really, but they help us understand what happens as a river works to maintain that ideal curve I mentioned. See if you can think of rules I miss."

"My first river rule is this: *Every rock has its number.* Let's walk off our sandbar to the water's edge, and I'll explain it to you."

The beach is plated with flat rocks, like big stone coins. I tell my companions to look closely at the stones before we disturb anything. I show them that these stones are arranged like shingles, each overlapping the next one downstream. The term for that, I say, is *imbricate*. They arrange themselves that way, I explain, because they are governed by the first river rule.

"When the stream carries a stone to this shore, the stone spins in the current, flipping over and over. It moves downstream, just so long as there is sufficient current to carry it. Then, as it moves away from the main current, it will spin into the last orientation that can move it. The lifting force just capable of moving the rock is the rock's number."

"The stone then moves into quieter water and settles," I continue, "overlapping the next stone below it. That overlap cancels the last effective lift the river can provide. The stone, you see, is held in the stall position, a lower number than can fly it."

"I've been told that one can hear that last adjustment of settling rocks—clack, clack, clack, clack—as the stones settle seriatim onto the bottom, overlapping one another."

"So, the stone's number defines when and where in a stream a rock will be deposited. You can read a stream bottom, or an outwash plain, or a gravel bank by knowing this rule. We'll try that in a minute."

"Flat stones, such as these on this beach, illustrate one factor in moving a rock downstream," I tell them. "Their very flatness turns them into little, submerged, airplane wings. The current running past them creates substantial lift, and they can fly a little in a current. Most of the rounder rocks in a river don't obtain as much lift, and typically they roll or, at best, bounce along the bottom. In a good storm right here on this bank, you would hear the boulders crash against each other as they move downstream."

We dig into a gravel bank to see if the fine gravel is laid down imbricate like the flat stones. Sure enough, though not so neatly arranged as the flat stones, the gravel proves to be imbricate too. We can tell the direction from which the now-disappeared stream had come, because we know the imbrication faces down-current like that of roof shingles.

We scale a few more stones, and Josh, with two monumental heaves, sends a couple skipping clear across the river. It is about the best stone-skipping country I have ever encountered, given the enormous ammunition supply, so we spend a few more minutes challenging Josh before we slide our boats back into the river again, mulling over the simplicities of the watershed.

"Let's head for River Rule No. 2," I say.

Steve and I race ahead in our canoes, the inflatables coming up behind. Downstream a mile or so, we nose our canoes onto a sunny gravel bar across the river from a tributary stream that enters the main channel. Fifty yards upstream, the tributary tumbles over a little five-foot waterfall.

"Lunchtime," I announce. We lie there in the warm sand, eating our sandwiches. The cliffs far back, the little waterfall, a field of new grass across the river, alder and willow groves lining the banks, flickering spring leaves, and our sunny sandbank define our little stage. Two mergansers fly by, going upstream low to the water; tiny newly transformed toads hop over the sand around us; and primordial-looking dragonflies hover and rush at each other over the horsetail rushes.

After lunch, I feel another sermon coming on. "That little waterfall strikes me as odd. Do you feel its oddness?" I ask. "Rivers react against such oddness," I tell them. "They concentrate their forces at such spots, then dig, swirl, and carve away until the oddness is gone, until they carve down to their magic curve."

Greg, who knows his physics, puts it simply: "You mean the river spends its kinetic energy at places such as waterfalls?"

"Exactly," I reply. Then, using the teacher's ancient strategy of shunting the tough stuff onto students, I ask: "Can you tell us what you mean by kinetic energy?"

Greg is ready for me. His definition goes like this: There are two energy states for any body—potential and kinetic. Potential energy is embodied in that rock balanced at the edge of the cliff. If the rock is pushed over, that energy becomes kinetic. The force is the force of gravity. The water going over that waterfall is in a kinetic energy state.

"Right on," I say.

I explain that the second of the "rules for rivers" relates to kinetic energy and how it is dissipated. It says: *Rivers tend to avoid storing energy.* Any time water goes downhill, it spends its kinetic energy as it falls, often in moving something.

I go on to explain that living processes don't always behave that way. Much energy in living systems is stored, usually in chemical form, like fat. And rivers do find themselves with much temporarily stored energy in the form of lakes or ponds, but the condition doesn't last. Stored energy is something the river ceaselessly works to release. It represents a little blip above the energy state of the magic curve.

"That's why that little waterfall seems strange to me, out of place. Something has happened over there."

I tell them a little story as we lie there on the sandbank: "I once tried to oppose a stream. I tried to build a little check dam across the creek below my house to impound water for our farm. Right away, the river went around the ends of my dam, almost toppled a big alder tree, flowed over, and swirled back under the concrete I had poured. It was almost as if the creek was angry. Three months later, my dam had been undermined so thoroughly that the creek flowed right under it, peaceful as could be. My concrete 'dam' stood a foot above the smoothly flowing water, balanced on the reinforcing bars

I had driven into the stream bottom. The river was reestablishing its golden curve."

"Before my dam was destroyed by Laguna Creek, I had slowed the stream behind it, and debris had begun to pile up in my new pond. The river just above the pond slowed a little too, and more gravel and stones piled up there. This prematurely deposited sediment was shaping a new riverbed curve."

"So, let's make a third rule for rivers: *In a river at peace with itself, tributaries enter the main stream at the river's level.*"

Jackie, sitting way at the end of the sandbar, sees the explanation. She tells everyone that the little waterfall goes over a man-made dam, which she can see from where she sits. I walk over and confirm her finding.

"I'll bet the farmer of the field above was trying to save his land, and he built a dam," I muse. "I hope he has better luck than I did."

"There is another truly important river rule I'll mention before we go back on the Mattole again. When my dam was undermined, the stream not only excavated under the dam, but in the resulting rush of water, the stream eroded tons of gravel at the upper head of my pond and sent all of it downstream in a rush. So, the fourth of our 'rules for rivers' is this: *Anytime a river overcomes an obstacle, the effects go both upstream and down to restore the mountain's curve.*"

"For civilized man, this rule is a powerful one," I say. "If you live at the mercy of a watershed, you should look both upstream and downstream if you want to know the damage a river can create. A watershed is an entire, interconnected, interacting thing, from its beginnings up high on the mountain to the ocean. Thinking about just one part of it is never enough."

Up ahead, I know, we will soon encounter big rocks, a couple of them three stories tall, right in the middle of the stream course. Around each one of them, we will find a deep pool, a place where the river scours deep. There the river is busy undercutting each rock with its gravel and stone teeth. It will be a long time in human terms before the river wins, and all that time the stream will bend aside around the rock, to spew out its load of cuttings onto a debris bar downstream. But, given the river's version of time, the rock will go and it won't be long.

Ann Marie, noting the entering tributary, suggests that the river becomes bigger as it flows toward the sea, and so we evolve Rule No. 5: *Rivers are the sum of their tributaries.* "A big river involves a huge amount of energy, vastly more than a little mountain stream. So a big river can move things a little one can't, and if a work of man gets in its way, it can cause enormous destruction. That's what Ann Marie's rule tells us."

A chilly afternoon breeze had picked up. We hurry back onto the river to rendezvous with Larry before wet clothes and cold air can get the better of us. The river carries us down a colonnade of tall douglas-firs and alders, some leaning clear over the stream, branches meshed together above. The water runs black. Shafts of slanting afternoon light play down through the broken canopy to flicker on greenish, river-bottom stones.

We nudge into the riverbank at the little village of Petrolia and pull our craft onto a sandbar. Steve leads us up the bank to the welcome warmth of the Hideaway Bar, a big, galvanized Quonset hut built next to the river. They serve nachos and draft and the finest sandwiches on the river. Knowing my student friends' penurious ways, I am ready for them: "The first check's on me. I'm trying to buy friendship." I see grateful looks flash between them—there is scarcely a nickel among my river friends.

Soon Larry comes in, having driven up from the river's mouth in the bus. He and the next group of river runners have already built us a camp on a grassy bench down close to the river mouth. With pride, he tells me about the outhouse they have built. He explains that it has a canvas roof and signal flags to let potential users know when it is occupied.

Larry drives us down the river-edge road and onto the broad gravel bar near the river mouth, the rubbley remnant of great storms past, made of stones of many sizes, interspersed with pebbles and sand.

"The number of that boulder must be pretty high," Jeff notes, looking at a four-foot-diameter monster. He reflects with awe about the powerful current required to roll it all the way down the mountain to where we stand.

"I doubt that is what happened," I comment. "Big rocks and most of the larger stones of the river seem to be moved long distances in mud flows. Mud is nearly the same density as the rock, so the big boulders almost float. But mudflows are rare events; hundreds of years may intervene between them. Perhaps only when a fire has denuded the watershed and all the water comes at once do they happen. But they do."

We walk across the bar and then wade the broad, shallow river to our camp. Already a driftwood fire blazes, big tarps are stretched between willows, and sweet Alisa strums quietly on her guitar. Later she will become a noted folksinger. A dotting of little tents shares the meadow.

Here on the Mattole, we all know we have to prepare for rain. Larry has located the tents on the highest ground that can be found, and each is ditched carefully.

"Looks wonderful, Larry," I say.

Next morning, Steve drives Larry and me to Petrolia. He returns to camp to take the camp crew out botanizing the hills, while Larry and I navigate the lower river.

"Life vests, everybody!" I emphasize the biggest hazard here: the willows. One by one, we peel off into the current. Not long afterward, the river breaks out onto the broad floodplain and into the welcome sun. It begins to wander from bank to bank in half-mile arcs through a vast accumulation of erosional debris from the mountain.

As the slope of the riverbed lessens further, the bends begin to tighten until they twist like a snake in meandering curves. We are far down the mountain's curve now. Larry and I nose our canoe onto a sloping sandbar located on the inner bend of a tight loop of the river. On the outer bend, the riverbank is an abrupt, curved cliff, dropping straight into deep water. The other boats soon beach alongside ours. We clamber atop the bar.

The warm sun is almost enough to make us take a snooze on the sand, right then and there. But there is still a lot of river yet to run, and right before us is a curious story.

"These meandering curves and this floodplain are a remarkable energy-compensation system." I tell them. "At a low-water time, the stream meanders, flowing slowly around each sharp curve. In a storm, when the river is bank-full, swirling and tearing along, it shaves away the bends and straightens out the channel."

I explain that, as the high-water river swings along, it spins off eddies that cut into the vertical banks, like the one opposite us. It can be dangerous to take a boat too close to such banks at swift-water time. They can become so undercut that they crash into the river—tons and tons of soil, gravel, and rocks in a single violent slump. I tell them of drifting along on another such river, the lower Colorado, where over and over we river runners heard the hollow boom of slumps, like distant cannon fire. "That undercutting and slumping is how a river moves its channel," I tell them. On a broad floodplain such as this, the channel will snake back and forth, all over the place."

We sit there envisioning what would happen when a storm hits. We build a picture of every little stream and rill upriver adding its contribution to the lazy stream before us. In hours, it will become a muddy juggernaut, overflowing its banks. A hundred-year storm would fill the half-mile-wide valley with mud, rocks, gravel, and water, bank to bank.

"That's the reason for there being a floodplain and for not building a house here," I note.

A vision of the dynamic river—sometimes powerful, sometimes a gentle pussycat of a stream—emerges from our spinnings of the wheel. We stitch together a vision of a mountain being carved down over time and carried toward the sea. We come to conceive of the slow, sinuous Mattole as a sleeping giant, waiting for its next pulse.

On down the river we go, looping around bend after bend, scaring up egrets and sandpipers who stalk the water's edge. It is a lovely drift in the welcome sun. Finally, down where the Mattole at last slides into the ocean, we stop again, this time alongside a mudflat. The surf, just out of sight over the cobbley beach berm ahead, pounds and spurts high. We can hear the beach stones hiss as the sea sluices over them, then their clatter as the water recedes.

To me, mudflats are beautiful things. They glisten in the sun; you can take off your shoes and wiggle your toes in them; crabs can dig burrows in them, carrying up little balls of mud held between the tips of their two claws. Such crabs always seem so serious to me. When they carry mud, they hold their claw tips together, elbows out, like a mother rocking a baby.

I ask my companions to look down into the now fifteen-foot-deep, clear river. About halfway to the bottom, the water somehow changes character. We seemed to be looking through a bad sheet of glass, like one of those very old windowpanes from a nineteenth-century house.

"Anybody know what we are seeing?" I ask. Silence, except for the breeze. "We need to sample the deep water, below what looks like window glass." From my pack I pull a corked bottle and a long piece of twine. "With this string and the bottle, I think we can sample that deep water from the bank. If I tie a rock on the bottle and a string on the cork... ."

"Let me swim down. It'll be easier," suggests Brock. In moments he strips to his shorts. I hand him the bottle, and he dives ten feet down into the river. He surfaces and hands me the full bottle, shaking off water like a spaniel.

"Taste it," I suggest. Leigh Ann tries it and pronounces it salty.

"That's why the mudflats are here," I say. "Dense seawater spilled over the berm by sea waves has slid under the lighter freshwater of the river. The interface between the two layers is the wavy glass we are seeing." I explain that the particles of clays are very small and don't become rounded the way river stones do. They're platy and are simply suspended in the roily water as the stream moves along. They settle out where freshwater meets salt because of electrical charges on the clay. "The result is mudflats at the mouths of many rivers that reach the sea," I say.

We walk at the edge of the river, over to the shining mud. As Larry and I pull our canoe along the river's edge, we encounter the opening phases of what will become known in Field Quarter lore as the "Mud Festival."

Erica and her pals had been wiggling their feet in the mud, releasing the water trapped in its layers. In minutes they had found themselves at the center of a lovely bathtub filled to the brim with purest liquid mud. They are up to their knees and going deeper as we pass. One or two have already taken the plunge and are glistening brown from head to toe, only eyes showing, as if through a mask.

Convincing myself they are in no danger, I comment as we go by: "Have fun, mud people." I know that they won't be trapped as they could be in quicksand. They can always lie down on the bank and wriggle out and that should be no problem for any of them. Larry and I continue back to camp to check on dinner preparations and hear how Steve has fared on his terrestrial ramblings.

Two days later, the rains sweep in. We watch the river, brown and roily, rise toward our grassy bench. The tents with their ditches stay dry; the outhouse proves a great protection and solace.

We had been able to run the Mattole and learn a little about the Most Elegant Thing on Earth—a river's system and the mountain range down which it runs. Elegant, I say, but also heedless of the skim of life laid over it. We had perceived that the watershed's imperatives spring from the rising mountains and the track of storms moving around the earth. Ultimately, humans can do little to evade the forces involved. It is most important for us to understand the rules of rivers. And those of mountains, too. We are the ones who must alter our behavior. Rivers won't. They have no brains.

After the drive home and a week in Santa Cruz for rest, research, and re-supply, we will load our bus, Old Blue, for another adventure. We will head for another river, Big Creek, to start our exploration of the ways in which life, in all its complication, lies like a blanket over the hills and will clean a river until it shines like blue-green crystal.

Ken Norris and student studying sand and pebbles on the Mattole River bank.

Looking across the opening of a canyon at Landels-Hill Big Creek Reserve.

A dragonfly emerges, observed by Field Quarter 1988 students at Redwood Camp, Landels-Hill Big Creek Reserve.

Chapter 5:
The Canyon

This wild canyon is full of 10,000 species—trees and bushes, insects, fungi, birds, reptiles, amphibians, mammals, and all the rest—all living together. So why is it that one can stop at the bank of the stream, listen intently for the sounds of life's activity, and hear nothing but the wind in the boughs above, the susurrant voice of the river, and a jay scolding far off? That's the question that seems to bubble up in my mind whenever I arrive at Big Creek.

The number 10,000 is a figure of speech; I've never tried to count everything that lives in this or any other wild canyon. What matters is that all the numberless lives mesh in a webwork that has somehow obviated the need for most sound and where the world is not degrading before one's eyes. There is perfection in such a place, an equipoise that converts the borings of insects into duff, leaves water and air clear and sweet, and perpetuates life itself.

I sometimes contrast the experience of being at Big Creek with a moment deep in one of our cities. In the city everything is dominated by just one species. There we have walled ourselves off from all wild places. The cacophony of traffic is matched by the sights, sounds, and smells of processes unfinished, the raw feel of energy loose and unchanneled. The air reeks from the bus that has just ground by; lights flood from hundreds of windows; such soil as has not been locked beneath pavement is acrid with undigested waste. Plants—weeds, we call them—struggle toward the sun from fissures in the pavement, and only a few tattered survivors can be there at all, doused as they are by a parade of dogs on leashes. A single row of trees, each tree with a fierce cheval-de-frise of pointed metal bars protecting it, lines the street edge—a curious statement of perfection lost, yet at the same time almost universally yearned for. The city is run by human clocks, all synchronized. Time has been regimented into a race, with everyone starting together. One can almost hear the crack of the starting pistol.

The many intersections of Mountain Time, so conspicuously absent from the city, are embodied by the wild things of this canyon and their many different life-cadences. With its comprehensible scale, elemental beauty, and quiet throbbing of 10,000 life-forces, Big Creek, on the Big Sur coast, is the real canyon I have in mind when I use the word *canyon* to conceptualize the interlocking, time-and-space matrix of Mountain Time.

And so we are here at Big Creek, to continue our exploration of wild California. We cross the concrete bridge that spans the mouth of the creek, just before it rushes down the cobbley beach and into the ocean waves of the little cove. I tell the students that, when they walk down there, they will have to look hard to tell the harbor seal and sea otter heads from the bulbs of giant kelp.

Steve unlocks and swings open the heavy iron-and-wood gate, then guides the bus down the narrow dirt road to the gravelly parking area. We load our gear into the reserve truck and follow behind as it wends its way up the canyon. The hard-packed dirt road parallels the conjoined waters of Big Creek and Devil's Creek, which have vaulted down the most precipitous mountain slope on the West Coast of the U.S. south of Alaska. Devil's Creek gathers as wet places and tiny springs on the flanks of Cone Peak, 5,155 feet high, before running, in a bit more than three miles (hawk distance), to the Big Sur seacoast. On the way, smaller streams join it to leap and slide in falls and cascades, and when it meets Big Creek, it takes the name of its slightly smaller sister and slows to long lovely runs cupped in smoothed rock, over shoals of washed gravel, until it merges into the Pacific's swell.

Our first camp is in a grove of ancient and scarred redwoods about a mile up the canyon. Layered in their deep fibrous bark is a red and black history of wild fires. In times past, often more than once per decade, fires have crackled and smoked across this forest floor. They lit the branch skirts of some redwoods and sent them flaming into giant torches, leaving apparently dead black spires behind. Not many weeks afterward, though, emerald-green shoots from the living inner bark appeared from within the black charcoal, and soon each snag was transformed into a green candle. With more time still, new branches formed from those buds, and then the fire receded into bark history.

With each such passage, fire, creeping deep and slow in the duff, had invaded the bases of some trees, digging in until it reached live wood, which charred and steamed; but another inch was gone. There is one such tree right in camp, a deep hollow carved in its base so that a precarious living shell is all that supports the ponderous tree towering above. Not far away, one like it has fallen—a middling giant, five and a half feet through its trunk. A long swath of forest floor was flattened by that climactic event, and now the fallen tree slowly merges into the dark soil.

Is such felling the time-pulse of these redwoods? I think not, because it is impossible to kill a redwood forest that way. They sprout again from the roots, and new trees grow. Instead, that span is probably determined by the slow shift of the climate. This canyon will one day harbor no redwoods at all if the incoming storm tracks shift a little to the north and the coastal fogs abate. Then needle drip from the redwoods themselves will no longer be sufficient to keep the soil moist. The southern limit of the coastal redwood species is just a dozen miles down the Big Sur coast. That's at Salmon Creek, which seems little different to my eyes from this canyon, just a little hotter and perhaps a little drier.

Up on Mining Ridge above camp, my wife, Phyl, and I once saw what keeps the redwoods here. Sitting there a thousand feet above the stream, we looked out the deep V of the canyon to the sea beyond. It was covered with cotton-batting clouds, and they came at the shore in enormous fluffy waves, now spilling over the ramparts of the canyon and sweeping up over the trees below, and a dozen minutes later, receding. In the roily air at the front of these huge impalpable waves, black swifts darted and dove, catching insects borne aloft by the misty turbulence.

The stately pulse of the redwood forest may mark the basic life's beat of this canyon; it may be the metronome. Most of the other 10,000 organisms seem to live at more rapid cadences, in counterpoint with the ancient forest. Among the shortest lived are the tiny insects who, dancing in the sun, swarm near the water. Some of these lay eggs in tree bark and repeat their life patterns again and again within a single year.

We reach the camp, set among these redwoods, throw our packs down and fall to organizing our gear. Sleeping bags are laid on soft mattings of fallen redwood fronds; wood is gathered, chopped, and piled for the evening fire; pots are placed on the plank tables of the camp, filled, and then set to simmer on the grills. The smoke from our cookfires is caught in the gentle down-canyon breeze, to skirt through the branches of willow and bay before dispersing over the stream. We set up our Parnassus in the library tent, and I sprinkle a little water on Miss Preen, who sits up and threatens to rap the knuckles of anyone who doesn't bring their books back on time.

For this trip, Larry has moved on, as students must, to graduate school. Now just Steve and I are left to savor our past times together. Ably filling Larry's shoes, however, is Don "Santiago" Usner. Lithe and indefatigable on the trail, he brings a fine combination of Irish bluffness—"get the camp cleaned up, we'll be ready to roll in twenty minutes"—and a deep feel for the land and those around him. The lineage of his Spanish mother reaches back in the New World to the walled plaza of Chimayo in the Rio Grande Valley of New Mexico—then back, perhaps, to the Seven Cities of Cibola. And he has brought his guitar.

In the last fading gold of afternoon, we eat our meal, chatter and joke with each other. As darkness falls, Santiago and Steve build the fire around which log seats are arrayed, and we gather there with firelight dancing on the huge dark columns behind us.

"Tomorrow," I announce, "is the day for soaking up the canyon's gestalt." It is to be our Little Kids Day. I give my little speech: "We all come to this canyon as little kids, but we have a new toy. We now know how to spin the wheel. So we'll use that new way of seeing to carry out the mission of the trip, the 'niche hunt.'"

I tell them to wander the canyon wherever they want, with the aim of picking out a couple of species they might want to spend more time with. "Then sketch in, as well as you can, the plant or animal's place in the life of this canyon. You may want to work in pairs, or even groups of three or four. It's up to you. But, it's also okay if you want to work alone."

My advice is to find a species that shows promise of giving up secrets easily. In the days ahead, I will suggest they attempt two—a plant and an animal, or even a linked pair. I point to a dead snag lined with little white ball-shaped fungi. "There is a beetle that lives inside the cavity of that fungus. What's it doing there?"

Plants, I suggest, offer the advantage of easily being seen over and over. They move at a slow pace, via pollen or seeds. "A plant can be sketch-mapped in a few hours. Pick apart a flower and find how it is built. Figure out how the plant spreads its leaves, and what those leaves are like. Examine the place the plant lives, how it is different from other places."

"Animals," I tell them, "are usually a more difficult challenge. One has to psyche out how they move and what they use movement for. What does their behavior mean?" I give them an example. "On the hedgenettle, *Stachys*, that's so common along the entry road in sunny places, a little spider spins its webs under the leaves up high on the plant, near the flowers." They could find out what the spider is doing up there, I suggest, why it rides on the plant, whether the two species range as one, where they range, and whether or not their lives are really linked.

"One of the things I would do, if given a challenge like this, would be to tap into the knowledge that already exists about the player or players in my search. Key them out. Read about their legs and fangs, their leaves and flowers, their webs, their seeds and roots, their color patterns, their life cycles, if you can. Steve and Santiago and I may know some of this stuff, but the Parnassus will likely know more. Don't hesitate to ask. The object is to figure out the creature, and we instructors are here to help as best we can."

I continue: "Most of what is going on in this canyon remains unknown. Many things that you will discover have never been written about by anyone. Imagine that! I have no doubt at all that, around our campfires these next few nights, we will describe some things that nobody in the history of the earth has written down! But don't expect to learn more than just fragments. Don't despair about the intricacy you begin to uncover. You will have the great excitement of original discovery going for you. You'll see!"

"At the end, we'll sit down together, tell our stories, and begin a 'canyon's quilt.' By then we will understand, much better than we do now, how these 10,000 patterns of life fit together. We may even see hints of larger patterns."

"So have a good time out there in Mountain Time," I tell them. "The three of us will try to find you wherever you settle down. We will enjoy sitting with you for a while to hear your tales. Right now, how about a song?"

"The wedding song?" someone asks.

"Okay," I reply. "Are you up for this, Steve?"

"Well, I don't know," he growls, in a voice that I recognize as that of Buffalo Boy.

Santiago hands me his guitar, and I strum out three of my six chords. "I'll take the woman's part—okay, Steve?" No reply; Steve is getting into his role, and it doesn't allow for easy communication. I begin, anyway, in my best falsetto:

"When we goin' to get married, get married, get married, dear Old Buffalo Boy?"

"Well, we'll get married next Tuesday, next Tuesday, next Tuesday—that's, if the weather is good," growls Steve, way off tune.

And so it goes. Several verses later, we come to the climax:

"Who you goin' to bring to the weddin', the weddin', the weddin', dear Old Buffalo Boy?"

"I'm gonna bring my children, my children, my children...."

"Well, I didn't know you had children, had children, had children, dear Old Buffalo Boy!"

"I got five children, five children, five children—six, if the weather is good."

"Well, there ain't gonna be no weddin', no weddin', no wedding'... not even if the weather is good!"

After we finish, I hand Santiago the guitar for a couple of songs. "How about 'The Monkey and the Engineer?'" I ask. And Steve adds, "Then give us one for these mountains: 'The South Coast Is a Wild Coast and Lonely.'"

The guitar goes round the circle, songs new and old are sung, and new contributors emerge to play. The fire burns down to coals, until only two students, journals tipped toward the fading light, remain, and soon they too find their way to tents or sleeping bags. A tiny triangle of stars twinkles through the high treetops. The rest—as it always is deep in a redwood grove—is blackest night.

Next day, it is no minor task for Steve, Santiago, and me to find our student friends. Three have hiked up the precipitous Ridge Trail and are lying spread-eagled under globe lilies, looking up to find out how the pollinators get in. Another group is down on the canyon road, watching hummingbirds pollinate the elegant red columbines. One student, alone, is halfway up a sycamore following ants. A lively cluster of students is down on the beach digging for pseudoscorpions in the dried kelp wrack. From each, we hear tiny stories.

Then I come across Teresa, who tells me about her snake. She is filled with obvious excitement. Sitting on a log that dips into the river, she noticed a little snake stretched out on the trunk right at the water's edge. She identified it as a western aquatic garter snake by looking it up in the field guide. She asks me if I know that they have red and black tongues.

"Yes," I reply, "black tips and a red base." I am familiar with the critter from my several years of work with reptiles. She tells me that this one stuck his head over the water and began to flick its tongue down into the water, not up and down the way they usually do. Some little fish were attracted to the moving tongue, she says, and the snake snapped one up, right while she was watching. I wonder if anybody has ever seen that before—a snake goin' fishing.

I find Nancy in a vale of wild cucumber vines, which are dotted with white blooms and hung with big hooked pods. She is testing the resilience of the springlike tendrils that suspend the vine in a coffeeberry bush. She expresses the notion that her vine is just a tree lying down, pointing out how long it is, not much shorter than a redwood tree is tall. I ask how sap gets from one end of the vine to the other, or to the top of a 200-foot redwood tree, for that matter. "Where's the pump?" I want to know.

"Look at this!" she says, brushing off my questions. "This vine is on springs—these tendrils here—that hang it up in shrubs, and no wind makes any difference." She shakes the coffeeberry bush and the vine hardly moves.

I ask if she knows the reason that wild cucumbers are called man-in-the-ground. She knows, and tells me of their huge root, as big as a man, and how it allows them to sprout right after a fire has passed through. I tell her that only a few days after a fire, right in this canyon, I'd seen the bright green vines of wild cucumbers running in the black ashes.

I move on and find Adam and his buddies—Daria, Erin, Serge, and Dawn—out in the middle of a little meadow, on their knees in a circle, all bent over looking at something. I can hear their exclamations and see the tautness in their bent-over forms as I approach.

"The spider stuck the insect right into the dewdrop!" someone comments. They tell me they are watching what they have tentatively identified as a dwarf spider, which has spun a horizontal, handkerchieflike web over part of a deer's hoofprint. An insect crawled beneath the web, they explain, and tried to escape by jumping up. It was immediately entangled, whereupon the tiny spider killed it.

Then, as they watched, the spider pushed its prey into one of the several shining globes of dew that hung down from the web.

I get down on hands and knees and look, too. The magnified eyes of the insect show red from inside the crystal sphere. "Maybe the spider stores food in dewdrops," someone says. Another comments that it looks like the spider equivalent of a beer cooler. Still another suggests that the insect might stew in the dewdrop, allowing the spider to drink the dewdrop later for nourishment. One student asks me what *I* think is going on.

"I have no idea," I reply. "Keep looking!"

Back at camp late in the day, I find Chris, finishing a drawing of an iris in her journal. That morning, she had approached me with an intriguing question: "How do all these things we are learning affect what we can see?"

"Do you mean that if you study a flower, you come to see it differently than before?" I had asked.

"Yes, exactly," she had replied. "And does the way you relate to the flower control what you see? Does a poet see nature differently than a field biologist? Is it okay with you if I do my niche hunt on these questions?" With my blessing, she had taken this imaginative approach to the day's activity, planning to make a series of three drawings.

She shows me her first drawing. It's of an iris on a hillside, completed before she read anything about irises or even looked at the plant up close. The drawing reveals the delicate nature of the flower, its motion in the breeze. Then she turns the page to show me the second drawing. It depicts the same iris, propped up in her water-filled hiking cup. This sketch, she tells me, was undertaken after she had examined the flower carefully, noting its elegant pattern of blue and white and yellow, the lines leading down into the flower's three throats, where the beards of colored hairs lie. It is much more detailed than the first drawing, though a less-free interpretation of what I think of as "iris-ness." Her first drawing has the motion and sweep of delicate petals held up in the air, glowing light against shadow. The second drawing does not.

Then she shows me her third drawing. Before making this one, she tells me, she went to our big red plant bible, Munz, and carefully read the detailed description of the Douglas iris, *Iris douglasiana*, with the flower in hand. She had learned about the three large showy bracts, or spathes, and the more vertical sepals, or falls, and had cut open the flower's three-compartmented seed chamber, full of little black seeds. This third representation of the iris is a diagram: it shows each part in precise detail, but it is graceless, like the work of a painter using too small a brush. The delicacy of the flower is submerged.

Chris, I think, drew the first iris as an artist and, by some magic mental process, expressed the essence of the iris-in-nature. Then she switched brain patterns to analyze what she was seeing, to depict it with the precision of a scientist.

"Many scientists want the process of science to be just the last two irises," I comment. "It's as if the right sides of their brains had no input. Just zero down through your hand lens or microscope is the implication—pick apart nature, line up the results in neat columns, put numbers on them, and voila! science. But I don't think that's enough. I think your first flower is needed if one is really to understand an iris, even as a scientist. Such an artist's vision sets the frame of the iris-in-nature. You have, in fact, sketched out the tension within science, the two sides that make it work."

After dark, a cluster of us make our way down to a big pool below camp to look for steelhead trout, fish that hatch in the gravel bars of this stream and then move downstream and out to sea. They remain at sea for a matter of years before they return to spawn. I suspect the steelhead are here, because on my walk earlier in the day I noticed that the rivermouth bar was gone, washed out in the freshet, and I saw a big flash of silver in the river above. Santiago carries a waterproof flashlight. Sure enough, when he shines the light below the water surface, the entire pool lights up like a diamond trapping light, and there is a ghostly two-foot fish darting this way and that. I want to know about the steelhead's piece of Mountain Time, and so there by the pool we discuss the ecological meaning of spawning in one world, but living and growing in another.

After two days at Redwood Camp, we head up the challenging trail toward Boronda Camp. There we will find ourselves in a new habitat—live oak woodland—in a grassy bowl tucked down just below the ridge crest. Almost immediately after leaving Redwood Camp, we scale steps cut into the spine of steep Mining Ridge and ascend the Cardiac Trail. Once over the crest, we move into the cool, north-facing forest of the Big Creek drainage. Single-filing along the springy earthen trail, we at last reach the creek, to drink our fill from the ice-cold water. A huge fallen tree serves as a bridge. From there, the trail leads up through redolent bay tree forest and, at last, out into the grassy bowl of Boronda Camp, high above the stream-bottom forest.

Lonely old Eduardo Boronda's redwood shake cabin and barn are nearby, abandoned sixty years before. With only corset adds from Godey's *Lady's Book* for wallpaper and jugs of red wine to keep him company, he had raised pigs. Then, alone, he had driven the pigs to market on a primitive trail over the main Santa Lucia ridge and down into King City. It seems a life so elemental and so lonely that I have difficulty connecting with it.

As I watch the file of students and teachers enter the grassy vale, I see us as interlopers. It is not possible for this wild stream canyon and these hills to support us, not nearly. We, in our numbers, are the eternal visitors, depending upon food systems that reach out around the world, not just from a canyon like this.

It is a flower year, just as it had been on the desert. The rounded ridges above are extravagantly cloaked with deep blue lupines, splotched here and there with fields of bright orange California poppies. But it has been a long climb. Rather than scampering up the hill to see the wildflower display, we shed our heavy packs gratefully and set up camp. I spread my tarp and sleeping bag in the shade of an oak tree. Then I begin to gather firewood for our evening circle.

After dinner, we gather around the campfire to stitch together our Mountain-Time crazy quilt, just as the spotted owl begins its curious evening call. I start by suggesting that the redwood might be our best candidate to beat out the basic cadence of life on these mountains. "But I am wary," I add. "Perhaps the lichens on the rock slabs are as old. What other candidates can you think of?" I ask.

Someone suggests the ponderosa pines at Gamboa Point. "I doubt it," I say. "The fires get them, and then their dead snags become dotted with those little globular white fungi we've seen. After that, the trees themselves decay and fall." I suggest that their seeds carry them through. I'd seen ponderosa seedlings in total profusion after a fire.

Another student nominates manzanita, one of those with a burl that can sprout back after a fire. Nancy asks about man-in-the-ground, noting that it must be very old to form that huge root. In the last analysis, we conclude, all life runs in streams. Seeds and buried roots are one part of it, and so are birds and lizards and trees, but life does not stop until a species is truly pinched out by extinction. It doesn't stop or start at birth, as our debate over abortion would have it. We humans tend to think about individual organisms as being the important measure. But are we? Isn't the dividing of life's stream into a species such as us just a strategy, a lineage of individuals who are born, reproduce, and die?

We can perceive the cadence of some individual packets of life, the longest probably measured in the low thousands of years. We come to suspect that life's beat might be limited by climate, by what happens to the earth itself. In the largest sense, life will not stop so long as there is water to imbibe and chemicals to feed its players—although the mix of players might change dramatically.

I ask if we can list some kinds of strategies that living things seem to play out here? I provide three examples to start with. The first is "waiting it out," typified by the redwood. "They send their roots into soil below the reach of fire and retreat into that impervious bark of theirs. Then they just stand there for a thousand years or more, producing seeds each year."

The second is "going quiescent." I talk of the many living species, plant and animal, that survive in difficult environments by retreating for a time when conditions are bad, shutting their metabolic engines down to "low," to emerge when things turn good again. "Most of the delicate life we found in the desert was doing this," I remind them. "By summer, most perennial desert plants are dormant. The annuals retreat into their seeds, and most of the animals go below ground."

The third strategy is "hanging on." I tell the students that tomorrow we will try to find our example in a tiny barren canyon three ridges back from the sea. "It is a little lizard called *Uta*—the side-blotched lizard. There may be fewer than a hundred in that little canyon." I explain that these aridity-loving lizards were probably isolated there when the Big Sur climate began to change. Perhaps they had arrived here before the birth of Christ, during the warm time that paleoclimatologists call the "climatic optimum." Now they just hang on waiting for aridity to return.

Olga proposes another strategy she calls "lives linked." She'd been among the crew looking at columbines and hummingbirds. That group had proposed that the way columbine flowers hang down is related to the ability of hummingbirds to hover and shoot their tongues up into the flowers dangling above. Columbine flowers hang down far apart and quite a distance above the ground, leaving enough space for a hummingbird's wings to beat outstretched, Olga says. Even then a long tongue is required to reach into the columbine's deep nectaries. Only a hummingbird seemed able to pollinate a columbine. "We watched them do it, over and over."

I admire her wonderful story, but present a possible complication. I'd seen the same columbine, *Aquilegia formosa*, in the Wrangell Mountains of Alaska, not far south of the Yukon River and the Arctic Circle. I ask: "Do hummingbirds go that far north? If not, who pollinates the Alaskan columbines?" I suggest we consult Miss Preen.

Erin replies that we've left Miss Preen's library back at Redwood Camp, but she's brought her own bird book. She leafs through the pages and then reads: "The rufous hummingbird breeds as far north as the southern Yukon!" Imagine that. Maybe these two species—the bird and the plant—are truly linked together.

Then Jim suggests a variation on this strategy that he calls "lives locked." He isn't thinking about columbines and hummingbirds, but about lichens, which are a tightly layered combination of an alga and a fungus, each one supporting and completely dependent upon the other.

Steve comments that almost every kind of life has some linkage with other kinds of life.[1] Thinking of the mycorrhizal fungi we'd first seen in the desert, he points to the meadow edge where a ring of mushrooms is coming up. "Fruiting bodies," he says. "Down below the soil surface you will find the mushroom's mycorrhizae. They look like pieces of hair. They are able to capture nitrogen, making the fertilizer that all plants need."

Everyone sits thinking. After a while, I shift the discussion a little. "Why are these streams so clear?" I ask. A silence falls over our circle, and firelight flickers on faces in thought. Finally, Dawn speaks up, suggesting that because the stream moves, life takes things out of the water faster than they go in. Impressed, I add that the little still pools at the edge of the stream are apt to be the most cluttered with debris and may even become cloudy. Maybe she has it right. We leave it at that.

Next day we hike out onto the flower-washed ridge and find our *Utas* in their little canyon, a tiny sunny nook protected from the sea winds. Then we skirt south along the ridge 2,000 feet up from the sea. The ridge is so steep-sided, it seems possible that one could tumble all the way to the water's edge.

Richard, in excitement, points beyond the kelp bed. "Are those killer whales?"

Grizz and I shade our eyes and look; then we see them, too. The killers are not alone. They close upon a pair of huge baleen whales,

California grays, making their way north. At this time of year, gray whale mother-and-young pairs travel northward, right up against the shore, often swimming among the beds of kelp. The whales are soon circled by the racing, dark-centered splashes of the killer whales. Everyone stops to watch, deep in awe at the visceral scene. We see the big whales lunge and slow; we can just make out the plunging, circling killers mobbing them. The gray whales soon stop as if their engines have failed, and then we think we can see a spreading stain of red in the water. Then all are gone, and only the dark patch remains to dissipate in the parading swells.

"Life from life," someone says quietly.

Neither blame nor innocence weighs in the scales of the Mountain Time world. The true equation is the mountain's passionless answer to whether or not a place may be found in Mountain Time that can be occupied. Even though many organisms live together in achieving such occupancy, this hard question does not change. *Right* and *wrong* are human terms made within our own ranks. They are not part of Mountain Time. Yet there is elemental beauty in the canyon and a kind of peace. Very long ago, we emerged from such lands.

Part II • From Desert to Ocean

Ken Norris writing up his daily field notes at Rancho Guivocaba, Mexico, August 1950.

Original field notes by Ken Norris, documenting his discovery of the two-legged "lizard," Bipes biporus, in Baja California, July 13, 1949.

Photos courtesy of the Norris Collection

Chapter 6:
The Two-legged Lizard

Within my working lifetime, the reigning conception of the earth has undergone a profound transformation—from a globe with fixed continents and oceans to one of mobile land masses and ocean-bottom crustal plates that dive, collide, and slide past one another with such unimaginable force that whole mountain ranges are no more than earth wrinkles left behind.

The new conception of the earth was only a handful of years ahead when, in 1949, Charlie Lowe and I sought out the two-legged lizard on the slim desert peninsula of Baja California, which stretches 800 miles south from the United States border to just below the Tropic of Cancer. Charlie and I had decided to assemble a treatise on the reptiles and amphibians of Baja, and the two-legged lizard was one of the peninsula's faunal mysteries: rarely seen, barely collected, its known localities oddly distant from those of its close relatives on the mainland. We were unaware that a dynamic model of geologic change would be necessary for understanding the two-legged lizard's present-day situation.

At the time, the peninsula seemed like true *terra incognita*. A single unpaved trace ran its length. To call it a "road" seemed like overkill. Nonetheless, that trace was an ancient road, sometimes of sand, sometimes a jarring path of lava cobbles. It linked lonely missions and isolated ranchos together, just as it had when the only traffic was men on horseback and long supply teams of mules snaking their way through the desert dust. At Bahia Concepción, we would find that the "road" ran half a foot below salt water at high tide. Schooling fish paraded back and forth in front of our truck and the stolid *botete*, the pufferfish, fanned its fins and darted for safety as we sloshed toward it.

Our particular traverse of the road began at the Alta California border in June and ended for Charlie, his wife, Arlene, and me when we returned in July, after forty-one days of sweaty jouncing travel, down and back.

Some days we saw only one other car, and whenever we wished to camp, we simply pulled off into the desert scrub, set up our tables, pumped up the lamps and stove, and made dinner. Then we worked past midnight to describe the colors and patterns of our collected specimens, matching them against a book of color standards we carried. We labeled our prizes using India ink written upon tags of parchmentlike paper, tied the tags on a hind leg or a neck, just so, snipped the specimens open with surgical scissors, and lay them out carefully on a bed of gauze soaked in pickling fluid to harden them. Then we stowed them away in gauze bundles, ever so carefully, to protect them against the incessant jouncing of the truck.

A major goal of our expedition was to find the two-legged lizard, *Bipes biporus*, and learn something of its still-mysterious life. Before our trip, only six specimens were known to science, having been collected by the almost mythic field collector of the California Academy of Sciences in San Francisco, Joseph Slevin.

We knew from our reading that there are two species of two-legged lizards, the Baja California form, and the not-very-different *Bipes canaliculatus*, which lives in the mountainous region behind Acapulco, far down on the tropical southern bend of mainland Mexico.[1]

Bipes isn't really a lizard, but instead an amphisbaenid reptile, an ancient animal whose little squarish scales run in rings all the way around its pinkish body, instead of being divided into belly and back scales the way lizards have them. It is also blind or, at best, only able to discriminate light and dark. All that remains of its eyes are two bluish spots showing through its head scales. What really distinguishes *Bipes* are two prominent, flat, five-clawed feet that protrude from the neck of the seven- to nine-inch animal and a total absence of any external hind legs.

Charlie and I had made a pilgrimage to the California Academy of Sciences in San Francisco to see these animals. Slevin, an old man by then, unsmiling and dressed in a starched white lab coat, laid two gauze-lined trays on the table before us and then retreated to the collection range to return with an alcohol-filled jar containing his precious specimens. He told us that he alone was to touch them, projecting a clear aura of distrust at we uncredentialed graduate students.

The specimens looked like big earthworms with mole feet. We queried about how he had collected them; they had been plowed up by farmers and brought to him, he said.

The puzzle that engaged Charlie and me was this: how to explain the divided distribution of this creature that lived buried in moist soil. Neither of the explanations we came up with seemed very convincing. Perhaps, we speculated, *Bipes* had somehow floated across the gap between the two species by sea. Over geologic time, impossible-seeming events can become likely, simply by long repetition and chance. The traverse we envisioned involved about 700 miles of open sea—Acapulco to Baja California. No, we reasoned, that explanation stretched the imagination no matter how you sliced it.

What seemed more probable was that the ancestors of *Bipes* had somehow spread up over the west coast of Mexico at a moister time, moving between the Acapulco area to the top of the Gulf of California and then down the length of Baja California—about 2,000 miles. If that story were true, however, why hadn't other populations been left all along the way?

For a while, even so, that seemed a plausible scenario. Charlie and I were tantalized by persistent reports of a two-legged lizard from the Santa Rita and Huachuca Mountains of southern Arizona, which would have made the story much more plausible, but to this day no specimen has been captured in these places, and the verbal descriptions given us of this elusive animal (who always somehow escaped) suggested front limbs far too small to be *Bipes*.[2]

Such was the state of the mystery when we set out in our new civilian jeep to collect reptiles and amphibians the length of Baja California.

About halfway down Baja, we traversed interminable miles of parched lava mesas and dry cactus-filled arroyos before the road abruptly descended the lava wall of a deep canyon and entered the lush palm oasis of San Ignacio. A more unlikely haven in the desert I have never entered—a canyon of deep reed-lined lagoons, backed by grove after grove of dark green date and fan palms.

In a nook of the arroyo protected from floods, we found a little village of about 2,000 isolated souls, clustered around a double-spired stone church, whose bells still peeled out the Angelus, embracing the entire village in their reverberant sound.

The church had been built of dressed lava blocks early in the 1700s by two European padres and their Indian workers. What a feat! Two padres, starting with very little in the way of tools, crossed the language barrier to train hunter-gatherer Indians in stone masonry, and then together they built a church. The strength of their faith was such that they knew there must be a worthy house for their God in that remote desert, if they were to do their central work. What was the journey of the bronze bells? Where had they been cast? I was sure someone knew, but we could only wonder.

No one at San Ignacio seemed to have heard of the two-legged lizard, including the dozens of curious little kids who thronged around us as we worked up our collections. They watched every move we made and then set out to collect lizards and snakes for us, in exchange for the coins we offered. Not that money seemed to mean all that much to these children. It was mostly the curious things we did that held them around us, watching, chattering, mimicking us when we looked away.

The kids told us of a turtle that lived in the long lagunas, saying that it stayed deep beneath the surface during the day. A turtle? Here in the middle of this desert? I wondered.

Charlie, who had been more thorough about his reading than I, already knew about the turtle. He offered the kids five pesos for one, a princely sum. No response. He called them *perezozo* (lazy), and they laughed and lay down in the dust to show us how lazy they were. One boy flung himself among the reeds, laughing even harder, to show that he was *really* lazy.

The turtle, it turned out, had been described by Dr. John Van Denburgh in 1895 (the real, corporeal Dr. Van Denburgh, not our patron saint of field trips). It had been captured by museum collectors from waterholes and slow streams from San Ignacio clear to the southern cape of the Baja California peninsula.

Turtles in the desert? There were almost as many conceptual difficulties in understanding the range of this turtle as that of *Bipes*, maybe more. Both were limited by water. Whatever had allowed one of them to travel probably was required of the other, and there we had to leave the matter dangling.

The road turned east toward the stifling, muggy Gulf of California. It had been suggested to us that we seek out an expatriate Scottish dentist, Dr. C. S. MacKinnon, who practiced in the mining town of Santa Rosalia, right at the edge of the gulf. He would help us with introductions to people further down the road, especially to guides who might take us into the remote mountains that lay ahead. And he might know about the two-legged lizard.

Santa Rosalia occupies a bleak fold of parched hills, just up from dark wharves that jut into the calm Gulf of California. From these, the manganese and copper ore of Santa Rosalia's nearby mines was loaded on ore carriers headed for distant ports.

It was afternoon when we joggled down into town and pulled to a stop at the edge of the city square. Young men and women in their best had begun to emerge from siesta to march and countermarch, now that the midday heat was abating.

"*Dentista?*" I asked. "*Allá*" ["Over there"], our informant said, pointing to a man working upon an aproned patient who sat in the open air in a portable dentist's chair. They were just beyond the gathering promenade. It was MacKinnon, alright, and he was operating the treadle of a dental drill with one foot. We could hear the whirr-whirr-whirr of his drill.

We approached and, between bouts of drilling, asked if it was he.

"Yes, just a few moments, and I'll be done here," he replied in the Aussie-accented English that marked one stop on his life-long passage around the world.

After he had finished with his patient, cleaned and stowed his tools, he scrawled out introductions to people ahead who might help us, using blank pages from my journal. Then he asked us if we had encountered a lizard with only two legs that the locals called "ocolote." (*Ajolote* is, I think, a better spelling.) He drew a crude picture of the animal, saying it was common on his ranch down near La Purissima. Hardly any doubt about it. He was talking of *Bipes*!

We left town, picked our way south on the cobbley road, then crossed the mountain spine of the peninsula again, this time going southwest into deliciously cool air blowing in off the Pacific Ocean. We rocked and swayed down a road that crossed and recrossed a little greenish stream, while above on each side thousand-foot promontories loomed. La Purissima! The garden of central Baja California whence in mission days came figs, wine, livestock, fruits, and vegetables.

With Arlene preparing and tying tags on the day's specimens, Charlie and I spent much of the night boiling water from the stream to refill our jerry cans. Late in the black night, we finally finished and collapsed into a sleep that would not be broken until midmorning.

"Don Santos Castro is your man," MacKinnon had told us. "Ocolotes should be common on his rancho, and he will help." After breakfast, we headed toward the canyon mouth and out onto the northern Magdalena Plain. We had no trouble locating Castro. His rancho was right on the main road. He welcomed us, breaking away from a conversation with his foreman to tell us about the two-legged lizard.

With quiet pride, he led us out among his fields. Far different from most ranchos we had seen, Castro's was a lush spread of well-tended plots of corn, beans, a grove of fig trees, trellised grape vines, with a big diesel engine pumping a clear stream of water from a hand-dug well, shored deep into the earth with heavy mesquite logs.

For a while, we tried digging in moist places where Castro suggested ajolotes might be living. No luck. Remembering Slevin's method of collecting, we left some empty coffee cans, lids, and a roll of tape to close them. Castro's workers could collect ajolotes for us while we traveled on toward the Cape of Baja California. Charlie said that we would return in about two weeks.

We returned to Castro's rancho about on schedule, dusty and tired from the long slog across Magdalena Plain. Don Santos told us: "Yes, we found ajolotes for you." With Castro in the seat beside us, we drove through his rancho to the farthest corner of the most distant field, stopping alongside a pile of brush. Castro pushed back the limbs and then dug with his hands into the loose soil. A few inches down, there were our cans, and in them were seven live ajolotes.

We each held one of these strange pink prizes in our fingers, feeling them wriggle through our grasp, concertina-fashion. In my notes, I described their locomotion:

> *When I placed one on the slick pages of my notebook, the front feet, which resemble those of a mole, are moved rather rapidly, dog-paddle fashion. Each has five toes ending in a sizeable claw. These two limbs are placed just posterior to the small head. The largest toe is the inner one, and all are bent inward like those of a badger. The limbs are very much flattened, and when folded back, each fits into a depression in the side of the body. During burrowing, the limbs are for the most part pressed against the body and used only sparingly. Burrowing appears to be accomplished mostly by lateral movements of the head, accompanied by concertina locomotion by the rest of the body. The curious hinged plates of the skin are used ratchet-fashion to secure purchase against the soil.*

Bipes appeared able to use all its modes of locomotion at once, digging or not with the little "hands," burrowing with the shovel-shaped head, and moving the rings of body scales toward or away from each other. It could move either backward or forward. What a strange creature!

I inquired why the ajolotes had been buried in a farthest corner of the ranch. Castro described a myth attached to the creature—that it would use those little hands to crawl up inside a person while he was relieving himself. I didn't wonder at the myth. The pink eyeless ajolote, with its little clawed mole-hands and the locomotory waves moving over its body, first one direction and then the other, was certainly the stuff of myth and capable of giving a nonzoologist the creeps. But I doubted the reality of the story. Don Santos said he did not believe the story either, but it kept the peace to store our specimens far from the house.

We thanked him, left money for the men who had captured the ajolotes for us, and made our way back to our old camp in La Purissima canyon. There some local boys brought us a dead specimen of the big Baja California turtle that we had sought at San Ignacio. I thought, How huge a turtle for this tiny stream! as we slipped it into the pickling fluid that now filled one of our empty three-gallon food tins, the only container we had big enough to accommodate it. How did it get here?

In the years immediately following this Baja California adventure, the reality of moving continents (plate tectonics) began its profound revision of how we viewed our world. The desert Baja California peninsula we had traversed was revealed to be a mere sliver of land that in very ancient times had first moved up the west side of Mexico, starting near modern Acapulco. Then, about five million years ago, the unimaginable forces of sea-floor spreading had opened the Gulf of California, moving the peninsula west and a little north, to take both reptile and turtle to their present locations.

Where this rafted land originally had been split away from mainland Mexico is the habitat of the second species of *Bipes*, and in the rivers of that coast also swim turtles much like those of Baja California.

So, both our mysterious turtle and the ajolote had probably gone on no self-propelled journey at all. They were simply passengers as their land moved from tropics to desert. Both the two-legged reptile and the turtle did no more than hang on in ever-dwindling habitat.

Right off, this story told me this: Nature really is the authority. Over and over again, when I have been patient, stories like this one have taken on clarity, until I could look up and say, "Oh, that's better. That's how it really happened!"

There is a still larger story, not just the puzzle of *Bipes*. Many of the living relatives of *Bipes*, other curious amphisbaenid reptiles, live scattered on islands and other continents. A few live to the south of Acapulco, ranging into South America. Some live on the Caribbean islands, and several are found distributed across parts of Africa to the Indian subcontinent.

If we give ourselves a lot of geologic time through which to think, these patterns become clearer. If we project our minds well back into the age of reptiles—say, 250 million years ago—we find the major continents aggregated and about to split apart. Africa was about to pull away from North and South America, opening a seaway that would become the Atlantic Ocean. Once again, all these curious reptiles had to do was to stay home and let the earth's surface do their traveling for them.

What none of us thought of before the idea was conceived that plates of the earth's crust moved was that these continental collisions, fusions, and separations did not just exchange the animals thus borne along. They also affected the very fabric of Mountain Time that had been elaborated on each block of land thus moved.

George Gaylord Simpson, perhaps the greatest mammalian paleontologist America has produced, seems to have been the first to see this.[3] He noted that, wherever two land masses came into contact and exchanged the mammals that had evolved on them, the animals from the larger land mass were typically the ones that overwhelmed the others. This happened when animals flooded both ways across the newly opened Bering land bridge between North America and Eurasia, and when Central America became a bridge between South and North America.

We might slide gracefully over this observation by saying that Asian mammals were more competitive than North American ones, or North American ones were superior to most South American ones. But to my knowledge, no one yet understands what such facile statements might truly mean, deeper down, down where the processes of Mountain Time work themselves out.[4]

Close-up of Bipes biporus, *the two-legged lizard.*

Bipes in situ.

Photos by Theodore J. Papenfuss

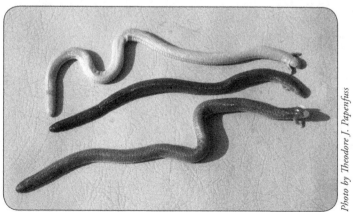

Three related species of Bipes: [top to bottom] Bipes biporus, Bipes tridactylus, *and* Bipes canaliculatus.

Mojave fringe-toed lizard, Uma scoparia. *Original art by Phil Schuyler.*

Chapter 7:
Adaptation

The vegetation thinned as Warren Porter[1] and I trekked up a sloping apron of uniform, pale peach-colored dunelands, ripple-marked by the wind. The dunes spread west of us for twenty miles, the same pale peach color the entire way. An animal living on these dunes and adapted for daytime concealment had to be pale peach colored or it would stand out like a sore thumb. We were there looking for just such an animal—the fringe-toed lizard, *Uma scoparia*. I wanted to show Warren the intriguing ways in which *Uma* had adapted to life in this unicolor environment. The lizards, I had surmised, used two means of concealment at once, each operative at a different distance.

We climbed higher on the dunes, into the hummocky zone where the bushes grew mostly down in blowouts—deep depressions in the dune front, where in summer the heat would become unbearable. Then, the blazing sun overhead and scalding walls of sand on every side would surround the hiker, or a lizard, with wavering walls of heat that could not be endured for long. Just ahead of us, the high peak of the Kelso Dunes rose, 550 feet of immaculate sand rising to an elegant mitre, sculpted in curves of sensuous perfection.

I stopped, grabbed a handful of the sand, and showed it to Warren. Close up, we could see that it was made up of yellow grains, rusty-colored grains, abundant black flecks of magnetite, and tiny near-spheres of quartz as clear as glass. The pale peach color was just the aggregate effect of all these constituents. "Warren," I said, "put this sand in a sandwich bag, and we'll look at it under the microscope back at the cabin."

We continued on in the direction of the peak. A six-inch-long *Uma*, unseen by us, watched as we approached. At first, the lizard hunkered down motionless, its pale peach-colored body a perfect match for the sand. The lizard's posture, head and body down tight against the sand, eliminated nearly all telltale shadows it might have cast. To a raven flying overhead, the lizard would be as invisible as it was to us.

Then Warren and I unknowingly entered an invisible circle that began about 15 feet from the animal. The *Uma* burst into flight, its long hind limbs reaching forward beyond its head in swift fluid strides. The hinged scales that margin its toes folded out flat atop the sand with each reach of its feet, serving as "sand shoes" on the soft dune surface. We watched the fleeing lizard rock from side to side as its much smaller front feet beat a rhythmic alternate tattoo on the sand, balancing the animal as it raced along. It ran fifty yards ahead of us and, in a sputter of flying sand, curved its path up behind a low bush and was gone. I, old *Uma* student that I am, trudged along, following the lizard's distinctive tracks. When we reached the bush, there was no lizard to be seen. Then I knelt back of the bush where the tracks ended, thrust my fingers into the sand and came up with the squirming *Uma*.[2]

Warren and I first took in the lizard's elegance and then, looking closer, noted the inset, pointed jaw that it uses to pierce the sand while running at full speed, the fringed "sand shoe" toes, the glittering eyes circled with lapped scales that help keep its eyes free of sand, the valved nostrils that can close to tiny openings, allowing the lizard to suck in air from between the sand grains while it is buried.

Warren, still a brand-new graduate student, began his own inspection of the lizard. He noticed that while *Uma* perfectly matched the color of the dune sand as it ran, from a couple of feet away it clearly wasn't painted a uniform sand color at all—its pebbly scales were of different colors, matching the fine-grain composition of the sand. *Uma*, it seemed, only matched the color of the dunes when seen from beyond a distance of about 15 feet, where the lizard's individual scales melded into the pale peach-colored blur. At a much closer distance, it was exquisitely multi-colored.

Most of the *Uma*'s encounters must be from this closer distance—when, for example, a snake or another larger lizard comes upon a partly buried *Uma* mere inches away. Then, the multi-colored adaptation takes effect: because dune sand up close is revealed to be made of those grains of many colors from many sources, the *Uma*'s outline is broken up, just as in the dim light of dusk a leopard up close is all but invisible because its spots break up any pattern that says "leopard." From that close distance, a homogeneously colored *Uma*, tinted like the overall color of the dunes, would stand out clearly, a unicolored space in a varicolored world.

We walked along, thinking about having two color strategies on the same animal at the same time. In addition to its fifteen-foot-radius outer circle of concealment, *Uma* seemed to have a much smaller inner circle of concealment. Within this circle, an *Uma* sitting quietly on the sand is difficult to perceive because its pattern of coloration mimics the sand as seen from close up. This adaptation disrupts the animal's outline, keeping it hidden from ground-level predators—or fooling prey into coming so close it can be snapped up. I let the lizard go, and it scurried off, fleeing to safety down the burrow of a desert kangaroo rat.

I looked over at Warren. What an amazing student he was—perceptive, a sponge for new knowledge, and overflowing with energy and good spirits. "Warren, would you be interested in exploring these color adaptation questions further with me? You could, if you wish, pick some part of the larger questions for a dissertation."

"I'd love to," said Warren.

I told Warren that I'd try to get a grant to buy us a machine I'd been dreaming about that would let us measure precisely the way in which light across the spectrum, from the ultraviolet way out into the infrared, reflected off the surface of *Uma* and the sand on which it lived. With the objective measurements of this machine, called a recording reflectance spectrophotometer, we could compare the actual colors of lizard and sand, and see exactly where in the spectrum they matched and diverged. The ability of the machine to measure in the infrared gave it another purpose as well. In my mind's eye, I saw the superheated sand of the dune habitat as a true obstacle course for a little ectothermic reptile like *Uma*. If we knew how the lizard interacted with light in the infrared—the portion of the spectrum experienced as heat—we would be much closer to understanding how the lizard could live in such an environment.

"Don't get your hopes too high," I told Warren. "Each one of those machines costs $12,000. I'll write a grant, but nobody thus far has ever presented me with $12,000." At that time, $12,000 was an almost unimaginable sum to a naturalist like me. I began to think my simple-seeming question was getting us in pretty deep!

The machine we sought worked by shining a beam of white light through a prism, which spread it into a rainbow, and then played the rainbow, one color at a time, over a sample, such as one of our lizards. The light that reflected off the sample was sent to a detector that measured the amount of each wavelength of light present. Then, miraculously, the machine would draw out a curve of all the reflected light it had detected, starting in the ultraviolet, the stuff of sunburns, tracing right through the visible spectrum and into the invisible world of heat, the near-infrared—such as the emanations that issue from the dark coals of last night's campfire and from the warm soil.

Pondering this, I realized that our tests could have a special elegance. There are very few uniform backgrounds in nature as extensive as a sand dune, all of a single color. On a dune, there is no confusing background of plant bark, leaves, and rocks for an animal to become concealed against. Instead there are simply animals living almost entirely exposed to their predators, upon the wholly uniform-colored sand of a vast dune. With this simplicity, we had a chance of seeing deeper into the process of adaptation than in almost any other circumstance, I thought.

A year later, quite miraculously, I was awarded the grant to cover the costs of our experiments, instrument included. The instrument arrived, a six-foot-long sprawling city of metal boxes, wires, and spheres. I was grateful that the factory sent out a technician, and that he and Warren, who seemed to love both instruments and numbers, assembled and showed me how to run the daunting creation.

I usually start out nervous around complicated instruments. Emotionally, I want as little as possible to intervene between Nature and me. But modern science has its imperatives, and two central ones are the need for impersonal precision and the requirement that observations be "quantified," so that the power of statistics can be brought to bear upon an idea. So it is often crucial for the human observer to go beyond what eyes and ears report, and to look at the measures produced by an instrument. This was just such a case.

In time, I would develop a kind of comradeship with that aggregate of metal, wires, and glass. I came to understand what it could do when asked, and now and then I patted it appreciatively on its integrating sphere. It was Warren's and my infallible set of eyes in the world of light, both visible and invisible.

First, I prepared a sample of Kelso Dunes sand from which an *Uma* had been taken, a little sandwich of sand held between two sheets of optical quartz. I taped this over the port of the spectrophotometer. The machine's pen dutifully began tracing a curve of sand color onto a big sheet of graph paper. The machine began its trace in the unseen ultraviolet, entered the visible, drew along into deep violet through blue, green, yellow, orange, red, and far out into the infrared. Then Warren and I readied an *Uma* from Kelso, warmed in my special lizard warmer. I taped a piece of quartz glass over machine's port and gently pressed the lizard's back against it. The machine's pen began to draw a second curve of light reflected from the lizard, right onto the same paper where the machine had just plotted the sand's color spectrum.

We watched enthralled. Initially, lizard and sand curves were essentially identical—the pen's two traces ran right over one another. The lizard's color seemed clearly to be matching the sand upon which it lived. What our eyes reported was real, according to the machine. The lizard really was invisible against the sand.

But, toward the end of the visible spectrum—at the tag end of the red wavelengths—the lizard's curve began to drop away from the sand curve. There was no longer a precise match of lizard to sand, but for some reason this departure didn't seem to disrupt—to my eyes—

Uma's exquisite color matching at all. How could that be? I named the place where there should be a match, but wasn't, a pseudomatch.

Warren and I removed our lizard partner from its warm bed and released it into the large sandy enclosure we had built on the building roof. We ruminated over these results all the way down the staircase. The lizard's visible match of skin to sand was far more precise than I had imagined it would be, except for that large deviation toward the red end of the visible spectrum.

Before we worked on the puzzle of this anomaly, we had to make sure our results were a real part of an *Uma*'s color. We ran many more sand and animal curves with other fringe-toed lizards from other dunes, many of somewhat different color, always with the same results. What our machine was recording in its mechanical way was real.

For some months, I circled around the questions our little test had raised. Perhaps, for some reason, a match wasn't as important out at the far end of the red as it was in the middle of the visible. I began to search through what physiologists had learned about the precision of color vision throughout the visible spectrum. In time, we learned that while vertebrate eyes can detect red light well enough, their ability to discriminate between the various hues of red becomes less and less precise the longer the wavelength. Apparently, it was imperceptible to the lizard's prey, its predators, or us that the two curves diverged at the red end of the spectrum to produce our pseudomatch. The lizard's effective protective coloration remained as perfect as if the pen's two lines had run right over one another.

This was all a tiny puzzle, you might think, but for me these events provided one small but important window to the way the living world has been fashioned. When we focused on the trace made by the spectrophotometer beyond the visible spectrum, in the near infrared, we began to realize that there was more than one agenda at work on the same animal at the same time. In the visible red, the curves of lizard and sand had begun to diverge, producing our pseudomatch, but just across the line into the infrared, color matching was lost altogether. The two curves spread dramatically away from each other, the sand becoming more and more reflective and the lizard less so. To a set of eyes sensitive only to infrared wavelengths, *Uma* would appear black against a dazzlingly white sand! So much for my vision of an infrared obstacle course: in the infrared, the lizard was colored to *maximize* heat absorption, not avoid it.

Why did *Uma* become a sponge for heat in the infrared? Before we had our machine, I expected that heat overload would be the problem for a desert lizard, but apparently that idea was backwards. What seemed to matter to *Uma* was the speed with which it could absorb heat. When it emerged cool and torpid from its burrow in the morning, it had to warm up quickly to escape its predators and carry out the other patterns of its life.

We began to realize that these results had a broader significance than proving my initial idea about heat avoidance wrong. The traces of lizard and sand across the spectrum suggested that the point at which the color of *Uma* began to diverge from the color of the sand had not been determined randomly, but instead by opposing selection pressures. That little dip in *Uma*'s reflectivity in the far visible red meant that Nature understood that vertebrate eyes were less precise in the red and contrived to take advantage of it. The pseudo-match in the visible spectrum was just the beginning of a response to an imperative directly opposed to that of concealment. In the infrared, with no eyes to watch, selection commanded that background matching be cast aside in favor of taking up heat quickly.

My head was reeling, especially when I began to recognize what this all meant for that entire cluster of animals with any concerns about catching *Uma*—all the hawks and snakes and coyotes, the animals that had forced *Uma* to evolve the adaptations of concealment. What was visible to me had to be visible to them, too. They all had to share the story with *Uma*, or else the whole thing wouldn't work. *Uma* would be caught every time. The lizards, the lizard's predators, and us, it seemed, were linked together through a chain of ancient eyes that had been shared by our common ancestors. Warren and I were looking at a scheme that had unfolded within the vertebrates themselves, and maybe even beyond, perhaps down into the invertebrates. We didn't know.

I wondered if *Uma* shared its dueling selection pressures with other lizards in similar circumstances. "Let's go looking for other pseudomatches," I suggested to Warren. "I think I know where there might be one—the White Sands of New Mexico." The dunes there are made of pure gypsum sand and are incredibly white. To walk them at all, one has to wear dark glasses. That means that our vertebrate eyes are failing. Yet lizards live out there—they are white as a sheet and all but invisible. There was even a white toad that lived on those dunes, and all one could see was its dark eyes!

My reading had told me that vertebrate eyes are poor at hue discrimination, not only in the red end of the spectrum, but also at very high light intensities. If an object reflects about 30 percent or less of the sunlight that hits it, we humans can discriminate its color very well, but in environments that reflect much more of the incoming sunlight—more than, say, 45 percent—we may fail dismally to perceive color differences at all. At the higher reflectivities, everything can appear washed out, as our eyes become saturated with light. I wanted to know if the high light intensities on the white dunes allowed the lizards there to use a pseuodomatch—to get away with a less-than-perfect match with the sand.

When colleagues Charles Lowe and Dick Zweifel and I had a chance to visit the White Sands dunes, I collected some of the blank white sand and some of the animals that lived on it. Back at the lab, we measured the color of the sand and of the lizards with our mechanical friend, the spectrophotometer, and found even more pronounced pseudomatching than Warren and I had encountered in the Kelso lizards![3] The little Earless Lizard of White Sands, *Holbrookia maculata*, for example—all but invisible to the humans trudging over those dunes—proved to have a color that diverged from that of the sand by as much as 30 percent. No spectrophotometer pen tracing right over the sand curve for them!

It seemed more and more remarkable to me that I was as easily fooled by the protective coloration of these lizards as any of the local predators they faced. If one asks, "Do our vertebrate eyes report true things about Nature?" the answer must be, "Well, only partly."

When on the White Sands, where I could hardly see at all because of blinding light intensity, my eyes and mind lied about color. The lizards and the sand seemed to be same color, but they weren't. The color-matching adaptation is based on what I and a lizard's predators make of what our eyes tell us. It is a mental relationship—a relationship of the reporting of brains.

Warren and I began to conceive that adaptation in general concerns the ancient adaptive shell of an animal, its *umwelt*, or how it perceives or faces the world. We concluded that the evolution of such adaptations as color-matching are based on what our mental equipment makes of the world after all the deeper processing has been done—after the light has been caught by my retina and information about that light passed through the various ganglia of my eyes, up through the nerves and lower brain centers, and finally to the cortex of my brain. That, I expect, must be how I, and every other animal with a semblance of a brain, faces the world. Embedded below this dance of life-to-life lie the ultimate truths of the physical world—the color of a dune, for example.

What evolutionists now conceive as driving this adaptive engine is what they term the fitness of a species. By this they mean that a given creature can survive in Nature only if the sum of its adaptations let it occupy a habitat in space and time capacious enough for its species to persist amidst the multitude of other contenders. In this sense, it is "fit." A species must prove fit within the broad context of Nature, as must every other living thing. That is the Mountain Time equation in a nutshell. The columbine must be fit, the redwood trees must be fit, and the killer whale and its prey, the gray whale, must also prove fit.

There is a point in such a tale as this when the worldviews of readers may begin to collide—the evolutionary view with the metaphysical view. On one side will be those who find truth in evolutionary stories, such as this one, and on the other side, those who feel that our lives and destinies are embraced by forces and relationships far larger than us, perhaps larger than we can hope to perceive, and that no evolutionary tale can ever suffice.

I formed my view of the world to include the idea that the organic evolution of life on Earth is a truth that must be accommodated.

To me, it is not a theory hanging fragile, up for being cast aside once various options are weighed. Many tests have modified how we have come to think the process of evolution works in detail. The story is not yet entirely told, but in my view the process of organic evolution on Earth is no longer up for grabs. Evidence for it is as robust as any concept about life on Earth, as strong as faith. To me, it is inconceivable that anything other than evolution could have lumped all the vertebrates together in what their eyes can do and how they can evade one another.

Yet the boundary between natural history and metaphysics is not one to be taken lightly, not to be dismissed out of hand. There is much that is deeply precious for those who hold each view. I finally came to think that these separate ways of viewing the operation of the world need not always collide and destroy each other in a clash of absolutes. But it seems clear as well that one cannot move from the natural history view of the world to the metaphysical view without giving up the former. I will return to my years-long exploration of faith systems later in the book, and there I will look as a naturalist at the metaphysical view of how the world works. Though I tried to give ample space for personal change, I was never able to shake aside the evolutionary reality and elegance of the story of lizard against sand.

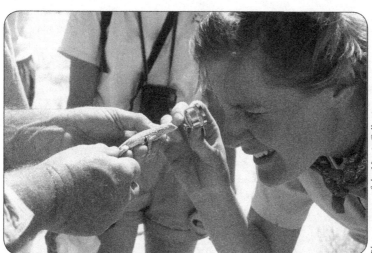
Mojave fringe-toed lizard patiently tolerates close examination by UC Santa Cruz Natural History Field Quarter Student Kim Glinka, 1988.

Desert iguana, Dipsosaurus dorsalis.

Chapter 8:
Desert Iguana

Right up to the edges of possibility, the arrangements of life play out their designs. It is near these edges that natural selection is fiercest and evolutionary change speeds fastest, and where life sometimes penetrates into a world in which it cannot long persist. In 1948, while I was a zoology graduate student at UCLA, my search for a dissertation subject took me to this kind of a marginal zone—the lowland floor of the Coachella Valley, a northern salient of the great Sonoran Desert, the hottest in America. There, I began to zero in on the desert iguana. This lizard, a sweet-faced vegetarian reptile about a foot long, was the most conspicuous animal of all on the Coachella's dunes. Its life was then all but unknown, so almost anything I could learn would be a plus.

I stopped my truck 3.7 miles east of Whelan's Drug Store in Palm Springs, California, amid a stretch of untenanted desert. This is far enough, I thought, no one will disturb anything. I painted a green band around a telephone pole to be sure I could find the exact place again. I didn't ask who owned the land. After all, almost the entire valley floor was unoccupied desert. I paced northward 300 feet, out among the wild accretion dunes that then covered much of the valley, essentially untouched by man. The little dunes were collected among the bases of big creosote bushes and there shaped by the wind. Where I walked, the prevailing wind came down the valley from the north, so each of these dunes had a long southerly tail of white sand that finally trailed off onto the hard-pan desert floor.

This was prime desert iguana habitat, the kind of place where, many times before, I had watched the lizards scurry and feed. I had seen them climb creosote bushes during spring days, to teeter out on branch ends where the yellow flowers are, gobbling whole mouthfuls, and licking their chops as if they had sampled the finest salad on earth. During much of the day, it seemed, these lizards could pick and choose where they ran and where they hunkered down. When the sand began to get really hot, they would occasionally wiggle their bellies from side to side to break through the surface and reach the cooler sand below, resting in the cool hollow for what seemed to be blissful minutes. In late morning, when no place on the exposed surface of a sand dune could be tolerated, I had watched the iguanas climb bushes and then hang festooned—sometimes several to a bush—in the upper cooler air, while they placidly cropped on leaves. Of all the Coachella's lizards, they seemed by far the most heat tolerant, eating that salad of theirs after every other animal had sought shelter. I had begun to form a question: What allows the desert iguana to remain out in the sun so long? I felt sure the answer would touch upon things we did not understand.

Deep in the dunes, I chose a point at random and pounded in a stake, the corner of what would be my football field-size study area. Walking the boundaries of my rectangle to set the other stakes, I took a mental inventory of the familiar animals and plants. A round-tailed ground squirrel family scurried ahead of me, the cute little babies tumbling into a burrow as I approached; a flat-tailed horned lizard hunkered down tight, motionless, and all but invisible against the sand.[1] I encountered a little sidewinder rattlesnake at the edge of a creosote's thin shade, coiled tight like a cow patty, partially buried in the sand. Even on that early spring day, the patterns of heat began to play, kaleidoscopelike, across the desert flats and across the little dunes.

On a paper map, I began to plot in every creosote clump and animal burrow in the study area, then settled down to observe the lives of my subjects. Today if an animal behaviorist tries to understand a society, such as that of the desert iguana, he or she will probably use the focal animal technique. The biologist simply learns to recognize a particular animal and then follows it through its day's activities, jotting down everything it does, including each encounter with another animal. This, needless to say, is much easier said than done. To understand a species, "focal follows" must include behavior trails for females, males, and young. In time, much of the life of a species can be sketched in this way: where it ranges; how, in a broadbrush way, its society works; what its relations are to other animals and to the environment. It is difficult, painstaking work, and more fun than any crossword puzzle. I began my work at a more primitive time in behavioral science, before focal animal technique had been invented, so I simply hauled my field notebook, a spotting scope, and a deck chair out into the dunes, set up a blind inside which I could work unnoticed, and began to record everything I saw a desert iguana do. Later, I would piece together my story from these unconnected parts.

In a month of fieldwork, I knew where most of the animals lived. The iguana population was spread out irregularly across the desert floor. Each of their burrows consisted of an ample chamber served by multiple entrances, each plugged tight with sand when the burrow was occupied. Try to grab an iguana in its burrow and it would burst through one of the closed entrances and race away. I supposed that this is what these lizards did when a red racer or a kit fox intruded into their quarters, searching for a meal.

I found that the desert iguana's day began when it pushed through the plug of sand that it had shoved into the burrow entrance last thing the evening before. It had slept curled up inside the blackness of its burrow. Then, by a magical internal clock, it awakened in midmorning (iguanas are late risers) and, as if its muscles were made of glue, slowly began to excavate its way out onto the desert surface again.

The lizard had gone into its burrow pale and whitish, a sign that it was warmed up to activity temperature; in the morning, it emerged dark gray, ready to accept a new supply of heat. Resting a third of the way out of its entrance, it was a dark form against the white sand. While I watched, the lizard began to lighten as its body picked up heat, and soon it emerged all the way, alert now, taking up a position on the open dune. Now whitish, it basked in the open sun for several minutes. It was, by then, on hair-trigger alert. I surmised that this behavioral sequence let the ectothermic lizard pass quickly from the torpor of sleep to full activity, in condition to evade a predator.

The little lizard tanked up with heat for perhaps half an hour, before moving off to forage among the dunes. Desert iguanas frequently lick the objects they encounter as they go along, and consequently ingest the darnedest collection of miscellanea—little bits of carrion, insects, bits of bone, and even their own droppings. The ingestion of this last substance is probably by design—it is sometimes called "the second harvest." Simply put, the passage of vegetable material through the lizard's inefficient gut leaves a lot of digestion to be done, so they often do it twice.

By midday, air temperatures had risen high enough that the attrition of most other animals had begun to take place. The ravens no longer croaked and flapped over the dunes looking for prey; hawks, roadrunners, and thrashers had disappeared. The sidewinder rattlesnake held out for a while, buried halfway in the sand, and then crawled into a cool rodent burrow. Predatory racers and gopher snakes did the same.

Soon, all that was left above ground were desert iguanas, and they seemed to know they were alone. Freed, they began to gambol like school kids in a play yard. They ran across the flats, toes curled backwards away from the searing soil. Up favored food bushes they went, especially a shrub named *Dicoria*. There they clasped the slim branchlets, nipping off the fuzzy new leaves. At midday in late spring, a single bush might host half a dozen iguanas blithely feeding, wholly in the open.

I began to take the body temperatures of these lizards using a delicate little Schultheis thermometer, which had an honored place clipped in my shirt pocket, just as it did in the pockets of many of my herpetologist colleagues. We called this activity "herpetothermometry," and it had become something like a religion among us. Few lizard or snake's temperatures went unrecorded, the rationale being that since they received their heat mostly from the sun, we had to record their body temperatures to understand their behavior. We simply grasped the lizard firmly by a leg, thrust the thermometer into its vent and waited a minute for the mercury to equilibrate.

This ritualistic temperature-taking revealed a considerable surprise to me. Those lizards up in the *Dicoria* bushes had body temperatures that would quickly kill a human. The highest body temperature I ever recorded from any lizard was from a desert iguana on my study plot, and it was a real shocker. One day in late spring, I happened upon a female desert iguana who had just emerged, gaunt and shrunken, from an egg-laying sortie down a burrow. (Gravid female desert iguanas become quite grotesquely deformed before they lay the dozen or more large leathery eggs they carry.) This lizard felt remarkably hot to my fingers, far hotter than my body. I inserted the thermometer into her vent and watched it climb to 115.5°F! This was at the time the highest voluntary body temperature that had ever been measured from a vertebrate animal.[2]

I became convinced that there is a link between these extreme body temperatures and the lizard's reduced wariness. It seemed that during torrid times when there are no other animals around to threaten them, their guard came down a little. Certainly, I seemed little threat to these gamboling lizards. I still am amazed that lizards in *Dicoria* bushes, or the deer in a National Park, seem to know they are safe. The closest I can come to an explanation is that they are much more aware of the world around them than we give them credit for.

Toward the end of spring, even the desert iguanas began to disappear. I suspected that they entered into summer hibernation (aestivation) below ground. This was one of the behaviors I should try to document, if I could. With the desert seemingly devoid of larger animal life, I, temporary exception that I was, trudged along, swathed in reflective layers of cloth that held a cocoon of cool vapor against me. So long as my body's water and salt reserves held out, I would be all right, but my time was obviously short.

One day I kept going as the midday air temperature (recorded in the standard five-foot weather shelter I'd set up) pushed toward

115°F and then beyond, creeping upward toward 120°F. Plant shapes jittered and danced in the heat. The glaring sand between the creosotes reflected like a mirror. Sweat poured from my skin and dried before it could trickle down, leaving a rime of salts behind. The salt pills that I took lost their acrid taste. Remarkably, they became a kind of candy.

Get out while you still can! I thought. My time here is nearly gone; this is no longer a place for a human. I slogged back to the road, slid onto the searing-hot seat of my waiting truck and turned for Whelan's drug store. I pushed through the door of the building-capsule, squatting there in the sun, into its chilly air-conditioned interior, slumped onto a stool, and ordered their specialty—a huge limeade, served in a tall ice-filled paper cup. At first, the drink was almost too much to tolerate. If I were incautious, my upper chest would shoot with pain at the descending ice. Soon it became easier, and then a matter of hungrily making up my water deficit with this green fluid, sucked from amid its slurry of ice chips.

As I pondered what I had learned in the field, a question formed. Here these lizards were, out in the wilting heat, stuffing their guts with succulent leaves, and yet what I had read about digestion suggested that these lizards should not be able to digest their stomachs' full of food. Digestive enzymes were found to be inactivated by high temperatures, temperatures far below those the desert iguanas endured every late spring day. If the iguana's enzymes were similar, then they couldn't digest the leaves they ate during the warmest part of a day.

I began to form the concept of the partial animal in my mind. The desert iguana seemed to have moved into the zone of body temperatures where it was no longer a completely functional creature. I began to speak of "entering the zone of tolerance," meaning that the lizard could not tolerate such temperatures permanently, but at least long enough to gather in the day's food.

This idea of an animal temporarily invading conditions where it is an incomplete animal intrigued me. I knew that many animals become torpid at low temperatures—bats, groundhogs, lizards, bears, amphibia, a few fish, and on and on. In a way, the hibernation or torpor of these animals seemed to be simply the other, low-temperature end of the same phenomenon I had begun to explore with desert iguanas. In either case, it told of creatures pressing hard against their physiological limits!

Was this inactivation-of-enzymes idea real? I shot a number of desert iguanas from road-edge bushes, using a .22 caliber shot pistol that most of we naturalists used, to see if the lizards were digesting the leaves they ingested. I thought little about such collection; it was what biologists of the day did when our questions required us to look inside an animal. How different a time from the world of today, when every such collection receives deep scrutiny, demanding that the animal be considered in our scientific machinations! Today is the better time.

What I found were lizard stomachs crammed impossibly full of *Dicoria* leaves. The packed leaves seemed to show few signs of digestion. So, at least it was a plausible idea that these lizards had become partial animals and that their sorties into extreme high temperatures might be a means of escaping for a short while into a predator-free world. But clearly I would have to dig deeper if I wanted to answer the question about enzymes.

One collateral fact made me suspicious that I might be right. Remember that these lizards are, first and foremost, vegetarians. A carnivore attempting to catch one up in those bushes had to be able to stay out as long the lizards did. But if the desert iguana could stand the extremes of heat better than its larger predator, even for a short while, it could feed with impunity in a predator-free world. Then, so my scenario went, it could retreat to its burrow, where its body temperature would decline and digestion could start.[3]

At one point in the spring, I had noticed half a dozen lath stakes pounded into the shoulder of the road down by the green-banded telephone pole, with unintelligible black writing scrawled on them. I hope whoever it is doesn't clean away all the *Dicoria* bushes that the iguanas love so much, I thought, assuming that a road crew was at work. But the coming events were to be much worse than that! On my next trip to the Coachella Desert, I was appalled to encounter a wide swath of planed-down desert—over half of my study area was vacant sand. Bulldozers had lumbered north off the road and flattened a long tract of hummock dunes. Creosote bushes lay in ragged, forlorn heaps on the bare sand. A large motor hotel soon sprang up on the cleared place. The Coachella Valley had begun its precipitous plunge into a world of golf courses, housing tracts, and condos. And it has not stopped yet.

When the bulldozers planed down that strip of dunes, my graduate research program was stopped cold. I was just beginning to know all the players out there in the dunes, their life patterns, their associates. It was no use continuing on that piece of desert. Soon traffic, pavement, visiting children, pets, and all the rest would rip apart the society of animals I had chosen to observe. How far into the dunes the effects would go was anybody's guess. I was dismayed, cast adrift.

Just before these events occurred, I had taken part in a long-term study of the fishes of the Gulf of California, Mexico, under Professor Boyd Walker, an even-handed field guy who knew his fishes as few people in the world do. On those trips, I was just a grunt, hauling nets and pulling on seine lines. But once the bulldozers struck, I took a closer look. Soon, with Walker's help, I was on my way to Scripps Institution of Oceanography at La Jolla, California, to finish my graduate career in the world of ichthyology—the study of fishes. Although I didn't understand it at the time, this new salient required me to look more broadly at the world. First in my personal unfolding had come geology, a view of the earth; it was followed by the life of the land. Now it was to be the sea.

A postscript: The catastrophe of the desert iguana study plot shook loose in me a clear and somber vision of the future of wildland

America. No question about it, the rapidly urbanizing United States would soon be a place where the natural land and its life would be embattled nearly everywhere.

As a graduate student, I listened many times to Doc Cowles' somber assessment of the future, especially about the disappearance of natural environments. He had watched, with obvious pain, as the wild places that supported his teaching and research disappeared. Several times, he had tried to convince the University to accept large tracts of wildland offered to him for these purposes; always officialdom had refused.

So when Doc Cowles retired in the early 1960s and I replaced him on the staff at UCLA, one of the very first things I tried to solve after substituting my junk for his in the office desk was this reluctance of the University about what seemed so obviously important to us. My conclusion was that there were nine UC campuses, and if the Regents approved a reserve for one, the other campuses would jump in, wanting their own lands.

So, as a brand-new assistant professor with no obvious inhibitions about what was and was not possible—I had no idea—I decided that the solution was a statewide plan, one with limits that administrators could hang their budgetary hats on. Plan it all at once for the whole state, I thought. And so I began an effort that still engages me.

I started by going to my ichthyology mentor, Dr. Boyd Walker, who seemed to know the byzantine University ropes. Good choice.

Boyd said that, first and foremost, I needed a very senior, very august committee to steer the effort, and it must come from all campuses. High-level academics can be used to impress high-level administrators. Oh, good idea! I never would have thought of that.

Then we needed a local committee that could draw up plans for the consideration of the more celestial group. We had to lay out what we wanted, and why, and where. Good idea, Boyd. I never would have thought of that.

Then somebody had to do the spadework. That proved to be me.

And so we did those things, and I found, right away, that there were scientists and teachers throughout California who saw the same future as I and who wanted to help. In time, I found that these same concerns were shared by thoughtful people throughout the state—businessmen, ranchers, people locked in cities, old families who saw their land going away, politicians, and especially new-minted students.

Thus we began. University President Clark Kerr liked the idea and knew just how to start. He designated seven natural lands that the University already held as the beginning nucleus of a reserve system. Then I asked my department for a spring's leave and a jeep to lay out the details of a statewide plan. With my sleeping bag and fishing rod and camping gear aboard, I visited every UC campus, asking the same questions of the field scientists on the staff: "What are your favorite wild places to teach and do research? Why?" And then we visited many of them.

A plan emerged that would encompass the ecological diversity of the state. We envisioned forty-four reserves: some near each campus for local teaching; other big, multihabitat reserves to serve a given ecological zone of the state; still other smaller, single-habitat reserves designed to include the especially important habitat types. The University of California Natural Reserve System (NRS) was the result. It now encompasses more than 100,000 acres in thirty-three reserves*, many with facilities and staff, and is by far the most complete, most magnificent such system dedicated to higher education and research in the world. It is certainly the most important thing I ever attempted to do. I gave the idea a push, and the will and very diverse skills of literally hundreds of other people have built and sustained it.

The NRS is still nascent in many ways. But it grows toward a future that can matter a great deal, and it has been built this far by people who care about our ecological future. California is huge—far and away, the most naturally diverse state in the nation—so the plan for the reserve system dealt with arctic-alpine habitats, rivers, lakes, islands, redwood forest, desert, and much more. What a time!

*By 2009, the UC NRS encompassed thirty-six natural reserves.

But people had to make all these dreams work, and a whole new cadre of talented and dedicated people came aboard. A statewide office was established, with a director, Roger Samuelsen, a small staff, and a systemwide steering committee, which began detailed planning. Roger proved to be a gem without price, a careful lawyer-outdoorsman, who took every new candidate land, encased it in watertight agreements, and presented them one by one to the Regents. I think it is true that he never lost a submission.

My botanist teacher and colleague, Mildred Mathias, entered and stayed with the NRS until her death many years later. A facilitator as well as a remarkable botanist, Mildred knew people throughout society and was respected by every one of them. Under her leadership, literally dozens of reserves were located and brought into the system.

To mention just one other person: Professor Bill Mayhew at UC Riverside, it was said by colleagues, wanted to walk on reserve lands from one border of the state to the other. With his accessible ways and great energy, he has left an indelible mark on wildlands teaching and research, and on the NRS. There are no more like him.

On and on, that story goes. The UC Natural Reserve System became a vast labor of love and commitment by an entire phalanx of people, and it still is.

Ken Norris with the "marvelous, wonderful, mysterious" ichthyothermi-taxitron that he built and used in his dissertation experiments.[1]

Chapter 9: Girella

How far back in the history of life do we have to go to find animals that lack all traces of consciousness? Here I relate an anecdote suggesting that a tiny tidepool fish might possess consciousness. And I go further, to write of one of the precursors to consciousness—volition.

I'd really lucked out. Professor Carl Hubbs, my new supervisor at Scripps Institution of Oceanography, had assigned me a little cubbyhole lab with a door that opened out onto the lawn above the La Jolla beach. A lab with a view! Sitting amid the old glassware of its former occupant, I began to contemplate my next steps. Very soon, I knew, I had to conjure up a research question and begin my work.

But, my past loves still held me. I found I couldn't simply leave my beloved desert and switch cold turkey to this new world of the sea, so I brought some desert red-spotted toads along and set up a terrarium where I could watch them under dim red light. I wanted to observe the details of their amplexus (clasping) and egg laying, which are the anuran counterparts of copulation and fertilization.

I knew that male red-spotted toads, small runty-looking fellows, usually emerge alongside their desert ponds just after dusk, to sit in the shallow water, trilling. It seems that this trilling gets them excited. At any rate, it isn't long until these males will leap upon anything that moves and clasp it tight. More than once, I tested this tendency by tossing small rocks into a desert pond. Each time, the male toads leapt aboard. Should more than one male emerge at a time, they clasped each other with grand abandon, sometimes four deep, all the while emitting release calls that said, "Get off my back!"

Alongside such a desert pond, I had watched the females emerge a little later than the males, swollen with eggs, like big ambulatory baking-powder biscuits, to be clasped forthwith by the nearest male. He would then begin his trilling call with real urgency, but this time with his throat pouch pressed right atop the female's head. Her head vibrated to the fervent beat until, after many minutes, her eyes took on a glazed and vaguely ethereal look. Then she would arch her back, close her eyes, and start spawning, paying out eggs with her hind toes.

At Scripps, I prepared little moist caves in the toad's terrarium, where every toad could retreat. I rigged up an artificial toad call, a water-filled bottle with a tin whistle on it. I could bubble air through the bottle and it would produce a reasonable facsimile of a red-spotted toad trill. My hope was that I could cause male toads to emerge, when I made my toad calls, and discern whether or not the females responded to the call.

I was about to test this primitive rig one evening when the campus cop, Mac, walked in. He often stopped by on his night rounds while I was setting up my lab.

"You want to see how steady I am, Ken?" he asked.

"Sure, Mac," I replied, not knowing what was coming next. Mac drew his .38 revolver, jacked the cartridges out of the cylinder, snapped it closed, balanced a fifty-cent piece on the barrel, and pulled the trigger six times. The coin remained balanced there.

"You're right, Mac, you're steady," I said in appreciation. "Do you have ten minutes to help me with a test?" I asked.

"No more than that," he replied. "I've got rounds to do."

I gave Mac the whistle and showed him how to produce nice long toad trills. I took up a notebook and a position where I could watch the toads. Mac trilled. One male toad emerged halfway out of its burrow. We tried again and again. No success.

"Okay, Mac, back to the drawing board."

"That's the first time I've been a madam to a bunch of goddamn toads," said Mac, as he moved off into the night.

The morning before, I'd walked up the beach in front of my office door, savoring the flights of shorebirds and the kelp wrack cast up by the waves. Half a mile down the beach, I'd come upon an acre of rocky tidepools, where little fish raced for cover at my approach. Here was a world I could watch.

Back at the lab the next day, I put the big terrarium in my truck, lined it with paper towels, soaked them dripping wet, and loaded in my toads. Then I drove to Pushawalla Oasis, where I had originally captured them. I let each toad go under the roots of a shaggy *Washingtonia* palm, whose overhead thatch sheltered the slow-moving pool from the sun.

Next day, I walked my beach again, down to the tidepools. I sat down on a rock to think. I knew that, below the high-tide line, there is one world—above it, pretty much another. The barrier, in fact, remains profound, even though various animals and plants have occasionally transgressed it in both directions. Below the tides, such players as bacteria, algae, corals, jellyfish, anemones, worms, crustaceans, tunicates, and fishes mark out the branches of an ancient tree that seems to lead back to the origins of life. On land is a newer and often different stream of life, one that started with a series of invasions of the land. In Earth terms, the vertebrate invasion of land was apparently rather recent, about four-fifths of Earth's history having passed before it began in earnest.

Between the two worlds ran the same intertidal band that stretched along my beach and through the little rocky reef. It is a line drawn around the planet, I thought. But it's not just a line. It's a band of transition. Many scientists have written about the emergence of life onto the land, but few seem to have looked at that barrier-band as a place of process, a place where two different versions of Mountain Time play out their relationships to two different cadences. I decided to watch this profound boundary, to spin the wheel there and see what I could see.

One animal that I wanted to check out was the opaleye perch, *Girella nigricans*. An earlier worker, Peter Doudoroff, had found that in the laboratory these little fish selected water of a very specific temperature: 79°F. With wonderful scientific integrity, Doudoroff checked and rechecked his findings, and could find nothing wrong with them, yet they seemed to make little sense. Even the highest sea temperatures recorded at Scripps weren't as warm as the 79°F that Doudoroff found. Nonetheless, he reported what he had recorded. Why should a fish select a temperature that it never encountered?

I poked around in the Scripps data files and found that Doudoroff had taken his seawater temperatures off the end of Scripps Pier, a short distance into the nearshore ocean. Young opaleyes, however, always lived in tidepools. There, I assumed, water temperatures should be very different than those off the end of a pier. Perhaps that was the answer.

I did three things. I walked down the beach to see if I could find opaleyes; I took water temperatures in the tidepools with my lizard thermometer; and finally, I built a chamber like the one Doudoroff had used to determine his 79°F. There were plenty of young opaleye in the intertidal pools, and they migrated up and down with the flooding and receding water. Sure enough, they swam in water of much higher temperature than that recorded off the pier. My newer version of Doudoroff's chamber was a fine complicated affair, in which I could place a fish and watch it move into the water temperature of its choice. I called the machine an ichthyothermitaxitron—*ichthyo* for fish, *therm* for temperature, *taxi* for movement or choice, and *tron* for marvelous, wonderful, mysterious machine. And I put a sign on my door to that effect.

I tested the opaleye's temperature selection in this machine, wondering if the behavior could be a guidepost in this tidal migration of theirs. It sure was. These little intertidal opaleyes consistently moved toward 79°F water, just as Doudoroff had found, and they did so it as if pulled by magnets. The effect, in nature, was to lure the little fish higher and higher up the intertidal reef, up where the rocks and pools are warmed by long exposure to the sun and where carpets of the opaleye's algal food are abundant. Along the shore, the boss metronome, I found, is the tide. Each flooding sets in motion a thousand stories, and as the water recedes, they cycle back to where they began.

Opaleye perch are spawned offshore in the kelp beds; the eggs hatch into beautiful little silvery fish, emerald green on their backs and bright silver on their flanks and bellies. These tiny fish gather in schools out in the kelp beds, up near the heaving sea surface. I began to perceive that "sea slicks" herd these little fishes toward the shore. On many calm days, one can see these slicks as wandering trails of smoothed water, not far out, running more or less parallel to the shore. They mark the crests of what oceanographers call "internal waves." These are the surface expressions of waves moving in a layer of water well below the sea surface. Slicks tend to move toward shore, just like surface waves do, and because they are warm on one side and cold on the other, they bathe the tails of the little fish swimming there in uncomfortably cold water, literally herding them into the intertidal pools.

There the fish undergo an almost miraculous transformation. Within a matter of days, the green and silver raiment is lost in favor of an olive drab mien, with iridescent blue fin margins and a bright white spot on either side of the little fish's back. They lose their slim shape, cease schooling, and flee from view to hide individually in underwater crevices among the rocks of tidepools.

I set up a canvas blind next to the pools and began to watch, just as I'd done with my desert iguanas. No fish emerged. In frustration, I took down my blind and moved to the other side of the reef, to watch through a little crevice that passed through the rocks and where I was sure my presence would not be detected. In minutes, the fish came out, nipping at particles floating on the pool surface. Unaware that they were being watched, they moved in leisurely fashion over the open sand bottom in the bright sun. They are truly wary little creatures!

I tested this wariness of theirs by placing two-foot squares of light-colored plywood on the dark rocks in full view of the fish. For a very long time, the fish didn't emerge. Almost anything out of the ordinary, it seemed, could cause the fish to hide. I'd seldom dealt with such wary subjects.

I watched the fish through my fissure in the rock as the tide came in. They milled at the head of their pool until wave wash began to fill the pools above. Then they rushed up through the upper connecting channel, like salmon breaching a cataract, racing into the higher pool. The little fish followed a zigzag course up the intertidal band until they and the tide reached the highest tidepools.

After several days of watching, I began to realize that the fish were not just going anywhere in their ascent through the mosaic of intertidal pools. They had a precise route, and they followed it each time. When I tried to catch specimens for the ichthyothermitaxitron, the fish raced to the upper head of the pool, and sometimes one would leap perhaps six inches over dry sand to land with a splash in the next pool above. A slight miscalculation in this seemingly blind leap, and the fish would have been flopping on the sand. They seemed to have a map of the pool series in their heads!

What did I really know about the mental world of this little fish? I wondered. How many of our facile human assumptions about such seemingly expressionless creatures were true, and how many were simply paper covering the walls of our own ignorance? I spun the naturalist's wheel again. Why should opaleyes make these daily migrations up through the intertidal zone and back? I'd noticed kiss marks on the rocky flats that intervened between intertidal pools, up near the high-tide line. The marks were peppered across the rocks, all over the place. They were made by the opaleyes when, using their peculiar hoelike teeth, they scraped off loose, encrusting algae and the tiny invertebrates enmeshed in the fronds.

Finally, I put it all together—my Global Field Theory of the Opaleye Perch. The opaleyes migrated up through this pool series, which they knew in great detail, until they reached the level of high tide. Then, as tidewater flooded out of the channels and pools and over the reef flat, the fish followed, abandoning the protection of their pools. As daylight faded, they swam freely over rocks recently warmed by the sun and there carried out their feeding. When the tide started to drop, the little fish retreated back to their pool series, retracing their paths back down to the cool subtidal—and presumably safer—sea.

All this allowed the little fish to follow a well-known channel where they not only seemed to know every rock and protective crevice in every pool, but every rock ashore that might harbor a heron intent on catching them.

How could ones so small, so new, have learned so much? There seemed to be the elegance of lock and key between tiny fish designs half revealed and that sward of boulders and channels. I wondered if these fish were acting like desert iguanas. They seemed to feed mostly where the warmest water spread over the high flat. That reminded me of lizards climbing a bush in the midafternoon sun to feed on leaves. Perhaps the little fish ate over the high-tide flats and, with full bellies, moved down the tidal series to carry out the digestion of their food at the cool end of this daily cycle of theirs, just as the lizards seemed to do.

This seemed to be exactly what they did. I held some little opaleyes in an aquarium tank at 79ºF and fed them. They ate compulsively. I've seldom seen an animal eat so compulsively. Well, maybe a sled dog acts about the same. I fed them; they ate. I fed them some more, and they kept eating as their little bodies swelled out in rotundity. They ate and ate until there was literally no more space for food, and even then a new piece of food was mouthed and held as if some adjustment of posture might create more space. I called it the temperature of maximum feeding, and the magic number was Doudoroff's temperature, 79ºF.

I'm getting closer to some truth that right now I only vaguely perceive, I thought. Do little *Girella* eat at high temperature and grow at low temperatures? I asked, spinning the wheel again. Sure enough: while they fed like hungry lions at 79ºF, they hardly put on any weight at all if held in water of that temperature. Almost all weight gain and growth was left to the cool-water, low-tide time.

Just like desert iguanas, I mused. Now what could that mean?

What it seemed to mean was that the life of a young opaleye is locked to the lunar cycle of tides, to the sun on the rocks, to the coolness of night, to a well-learned pool path, and that it is shaped, like the desert iguana's life, by a watchful dance with its predators. The little *Girella* watched vigilantly for the heron whose beak would dart or the predatory fish whose jaws would snap.[2]

What did the little fish do at the low-temperature end of their migration? Did they hide in crevices or burrows, like the lizard? I never found out.

Now, here's the take-home message: I thought I saw the sparks of consciousness in the opaleye, though I could not prove it. I thought I discerned an animal taking in the myriad details of the little world that surrounds it and making rapid and precise one-of-a-kind decisions about a course of action. Catching an opaleye with a net was no simple business. They raced this way and that, flowed around the tiny topography of a pool, leapt, and hid in crevices. They appeared to possess an *umwelt*, a perceived and changing world that followed them as they moved.

That's the way our perceptive envelope is arranged, too. Having an *umwelt* allows an animal to react to danger anywhere the senses reach and to change strategy opportunistically as it moves. The *umwelt* appears to be based upon a very specific, learned understanding of the world.

The opaleye's wariness in the presence of those squares of plywood or my carelessly placed blind was the result, it seemed, of glaring discontinuities in their *umwelts*. What opaleyes *didn't* seem to be doing was reacting to a fixed internal program that mechanically steered them through the world. The little fish were far too flexible, too immediately responsive to the always-changing conditions that they faced. *Flexibility*—that's the overall word for what I think I saw.

I thought I detected opaleyes using a map sense as they swam up and back through their strings of pools. When they moved zigzag, from pool to pool, and even jumped over dry land to the next pool, they seemed to "know" the route with great thoroughness, to be aware of their precise location on the route, and to factor in the direction from which a threat was coming. When I tried to catch individuals for my tests, their elusiveness seemed like no mere mechanism that I could conceive of.

But I couldn't prove that the opaleyes were operating at a level beyond the mechanistic, anymore than I could conclusively prove that you are conscious. I have mostly your spoken insistence that you are conscious to go by. The fish didn't speak up.

So, let's put this question of animal consciousness the other way around; maybe that will be easier. I challenge some bright young naturalist to provide reasonable proof that the opaleye *isn't* conscious. I don't want to hear the old litany that the opaleye is just a little fish, only weeks past hatching from an egg, or that its brain is very small and lacking a modern cortex. And I don't want to hear, "Does anybody but you extend consciousness so deep into the phylogenetic scale?" I'd rather not have to deal with the grotesque but firmly entrenched notion that only we humans have consciousness.

No, let's look directly at the fish, define our criteria for judging consciousness, and see what we get. The mechanistic explanation may well fit for animals tinier than opaleyes, those with space for just a few neurons to apply to any problem. But the opaleye seems too flexible an animal to be a pure mechanism.

The question of animal consciousness remains a profound problem, immersed in controversy. The mechanistic view still holds enough sway in the natural sciences to be an unacknowledged basis for the skepticism that often greets ideas such those I am proposing here.

The mechanists rose to prominence early in the history of behavioral science, in response to the excesses of quasi naturalists who invested their animals with human traits, making such formulations as "Sergeant Jay flew to the forest floor, calling his troops to order" without intending a metaphorical comparison. The mechanists were right in objecting. But with their own human-centered solution to the problem, they forgot their science. They said in effect: "The animal mind is unknowable. Therefore, we must regard it as a black box, and we must hew to the simplest possible explanation—that these responses we see are all mechanical. In this scheme, we humans alone have consciousness." The mechanists' solution of avoiding attempts at explanation still hangs as a dark pall over some camps within science today. Down deep, it seems to reflect a profound wordless need of humans to be special, to be the master in the presence of lowly vassals. If we were to allow all these others to join us, it seems to say, we are thereby degraded.

The typological view of brain evolution is one of the touchstones of the mechanistic view in the neural sciences. It says that the layers of the brain were built atop one another, one at a time, as higher mental functions arrived, each layer maintaining its old functions in the process. In this view, the opaleye cannot possess consciousness because of its rather simple brain, one with no hint of a modern cortex.

The pioneering neurophysiologist Antonio Damasio, however, has handed the mechanists a key defeat by showing this view to be erroneous. He espouses that consciousness in the human brain is not lodged only in regions concerned with language—a feature most people regard as ours alone—but also in the early sensory cortices and deeper still in the subcortical brain regions, such as the thalamus and the basal ganglia. This effectively makes it possible for consciousness to be ancient, to have been present in fish time, just as I have suggested here. And it suggests a more probable evolution of the brain: that various functions, perhaps including some beginnings of consciousness, appeared early, and their representations moved upward during evolutionary history, finally to become heavily represented on the cortices of animals like you and me. This could allow *Girella* the modicum of consciousness I thought I saw.

Also arguing against the mechanists, along with the opaleyes, is my dog Liza, who lights up when my daughter Sus picks up her shoes to take a walk in the forest or when Sus utters one of several words meaning "walk." Liza starts racing around the house, sliding rugs before her. Then in the evening after the walk is over, she creeps up into my lap in front of the fire, licks my face, and then settles down in obvious togetherness with the family of us. What a remarkable mechanical dog!

One last shot. The mechanist's explanation requires that consciousness arose full-blown in man. The sheer arrogance of that idea leaves me breathless. How can any one of us, with all we now know of the antiquity of complicated things, propose that the measured processes of evolution could have been so vastly speeded up for the hominids that this single precious and deeply complicated capability could be all our own? It literally makes no evolutionary sense, none at all.

Pushing aside for a moment the question of consciousness, let me talk of a new subdivision of creatures—the volitional animals. By this term, I mean creatures that somehow choose their way through the world. Think of trying to swat a fly. Now there might be a volitional animal. Somehow the fly is amazingly responsive to our attempts to squash it, and should we let our guard down just a little, it and its kind are all over us. Is this consciousness, or are we watching something simpler, more basic than we are willing to call consciousness? Maybe this will get us over our hang-up that consciousness is ours alone and not the result of a very long unfolding. Maybe, since I don't know how to separate a conscious animal from a volitional one, somebody will make the next advance by figuring out what is different between them.

My two terms, *conscious animals* and *volitional animals*, do not imply that there are two kinds of perception. They merely indicate that consciousness seems to have come from simple beginnings—in particular an awareness of the environment and the distinction between it and one's body. Damasio writes of such a simple beginning. He suggests that some kind of body sense had to exist for internal representations of the surrounding world to work. You can't make sense of the world beyond your body, he says, if your senses are not supported by self-knowledge—an internal *umwelt*, if you will. Some level of body–environment awareness, so far as I can see, goes back at least to the time when animals became bilateral—built to point in a given direction—with organs on their front ends that sensed the world and the direction in which they will move. That takes us down the evolutionary ladder at least to flatworms, and maybe even to *Paramecia*, those zippy little single-celled organisms that won't stay put under our microscopes.

Somewhere, some time, animals with awareness of their environment began to "make up their own minds," thus becoming volitional animals. Their behavior became more than just a simple integration of the raw input of sense organs to steer them. With that step, there appeared the first glimmerings of what we might be willing to call consciousness. The question of when volition became consciousness simply remains moot. We don't know how to subdivide and think about this ancient stream to everyone's satisfaction.

If the beginnings of consciousness are as ancient as I contend they are, think what that means. It means we are surrounded by many different shades and sorts of conscious beings. This, of course, is what the Hindus have contended all along. The naturalist, however, does not expect human mentality to be found in a fish, as the Hindu might, but instead a simpler consciousness, closer to its shadowy origins.[3] After my experiences with *Uma* and *Girella* and all the rest, I am remarkably accepting of a world full of such varied consciousnesses. It seems so obvious to me, so explanatory. The idea makes sense of so much of the world that before was blanked out by our own insistence that we humans are somehow above Nature.

Opaleye, Girella nigricans.

Al Allanson ready to dive off the coast of Baja California. He was one of the first deep-sea divers for the UC San Diego Scripps Institution of Oceanography, where he and Ken Norris met and became life-long friends.

Photo by Sibyl Allanson, reprinted courtesy of the Sweeney Granite Mountains Desert Research Center

Chapter 10:
The Blessed Frogs of Hidden Spring

Al Allanson ran the net locker at Scripps Institution, a big loft full of skiffs, nets, and camping gear. He and I were the field guys for our boss, Professor Hubbs. I loved fieldwork with Al. His gear always worked, and he had a puckish sense of humor that leavened even the most difficult adventure. Al was also an amateur archaeologist, what today's professionals derisively term a "pot hunter." Today we know to leave these sacred artifacts alone, but then it was just adventure, with never a thought that anyone should care.

"Ken, are you up for a hike to the Spindle Whorl Site?" Al asked one day.

"Sure," I replied. "What's a spindle whorl?"

Al explained that they were aboriginal artifacts, little rock doughnuts that were slid over a wooden shaft to help it spin. The Indians used them, Al said, to provide momentum to the spinning shaft, when they started a fire by friction, or to a spindle when spinning twine. He knew of a site on the side of remote Santa Rosa Peak said to be strewn with them.

So, not long after midnight on a May morning, we slid our hiking gear into the truck and left La Jolla for the rugged Santa Rosa Mountains, part of the Peninsular Ranges. Just at dawn, Al pulled up under live oaks, shut off the engine, and pocketed the keys. We swung on our packs and set out on foot around the great shoulder of 8,070-foot Santa Rosa Mountain. The trail, such as it was, led around to the southeast into head-high redshank and scattered yellow pine, and a few miles later gave out in a tangle of animal trails. Now and then, we could look down across the dun Borrego Desert, five thousand feet below. I could see the white disc of Clark Dry Lake, just above sea level.

"You ever been down there, Al?"

"No, have you?"

I described collecting lizards there and remembered that it was very hot in summer, but in spring it could be a garden of wild flowers.

We hiked on, keeping to an indistinct bench that seemed to lead around the face of the mountain. We were out about ten miles, I'd guess, when I tried to let myself down off a crumbling rocky ledge into a sandy streambed six feet below. I poked my agave walking stick into the dry gravel, and it slid over a buried rock. I tumbled down and felt my ankle twist and pop as I landed in a heap on the sand. I let out a cry as the searing pain swept over me, so strong it brought tears to my eyes, making me catch my breath in a spasm.

"You okay, Ken?" Al called.

"I don't think so," I gasped, clasping my ankle with both hands, curled up like an armadillo on the sand. Al hurried over and stood silently over me, taking in our mutual situation. I propped myself against the rock wall, calming a little. No bones broken. I found I could get up and hobble over the sand, but every time I tried to take a step uphill the pain swept over me. Going downhill, I found, was lots easier. I could poke my agave walking stick ahead of me to take up some of my weight. If I was careful and the hill not too steep, I could walk.

"Haul out the topo sheet, Al. Let's see where we are. Maybe we can go down instead of back the way we came."

"We're here," said Al, pointing his finger at a spot on Buck Ridge. I traced a possible path down Dry Wash. After that, the way looked pretty gentle, except for a sharp drop-off just above Hidden Spring. Then it was a straight shot to Clark Dry Lake and, after that, the Borrego Valley and civilization.

"I wonder what's at Hidden Spring," I commented. "It must be pure desert down there."

"It's about fifteen miles to Clark Dry Lake," Al said. "Could you make that?"

"Well, I think so, Al." I'd hiked on bad ankles before, but none as bad as this one. If I laced my boot up tight, the ankle would swell up and grow kind of numb.

"I sure don't want to go up."

As I look back on it now, I don't remember being afraid, even though I probably should have been. At such times, I seem to become clothed in a kind of innocent acceptance that pushes back fear. The idea of losing my life during an adventure never seems to enter my mind.

I hobbled around, testing the ankle. The biggest problem was that the ankle was weak and wouldn't steer right. I had to concentrate on every step. We threaded our way slowly down out of the chaparral and into high-desert vegetation, the spiny wands of ocotillo taking over where yerba santa left off. The day wore on, warming as we descended, until we gleamed with sweat. Both Al and I became acutely aware that we had started with only a pint of water each. We began to sequester it like the gold it was.

"Have you ever eaten lizards, Al?" I asked.

"Nope, have you?"

"I cooked a chuckwalla once. Not bad, but not much on them. Maybe we should try. It's going to be a long hike with just that bread and cheese we brought along. We're not going to get out of this until tomorrow at the speed I'm going."

I carried a long-barreled .22 caliber shot pistol with me in those days, to shoot reptiles for the UCLA herpetology museum. Pioneer California naturalist Loye Miller had made it for me, and I treasured it more than almost anything else I owned. Spotting a desert scaly lizard poking its head above a granite boulder, I sneaked up close, pointed the pistol, and blew it off the rock. I picked up the tattered seven-inch body, turned it this way and that. Its intestines bulged through its body wall, and blood seeped from a dozen wounds. Its pointed scales pricked my fingers. How, I wondered, are we going to eat this thing? I tucked it in the outer pocket of my pack.

Water had become the more urgent need. A pint is not nearly enough for a day in the desert in May. "The map says Hidden Spring is about five miles ahead," commented Al. We found the spring on the chart, marked with a symbol like a tadpole with a wiggly tail, and next to it a notation I'd never seen on a topographic map before—a line of tiny dots that said "Ancient aboriginal trail." And the trail led right to Hidden Spring.

The shadows grew longer as we trudged down the wide arroyo bottom. Dusk began to creep in with still a mile to go before Rockhouse Canyon and this mythical Hidden Spring. I wondered how we would find anything in the dark. Then, as we walked among blue-shadowed bushes, the granite cobbles turning to indistinct white patches in the gloom, I looked ahead and saw a great squat boulder, ten feet high. Atop it, silhouetted against the fading sky, was a cairn of three perched cobbles.

"The aboriginal trail?" queried Al.

"I wish and I hope," I replied.

We rounded the boulder and found ourselves at the brink of a chasm three hundred feet deep. "I see the trail!" exulted Al. "It's right in front of me. Steep though; watch your step."

I moved up right behind Al and put one hand on his shoulder. "Take it slow," he advised. Down the face of the chasm we went, me probing anxiously for solid purchase with my walking stick. Halfway down, we began to hear night noises that soon resolved themselves into a frog chorus, racketing louder and louder. It proved no problem at all to find Hidden Spring in the dark.

The spring was very small, about the size of three or four bathtubs set side by side, right up against a steep cliff. The frogs shut up tight as we prostrated ourselves at the pool edge. Pushing back the algal mat, we drank up a significant portion of the spring and then filled our all-but-dry canteens.

"Al, first we thank the frogs, then we build a little fire, then we pull off our boots and have a little dinner." It was luxurious to free my puffed-up foot, but I wondered about getting the boot on again. Right then, I thought: To hell with it—live for these delicious moments!

"Break out the cheese, Al," I said, lying back against a boulder on which firelight flickered.

"I don't have any cheese, Ken. I thought you had the cheese."

"I don't have any cheese, Al. Break out the French bread, then."

The Blessed Frogs of Hidden Spring

No French bread, no cheese. I found two crusts from a previous hike in my pack and a packet of chewing gum. Al looked balefully at me, reality soaking in. Then he got up and danced around the fire, chanting, "This is what I call living! A hard day's work, a crust of bread and two Chiclets! Beat's working, doesn't it, Ken?"

"I don't think we dented the water supply of the frogs, did we? " I said out loud. Then I wondered to myself: How did they get here, surrounded by a totally inhospitable environment?

Half an hour later, I suggested to Al that we get going again. "Let's see how much of the hike out we can do at night." So, taking a last fill of Hidden Spring water and forcing my ankle back into its straitjacket, we rose and trudged off down the wash. Fortunately, the moon was up by then, and we could see enough to walk. Well past midnight after the moon had set, we called it quits. Al and I each dug a little depression in the sand, to ward away the down-canyon breeze, and hunkered down to sleep, if we could.

It worked a little. We managed perhaps four hours of fitful rest before we got up again and began the trek anew. The stars were snapping bright, the shadows like blackest ink, and only faint sky light let us find our way. Dawn came as we swung along; first it paled out the winking stars, and then ahead the merest hint of rose tinted the eastern hills. The blazing glory of the sun seemed to rise very quickly, directly ahead of us, sending long shafts of apricot-red light across the bushes and facing the two of us with ruddy light. I could feel the first hints of heat.

"Shut up, stomach," said Al. "I'm as hungry as you."

About 8 a.m., we walked into the low forest of palo verde and mesquite trees that margin Clark Dry Lake. Rounding a sprawling mesquite already humming with bees, we came suddenly upon an ancient Pierce Arrow automobile—the kind with headlights built into the front fenders. The car had an early, handmade version of a camper built on its back. An old codger holding a dish pan in one hand walked slowly toward it.

"Hey, hello!" Al called, thinking that the man could refresh our dwindling water and perhaps give us a lift into town. He did nothing of the kind. He startled at Al's voice, looked full at us, and hurried into his camper. We heard the click of a lock being snapped closed. Al circled the old vehicle in frustration. "My buddy's hurt, and we badly need some water," he said to the silent vehicle. No answer, just the rising breeze in the mesquites. We looked for water barrels. There were none.

Al said, "Ken, we better get going. I don't know what's wrong with him, but we better get going." I knew that the hot part lay ahead. I suggested that, if we didn't make it over the divide and into the Borrego Valley by 10 a.m., we'd have to hole up under the biggest creosote bush we could find and wait for evening. "Yes," said Al, with resignation.

That last couple of miles out of Clark Lake Valley were the worst of the hike. The washboard road danced in the rising heat. We lowered our heads, talk stopped, and we moved mechanically toward the crest. We heard a car coming behind us. It was the Pierce Arrow. We signaled frantically to the driver. He drove right by in a cloud of dust, waving as he went. We watched until the car became very small and then disappeared over the crest. We felt very alone. There was no one behind us any more.

Just at 9:30 a.m., we stood on the crest and looked down into the Borrego Valley. There were two houses half a mile ahead, each way back from the road. "You go for that one, Al, okay? I'll take the white one over there. The first one to get a ride into town picks up the other."

I walked up to my house to behold a family sitting down to late breakfast. The odors of bacon and eggs and coffee floated over the desert scrub. Seeing me, one member rose and antiseptically latched the door closed, then sat down to eat again. They were silent as statues. Silverware and crockery clicked as they continued to eat. A murmur of voices too low to understand traveled between them. In my desperation, I made up my mind not to leave the porch no matter what they did.

I told my story through the screen. More voices. Finally, a woman said, "Would you like a cup of coffee?"

"Ma'am," I said, hands cupped together in front of me as if in prayer, "you can hardly image how I would like a cup of coffee." She handed it through the door. I had used the posture of supplicants the world over, without even knowing it.

Then came a plate of eggs and bacon. Then the suggestion that they drive me into town. We found Al beside the road under a creosote. He'd never made it to his house. The driver said, "You know, we folks out away from town have been afraid of strangers this last week." Two robbers, he explained, had been seen out their way only a week before.

He dropped the two of us off at the Prospector's Bar and Grill, an old Quonset hut with a Toonerville Trolley chimney wafting smoke over the desert. We slid into a booth, and a motherly waitress came up to us. "What would you boys like to eat?" she asked.

"Page two," said Al.

We each ordered and summarily ate a huge breakfast, then called the waitress back. "What's the biggest thing on the menu?" asked Al.

"The Prospector's Special—hominy, pancakes, sausage, eggs, cream gravy, biscuits... ."

"Two of those," said Al.

With an immortal line that still rings in my head, the waitress replied, "I sure do like to serve boys who like to eat."

We called Al's wife, and four hours later she arrived to drive us to the truck parked on the mountain, then to head for home.

Ten years later, I drove to Clark Dry Lake by myself and hiked up the long, long wash to Hidden Spring. What a remote little puddle it is, surrounded a long way by dry-as-dust desert!

How did the frogs get there, and what were their prospects? I wondered. That story, I decided, must have been an ancient one, one of shifting climates, of moister times long past. I sat by the pond's edge and watched a dozen little froglets, each with the remnants of a tadpole's tail, hopping on the moist sand. I looked along the tiny overflow rivulet, seeing it sink into the sand three dozen yards beyond the pond. More froglets were out there in the moss. Further still, on the dry desert that embraced Hidden Spring, I found the dried carcasses of a dozen more, parched like corn chips. Their hike toward other water is impossibly long, I thought, longer by far than mine had been.

I tried to conceive of the frog species as a whole. In its center, someplace far away, were dense populations of frogs where the presence of water was never a problem. Then toward the edges of the frog's range, populations became fewer and smaller, occurring only now and then where there was sufficient water, until here at Hidden Spring I sat at the very edge of the possible for these frogs. They lived in a precarious outpost at the edge of desolation. Their whole enterprise depended upon that pond and the hidden conduits of the rock that supplied Hidden Spring with water.

For a frog from Hidden Spring, there is no escape. Yet each year the frog's life force pours out its tokens onto the dry sand as if there were someplace to go. They hop away and die while the spring population fills its tiny space.

That fitting is a subtle process. How to trim a population to a pond's size, without driving the frogs to extinction, is the problem. No hammer that affects each frog equally will do, for then the frogs might simply disappear. More likely, it might be internal parasites that do the refined trimming. They leave wide difference between one froglet and another: some so infested they die, and some still strong. So, as the frog population increases, it is trimmed back and the pond-with-frogs persists. Or it could be the compass that keeps the frog population in check. Some may be vagrants, explorers who don't treasure water enough, and hop away to die.

Every year, I supposed, this drama goes on, this fitting of numbers to a world that can hold no more. The frog's relentless reproductive force keeps their tiny world filled. Always. Should the climate of the Santa Rosa Mountains change, the frog population could go two ways. The weather becomes drier, and Hidden Spring pinches out, a failed frog outlier. Or it becomes more moist, and other rivulets and springs appear on the mountain face, allowing the vagrant frogs to spread up Rockhouse Canyon and around the base of Santa Rosa Mountain. Then, maybe they could make their way through valley after valley and up mountain after mountain, until every canyon echoed with the reverberant sound of their springtime voices. Finally, they might meet another kind of frog or a frog predator and a seesaw battle for space would ensue.

But always the reproductive force pushes them on. Success is not its aim. In truth, there is no aim, there is merely adjustment. This adjustment of reproductive force settles at some percentage higher than the pond will hold, allowing Nature to trim numbers to the size of the pond.

I realized that reproduction is not just about families and children. It is even more centrally about space and the resources for life. The froglets are pawns in a statistical game. Their lives and deaths are integral parts of a larger process. Some wander beyond the water and die on the dry sand, thereby allowing the lonely outpost of Hidden Spring to wait for another spring. And another. We tend to ignore these contextual things and think only of the immediate tale of life and death in a frog pond, forgetting that we, too, are pawns in a similar story.

California tree frog (or California chorus frog), Pseudacris cadaverina *(formerly,* Hyla cadaverina*).*

Newly constructed Marineland of the Pacific, circa 1953.

Ken Norris working with a porpoise at Marineland of the Pacific, 1954.

Photos courtesy of the Norris Collection

Chapter 11:
Mabel, Myrtle, Frank, and Floyd

When, 65 million years ago, a five and a half-mile-long asteroid powered into the tip of the Yucatan Peninsula of Mexico, a pall of acrid gas and smoke blotted out the sun for weeks and killed much of the earth's life, including the last of the dinosaurs. A relative handful of mammals survived, many of them nocturnal. About 15 million years of evolution and diversification later, one branch of mammaldom began reentry into the sea. Over much time, these invaders became the Cetacea—the whales and dolphins. Since seals and sea lions invaded the sea millions of years later, and the manatees and dugongs, being vegetarian, pottered along the shore where marine plants grew, the cetacean's isolation from other mammals was all but complete.

What did they become during their 50 million years alone in the sea? I had no inkling of it at the time, but when I applied to be the curator of what would soon be the world's biggest ocean exhibit, I was opening the door to a career that would afford me the opportunity to consider this question in more depth than anyone could possibly have imagined, and to find some fascinating answers to it as well.

When first I learned of the opportunity at the brand-new Marineland of the Pacific, then being built on a bluff above the sea south of Los Angeles, the job seemed simply too grand to pass up. A full-time job going fishing! So I pushed aside my PhD research at Scripps Institution of Oceanography, saying to myself that I would finish it at home. Before I went for my job interview, I bought myself a new chalk-striped suit with wide lapels, *de rigueur* for the upwardly mobile young man of the time, reeved a 1953 version of a power tie under my collar, and ventured to downtown Los Angeles where the new manager's office was located. I was nervous and starchily scientific. I hardly saw the affable man across the table. What I didn't comprehend at all was that the feeling was mutual. Later I learned that the manager was a little intimidated by me, but since I had come on good recommendation, he decided to take me on faith.

I threw myself into the huge formless task of collecting an exhibit for the oceanarium. First came locating and hiring my team. I started with my old Scripps buddy Al Allanson, of "Blessed Frogs" days, making him Supervisor of Collections. Al searched out a commercial fisherman who knew the local waters. Frank Brocato seemed to know where each kind of fish lived and seemed able to catch them all. Part of the deal was the purchase of Frank's trim little 37-foot gillnetter, the *Geronimo*. Imagine that! A sweet little fishing vessel at my beck and call!

Then came a meeting with the upstairs brass in which I was shaken loose from my preconception of the oceanarium as a giant fish collection. The manager started right out: "What people mostly come to see at Marineland of Florida are the dolphins. Dolphins can be trained to do tricks," he said, looking hard at me. "People think they're fish. We have to have trained dolphins." I confessed I had no idea how to catch or train a dolphin. The manager thought for a while and said, "Let's see if I can get the Florida people to sell or loan us some."

And so four bottlenose dolphins—Mabel, Myrtle, Frank, and Floyd by name—were flown out from Florida. We met the plane at Los Angeles Airport and knew at once that we had been had. There they lay: four huge, lumpy, scratched-up, old, gray animals, puffing periodically and goggling their weepy eyes up at us. Our success will depend on them? I wondered.[1] Although these four were to open for me an exploration of one of life's most remarkable avenues, a story that often faced me with surprising discovery and challenged my typical human hubris that we had unfolded the last page of what life could become, no such thoughts entered my mind at the time.

We slid the four into the big circular tank and watched them form a loose school, circling and peering curiously at their new world. Now what? I thought to myself. The four dolphins had not been part of the cast of performers at their former home. They needed to be trained. I could contribute all the skills I had developed teaching my two dogs to sit up. I plunged ahead, anyway.

On a piece of paper, I drew a basketball hoop that we could hang over the water, and asked Frank to build it. I cornered Ray Valenzuela, the fish cutter, who worked in the freezer room where we stored animal food. The two of us walked up to the tank edge. "A buck if you can get one of those dolphins to toss that basketball through the hoop," I said.

I told Ray what I would do. "I'd have a bucketful of fish, and if one of the dolphins did anything remotely like throwing the ball, I'd toss it one. Be sure you toss the fish to the dolphin that did what you wanted. Let me demonstrate." I threw the ball in the tank, and when one of the dolphins nosed it, I quickly threw the big animal a fish. My speed about the reward, I thought, was necessary so the dolphin would understand what the fish was for. The dolphin mouthed the fish, rearranging it in its jaws before swallowing it, and right away bumped the ball again. I threw it another fish. These animals are really quick, I thought.

Thinking hard, I instructed, "Now, Ray, two more things. First, reward a dolphin only when it bumps the ball." I was making this rule up out of sheer common sense. "And be sure you reward the right dolphin. I have two dogs at home, and when I tried to teach one to sit up, the other always tried to steal the dog biscuit." I reflected on the task a few more seconds. "Oh yes, one final thing—maybe the most important: every time you reward a dolphin and it does what you want, be a little more demanding the next time. For example, on the first try, give it a fish when it bumps the ball. Then, reward the dolphin only when it bumps the ball closer to the hoop. If you keep at it, they might play basketball for you. Let's try it." Ray and I spent the next hour trying to train the ancient four. Ray got the hang of it right away. In just that first hour, the dolphins had bumped the ball closer and closer to the hoop.

I left Ray with his fish bucket, the dolphins gathered around him at the tank edge. Down deep, I didn't expect much to happen. After all, the people in Florida had rejected these animals, and they knew a lot more about both dolphins and training than we did.

A day later, I found Ray hanging around my office door. I was sure he'd given up, but no, he held out his hand—he wanted his dollar. We climbed to the tank edge to see. Given the ball, the dolphins performed with obvious enthusiasm, poking the ball toward the net like a scrub team in a gymnasium. Sometimes they even pushed it in. Fish rewards arced into the water.

All the way home I thought about what had happened. Ray had certainly exceeded my expectations. Bless him for the vital help he was giving me. But it was the dolphins that invoked the most wonder. Old and beat-up our dolphins surely were, but it was their obvious mentality that struck me.

To make a long and remarkable story short, under my primitive direction, Ray and soon others of the newly hired training staff induced the old dolphins to unfold trick after trick. Soon, as if by some occult hand, they were doing everything the Florida show animals were doing. Our dolphins leaped and touched a tethered ball suspended 18 feet in the air. They burst from the water at high speed, arcing gracefully over high hurdles, one animal at a time. Ray even got a dolphin to leap and take a fish from his mouth. To do this, Ray swabbed the mucus off a fish's tail, leaned out over the water ten feet up on a platform we'd built, and bit down. The huge mammal rose below him and ever so delicately took its reward. That performance, I thought, required as much from Ray as it did the dolphins. Another day, another dollar! In total, our opening day show cost me about twenty bucks out of pocket, but Ray, the dolphins, and the other trainers had saved us all.

I kept puzzling about those dolphins. When a dolphin stationed itself in front of the training platform, sculling slowly in the water with its broad tail, I was sure I could sense it waiting for the trainer to get his act together. The big animal seemed to know in advance what we were after, and maybe it did. I began to piece together an unlikely seeming scenario. These dolphins, I reasoned, couldn't have caught on as quickly as they did unless they knew in advance what we expected of them.

Perhaps our four had been socially subordinate in the dolphin society of the Florida oceanarium, I began to think. Could it have been that the other dolphins in Florida had kept them from performing, even though they knew all the routines? If my idea was correct, and I believe it may well have been, it required our ancient four to have learned most of our new show simply by observing the other Florida dolphins, since reportedly they had never performed. That's called "observational learning" and is supposedly a high-order kind of behavior, apparently the property of just a few kinds of higher animals. If true, the idea said a lot about dolphins and their shadowy society.

My idea seemed to require them to remember the elements of a performance for many months, all during their isolation in the storage pond. Most of that time, they apparently had no contact with the elite Florida show dolphins at all.

While working with the four, we almost forgot that we were in the company of wild animals. They never snarled at us; they didn't charge at us when we came to the tank edge in the morning, teeth exposed and threatening. Instead, they let us stroke their rubbery skin and gently took their fish rewards from our fingers. What kind of wild animals were these? How could a life swimming amidst implacable sharks produce creatures like these? What could possibly explain such friendliness between our two alien species? I wondered, too, how that obvious intelligence of theirs would match up against our own. I wondered how they used it in their seemingly peaceful lives.

Over nearly three decades of almost daily contact with dolphins, my colleagues and I would chip away at this puzzle. I was to have many face-to-face, mind-to-mind experiences with dolphins, each giving little hints that suggested a high-order mental flexibility and retentiveness in these alien mammals.

Very quickly, our little company of the first few dolphin biologists was joined by scientists of many persuasions—psychologists, anatomists, acousticians, hydrodynamicists, physiologists, students of wild populations, and animal trainers. Our many-faceted exploration began to paint in the shape of a dolphin's life and mind. Even today, this picture is just outlines, but there is enough known to propose why dolphins seem so peaceful, and what functions are served by those minds of theirs.

A key dimension of the puzzle was first laid before us in the late 1950s when a group of neural scientists from the National Institutes of Health began to investigate the dolphin brain. To their considerable puzzlement, this brain proved to rival our own in size. In fact, the bottlenose dolphin was found to possess one of the largest brains in relation to its body size of any mammal, just a little smaller on average than that of a human. It was also as convoluted as any brain known. The surface area of the brain had grown too large to be contained as a smooth sheet within the animal's skull, and had therefore become folded and wrinkled so that more cortical processing area could be housed in the same space. So those dolphins of ours were operating some pretty powerful equipment.

Clearly this greatly enlarged brain had developed mostly since dolphins had first gone to sea. Their antelopelike land ancestors had modest-sized brains, judging from fossils, a fraction as large as that of a modern bottlenose dolphin. Why had dolphins' brains grown considerably larger during their time in the ocean? What was it about a life at sea that seemed to require a special and obviously complex brain?

To me, it seemed a wonder that a long-lived, air-breathing mammal could subsist out there in the ocean at all. Later this wonder was reinforced tenfold when I stood on the deck of a tuna seiner in the open tropical Pacific amid a dense population of dolphins and cast a fishing lure into the sea. The fishing was great. I hooked skipjack tuna time after time, but only rarely could I bring one aboard because of the swarming sharks that snapped them in two before I could reel the fish in. Somehow, dolphins managed to live in such a sea. What did thinking have to do with their survival?

It began to emerge that there are two quite different sides to a dolphin's mentality. First, their societies hold many parallels to those of mammals ashore. Dolphins caress and court, they gather into family groups centered around the mother. Dolphin mothers care for their young as attentively as any mammal does. Old female bottlenoses emerge as the bossy centers of dolphin families. Young dolphins of both sexes struggle through puberty. Young male dolphins hang out together and then wander away from their home school, only to return and mate whenever the season and the chance are right.

What was new in dolphins were all the ways they coped with life at sea. How did they find their way around? How did they evade their predators, dive and catch their food? Many discovery-filled years would have to pass before dolphin biologists could see this new picture very clearly.

One feature quickly became evident: for a mammal gone to sea, access to air is vital and immediate; a dolphin must breathe or die. You might not think this would have anything much to do with brain complexity, but I came to disagree. We realized that any debilitating sickness or an accident can kill a dolphin if it becomes weak enough so that it cannot follow its school or, even more immediate, if it can no longer rise to the surface to breathe.

Now and then, the dolphins shared their solution with us. Simply put, they helped each other, sometimes to such an extreme degree that the lives—and deaths—of both the helped and the helper appeared to hang in the balance. They were joined in deeply cooperative societies that they never left, all through their long lives.

Let me tell you a little story about such cooperation. One time I watched through an oceanarium port as a common dolphin swam under its sick, lethargic partner, pressing it toward the surface for each breath. The helping dolphin continued to do this, almost without feeding, day after day—for so long that we observers began to wonder if the helpmate dolphin itself would die. Only once did my trainers attempt to intervene. The pair somehow eluded them. We stopped in frustration, knowing that each such evasion by the animals must have been a supreme effort. A couple of days later, the sick one inhaled water, slipped away, and sank, while the remaining animal circled above, whistling, whistling. No one could escape the poignancy. Some of us wiped tears away.

I have seen this helpmate pattern again and again. One black overcast night, out on the choppy San Pedro Channel off Southern California, we winched a netted thirteen-foot pilot whale toward the *Geronimo*. An accompanying school of little, bouncy, six- to seven-foot Pacific white-sided dolphins cut around the whale. They pressed the captive away. I could feel the bump, bump, bump on the whale's restraining line as they pushed. These small dolphins were attempting to lend assistance to another species several times their size! What, I wondered, could induce these little dolphins to come to the aid of so different an animal? Yet they did. The little dolphins accompanied the whale right up to the time we hoisted her aboard and swam by almost within touching distance of my outstretched hand, a thing they never did under normal circumstances.

In time, and with several other examples to ponder, we began to wonder if this epimeletic behavior—assistance of one animal by another—might be ubiquitous among cetaceans, including both the whales and dolphins. A thorough survey of the scientific literature suggests that this suspicion is probably correct. We should not forget that our own species also shows such behavior. That's what we give Congressional Medals of Honor for, at the same time as we hold up the self-sacrifice as especially honorable.

The real puzzle for me, and one I returned to again and again, was that this helping tendency seemed to be a general concept to the dolphins, one that extended beyond the boundaries of their species. This giving of oneself in the assistance of another, especially between different species, presses hard against the prevalent evolutionary doctrine of selfish behavior as the driving force in evolution.

I began to wonder if the notion of "selfishness" wasn't just one facet of a larger puzzle, a limited concept that could mislead as well as explain. I now believe that this epimeletic behavior results from a level of social organization above the selfish individual one, and in those who possess such group organization the concept of distress may be invoked regardless of the players. This idea says that in them the concept of helping has become just that, a concept, and that such altruistic behavior cannot easily be turned off just because the participants are not of the helper's species or are from outside its immediate family.

It is the case of a young boy raising a baby bird that has fallen from its nest, his feeling the embracing love that a mother would extend to her child. In the case of the dolphins, this seems to be played out in the vast ocean in the life-long company of its own kind, and among others that are somehow like it. For the boy, failing in his attempt to assist has no direct consequences for him, but for the dolphins this may not be true. Their lives are at stake. They can no longer swim alone.

Such a concept of distress is a complicated thing. It cannot be carried in the mind the way a simple fact can. It is, instead, a surround that embraces a set of facts, that orders them. We use such concepts all the time and never think a thing about it. But their use has been demonstrated in only a few other animals.

The more I thought about this relationship of helping, the more widely concept formation seemed to be exist among mammals. It came to seem not rare at all, but instead another of those capabilities that, once the groundwork had been laid far back in evolutionary history, could appear over and over. Even dogs, who most of us assign as our clear mental inferiors, show signs of having reached this cultural level of organization.

Because I feel this idea is so important to my story, I offer a common tale about a dog that demonstrates the abstract thinking that I believe typifies cultural creatures, both us and them. I don't mean by this story that we and the dogs are the same. We have taken concept formation much further than they do. My basic contention is that dog hierarchies are partly organized by guilt—guilt at breaking dog rules (or, when they live with us, those rules laid down by us as "top dog"). Guilt, like innovation, is a second-order phenomenon. It is commentary on the violation of a social arrangement. From time to time, scientists have challenged this view, saying dogs act more simply, more automatically. I think these observers have not watched carefully enough. I have spun the wheel with my dogs over many years, and I believe I understand how dog guilt works.

We have a dog door in our pantry that lets our three dogs out into the meadow where, by producing an awful ruckus, they protect our chickens (who roost in trees) from the attacks of raccoons, coyotes, and owls. A big yellow dog, Lucy, visits us now and then, but she won't fit through the dog door. So she can't get out to relieve herself. After several mistakes, she quite spontaneously learned to come to my bedside and utter a soft little whine in my ear that means, "Please get up and let me out." I stumble out of bed, grope open the front door, and stand there at 3 a.m., my teeth chattering, waiting for her to perform. Then we both go back to bed. Ah, the pains of leadership!

Sometimes I arose, unbidden by Lucy, to find noisome piles on the floor. Each such time, I took Lucy over to these deposits and went on and on about the rules of the house, like a mother-in-law pouring it on, waving my arms and pointing. Lucy cringed, creeping on the floor, and rolling over before I took her out. But a few times—and here is the crux—I came downstairs at night not knowing Lucy had failed, and I would find her abject, crawling low to the floor, even though I had not yet encountered the fecal pile.

She knew full well she had violated the rules of the house, and massive, cringing guilt, along with the awful certainty of punishment, was the result. I had said nothing at all to her or even thought it. Lucy clearly was acting from her own sense of guilt over an internal, second-order rule certainly wrought much earlier in other contexts in dog society, and she was transferring it over to the human society in which she now lived. That transfer of hers, too, was built on a matrix of second-order relationships, even more complex than just the immediate guilt she expressed over the noxious pile on the floor.

So, dolphins, dogs, and us (and certainly a good many other mammals) have passed a deeply important threshold—we all have come to use concepts in the arrangements of our lives. We all have vaulted into a new domain of communication and understanding.

The dolphins had another secret that only slowly unfolded before us. Over much time, we began to understand that, during their millions-of-years-long transition back into the ocean, they had developed a quite magical sense. They had learned to read the echoes of their own sounds. They had become able to make trains of sharp clicks, shoot them at objects, and listen for the faint echoes that returned. In this way, they became able to "see" right through water so murky a human couldn't see six inches into it.

My awareness of this exotic capability began to dawn when we began attempting to capture local dolphins. With insouciant ease, they eluded our nets no matter when or how we set them. Just as we strained to close the remaining opening of the encircling net, the dolphins raced through, then slowed, and began to swim quietly nearby. Dolphins don't let themselves get trapped—that was the message—and it's no big deal.

During the course of my discovery of dolphins' echolocation, I learned that the collectors at the Florida oceanarium had experienced the same problem as we had when attempting to net dolphins. They had solved the problem brilliantly by making their nets of larger mesh size—nine-inch squares instead of six. The larger mesh seemed to fool the dolphins into thinking there was no net there, and encirclement often worked. Puzzling over why this was the case, I began to flirt with the notion that dolphins could be echolocators like the bats, who shoot little clicks out ahead of them and manage in that swooping flight of theirs to catch flying insects. Dark or murky water seemed not to faze dolphins in the least. Maybe they, too, made special sounds and navigated by the echoes that came back.

I teamed up with young John Prescott,[2] the new head of the oceanarium lab, to run an experiment to see if this curious echosense really existed in dolphins. A peppery young bottlenose dolphin named Kathy was assigned to the task. I reasoned that, if we could somehow block Kathy's sight, she might demonstrate echolocation for us. John and I tried everything we could think of—blinders built like big eye-muffs, taped-on eye covers, a rubber hood—nothing would stick to her slick rubbery skin. Every time we tried to put the hood on her, she swam out into the center of the tank and shook it off, then dutifully brought it back to us. That's a dolphin for you! That deep streak of cooperation, that joining into human games, seems always to be there.

Finally, one of us thought of suction cups, like the ones used to hold ski racks on the tops of automobiles. Maybe we could place these over her eyes and they would stay in place. We decided to cast our own cups out of latex so they would fit correctly over the contours of Kathy's face. What would we use for a form? One of us thought of falsies—and so it was that the first successful dolphin blindfolds were cast over a pair of Jr. Teen-sized falsies, which, needless to say, was the subject of conversation for a long time.

John came bursting in to my office. "They work!" he said.

"What works?" I asked.

"The blindfolds—and you can't believe what she's doing. Come see," he said, pulling me by the arm.

Magic! Kathy seemed totally unfazed by having her vision shut off. She swam as fast as ever, cutting around the tank with total confidence and coming to poolside when we slapped the tank wall to have her blindfolds taken off. John and I were deep in wonder. You might think the development of dolphin blindfolds was a trivial thing, but not so. They have been used since in most of the dozens of experiments that followed, and much of our unfolding understanding of the dolphin echolocation system has been aided by them.

We built a maze of two lines of air-filled aluminum poles, set ten feet apart and hung vertically from overhead clotheslines. We could move the lines back and forth on pulleys to produce a new arrangement of pipes each time we asked Kathy to pass through. We stretched the contraption across her pool. She negotiated this pole barrier dozens of times, zigzagging in and out, no matter how we arranged it, without so much as touching a pole. On the last pass before we took the rig out of the pool, petulant Kathy swam through and whacked the poles with her flukes, as if to say, "So there, you demanding guys, take that! Right in your data set!" No wonder all those dolphins had escaped our encircling nets. It was a piece of cake for an animal with a good echo-sense.

John and I posed the most difficult questions we could think of. We asked Kathy to find and touch a small disc of plywood pressed against the tank wall. We asked her to discriminate between a slowly drifting, gelatin capsule filled with fish flesh from one filled with water. Neither of these problems seemed to daunt her at all.

Paul Asadorian and Paul Perkins, from a nearby Navy lab, helped us listen and record her sounds through all this experimentation. During every task, Kathy emitted long, whining trains of high-frequency clicks, far above the level of human hearing and much like the sounds bats use to catch insects in the dark. She literally shot out a beam of such clicks and scanned it around like a flashlight in the dark. Curiously, these clicks seemed to emanate from her forehead, which later study showed to be the case. Two pairs of little clappers located on each side of a dolphin's upper airway have been pinpointed as the sources of these sounds.

About this time, John and I learned that two other scientists, Bill and Barbara Schevill of Woods Hole Oceanographic Institution, Massachusetts, had already demonstrated dolphin echolocation by a much simpler test. At a pool dug back of a Cape Cod beach and filled with muddy water, they had asked an old, nearly blind bottlenose dolphin to choose which side of a long, projecting wall of net it must go to to receive a fish dangled below water. The dolphin responded easily, all the while emitting its "rusty hinge" click trains.[3]

In the decades that followed, our understanding of dolphin echolocation was filled in bit by bit. Dr. Bill Evans and Bill Powell of the U.S. Navy dolphin research facility discovered that a dolphin could "see into things with its sound," exploiting the fact that in water, sounds easily penetrate into objects, producing internal vibrations that vary depending on the object's composition. They painted a series of plates of different kinds of metal batttleship gray, hung mixed pairs of these plates—aluminum and steel, for example—before a dolphin. Then they asked the dolphin to tell the plates apart. The dolphin did so with high accuracy, discriminating copper from steel from aluminum and more.[4]

These were all close-up capabilities of the echo-sense. We still had no real idea of the dolphin's echolocation capability at long distance, where its vital role as an early warning system of danger should lie. Dr. Whitlow Au and his colleagues at the U.S. Navy lab in Hawaii took up this question. They stretched a pulley system between poles set in the sea bottom, way out across the open bay right next to their dolphin enclosures. They were then able to run an echolocation target out to any desired distance, lower it into the water (or not), and ask the dolphin if it detected anything. Their dolphins correctly reported the presence of a target about the size of a tangerine hung more than a football field's distance away!

The clicks Au's dolphins used proved to be less than a thousandth of a second long, but they were sometimes of almost incredible intensity—invading what physicists call the finite limit of sound, the range in which providing more energy to the sound generator begins to produce heat and not a louder sound. These little clicks were about as intense as the sound of a jet engine going full blast!

Think for a moment about the feat Au's dolphin had performed. The dolphin had rapped out its string of clicks, composed of sounds far higher in pitch than a human can hear. It sent these tiny packets of sound rocketing into the opaque world around it, and nearly all of the sound was simply lost, spread out in the open water ahead of the dolphin, scintillating away from objects of no interest and then spreading away into oblivion. But from one little object almost impossibly far away an echo of vanishing faintness returned, over and over. Even at the target sphere, the sound was so faint and high that none of us could hear it. And yet the dolphin listened and then gave the right answer.

I wondered: Isn't this the dolphins' key adaptation, the one that allows them to swim so freely for such long lives with so trivial a set of weapons in the hostile world of the open sea? This must be the early warning system without which they never could have invaded that domain.

My understanding of the remarkable nature of the dolphin mind continued when I moved to Hawaii to help build Sea Life Park

Oceanarium, right on the magnificent Hawaiian shore, and to head its research arm, the Oceanic Institute. This time the dolphin training was Karen Pryor's job, not my own. Karen, a crackling-bright young woman, had some animal training experience to guide her, unlike my Marineland colleagues and I. She had trained Welsh ponies as an avocation. In time, she would become the world's premier dolphin trainer, and I don't wonder. She is a person who sees through the intentions of animals as if she were gazing through window glass.

One day, word flashed around the new oceanarium: "You ought to see what Karen's done with her dolphins now, up at the theatre tank." Gregory Bateson, a renowned scientist whose specialty was animal and human communication, was working with us at the time. He and I trooped up to the tank and found Karen at tankside, her big rough-tooth dolphin Malia stationed expectantly in front of Karen, head out of the water, sculling. Karen waited, fish in hand and whistle in mouth, ready to produce a sound should Malia do what she wanted. (Karen used that whistle to signal her approval to the dolphin; an instant blast sealed the message, unlike our early attempts to throw a reward fish quickly enough for the dolphin to remember what it was for.) Karen asked Malia to "do something new." Malia understood what Karen was asking and, while we watched, proceeded to invent one new behavior pattern after another.

In that one day, Malia poured out a long string of new patterns that no one had seen before—long barrel rolls underwater, a beautiful arching back gainer that took the dolphin several feet above the water, a long surf on its chin part way across the pool, and more. The training process, Karen explained, had been a very difficult one as the animal edged on frustration, not understanding what Karen was requiring of her. But then, as if the light bulb had gone on over her head, she began to invent new patterns, and a fish reward splashed in the water each time.

"My God," said Gregory, "she's demonstrated a capacity for abstract thought in a dolphin." What Gregory meant was that the dolphin had understood the context of a communication, in this case the idea of "new." Such capability had been long thought the sole property of humans and the highest primates. Gregory called what Malia had shown "deuterolearning," or learning-to-learn.[5] All those puzzling observations of dolphins and whales helping each other began to fall in place. These animals seemed able to order their lives on the basis of concepts!

About this time, experimental psychologist Louis Herman from the University of Hawaii, over the hill in Honolulu, began to appear at tankside as Karen and her trainers worked with the dolphins. He soon became immersed in the vista of discovery presented by the dolphin mind. It would become his lifetime work.

Herman began systematically uncovering feature after feature of the dolphin mind. He taught dolphins to use symbols—much like human words. They responded to his questions with wonderful cooperative spirit, but unlike some chimpanzees, they did not take up this new language themselves. Hints of the complexity of dolphin life lay in Herman's findings. His dolphins proved to have remarkable "list memory," the ability to remember unrelated things, such as numbers in strings, and to do so a little better than humans.

Why should a dolphin be good at remembering zip codes? Well, the capacity also says the dolphin should be able to keep track of many unrelated events all at once, like, for example, the doings of two dozen schoolmates, as told from their sounds emitted at night in the black sea.

Herman and his colleagues found that dolphins are high-speed mimics. They can begin to mimic a sound before the sending animal has finished emitting it. That is also a key feature of our use of language, because we humans form a mental template of each word we wish to speak and then produce it as we babble along, though Herman will adamantly tell you that he found no evidence that dolphins actually use a language.[6]

I agree. I see no such evidence, either. Dolphins are themselves. They are not like humans. The ocean half of their adaptation has indeed produced a mammal like no other.

To begin to understand how these pieces fit together, I had to go back to sea with a wild spinner dolphin school and there spin the wheel. This work went on for two decades and a half. Only then did my colleagues and I come close to an explanation of this curious dolphin capability of high-speed mimicry, of the dolphins' deep cooperation, and their remarkable mental capabilities. What we found with those spinners, just as Herman had insisted, was not language as we know it, but an entirely different means of getting their intentions across. They used something like a musical score, and they played it out in both time and space.

Melia takes a somersaulting leap at Sea Life Park, Oahu, Hawaii, 1965.

Wild Hawaiian spinner dolphins off the Big Island coast, September 1980.

Photo by Randy Wells

Chapter 12:
Dolphin Jazz

We showed up for the luau all wearing our new Shannon Brownlee-designed T-shirts, which displayed the letters of our project name—Hana Nai'a—wrapped around a leaping spinner dolphin. We stopped by the garage to pay our respects to the *tutus*, the grandmothers, sitting there massive in their colorful *muumuus*, holding court. One of them put down her Primo beer and, with a sly look on her face, asked us, "You know what *hana nai'a* means?"

"Sure," one of us replied, "It means 'dolphin work.'"

The old lady rolled her eyes suggestively and told us to look down on a school of dolphins sometime, then we would know what *hana nai'a* really meant. We took this innuendo to mean that, among dolphins, sex was a way of life. The story was that whenever you looked at a wild dolphin school, you'd see some of the animals caressing in long exchanges, missing no body part as the pectoral fin of one slid over the neighbor's anatomy. It was not long before my colleagues and I would corroborate the tutu's assessment of almost continual caressing in active spinner dolphin schools. What it meant was a different matter, and that only became clear after many months of observation.

When I first hatched the idea of studying a wild dolphin society, my major problem was finding a place where I could watch dolphins over and over, for months at a time. Beyond that, I needed to find dolphins in water clear enough to see all the details of their interactions. Even in Hawaii, that was not an easily solved problem. But one morning a surfer friend dropped by my office and talked of a school of spinner dolphins that lived in Kealake'akua Bay, on the Big Island of Hawaii. "I swam right in among them," he told me. "I could feel their sounds tickle across my chest. The water was clear as glass."

Excited by all this, my assistant, Tom Dohl, and I made our way to Kealake'akua. Sure enough, beneath a somber 500-foot cliff of black lava lay a calm emerald-and-blue jewel of a bay. In the bay that morning were about forty spinner dolphins. They swam lazily back and forth in glassy water, over a patch of white sand bottom, thirty feet down, coming as close as about 200 feet to the shore. With my binoculars, I could just make out a few details of their fins and backs as they rose to the surface to breathe.

Not long afterward, the Hana Nai'a project team took up residence in a rented house right on Kealake'akua Bay, with our program vessel, the 25-foot *Nai'a*, moored close enough offshore that we could row or swim out to her. Rocking gently on another buoy nearby was our ungainly underwater-viewing vessel, the *Maka Ala*, whose name meant "the watchful one."

My hope for Project Hana Nai'a was simple enough: I wanted to see if it was possible to assemble the natural history of a wild dolphin species at sea. I wanted to keep our eyes wide open and spin the wheel, and, like good scientists, measure whatever we could measure, getting it all down on paper, recording tape, or film.

Spinners are lovely creatures, dressed in a dark charcoal cape above, with pearl gray flanks and an immaculate white belly. Their long, black-tipped beak is lined with delicate little teeth that suggest they wouldn't hurt a soul. There is a kind of graceful gentility about them and it shows in their faces, especially in those of their sleek tunalike young. The word *innocence* seems designed for those littlest of spinners.

The name *spinner* is derived from the dolphin's habit of making spinning leaps. Scattered throughout their school as it moves along are individuals that leap and rotate in a blur of fins, flukes, and flying water, to fall back again in a crash of spray and then to spin down deep into the water amid a spiral of bubbles.[1] In his whaling days, Herman Melville knew the spinners well. In *Moby Dick*, he called them "Huzza Porpoises," describing them as swimming "in hilarious shoals" and being in the habit of "tossing themselves to heaven like caps in a Fourth-of-July crowd."

In making any attempt to understand a population such as the spinner dolpins' in the wild, there are key life-patterns that need to be described because they embrace everything else. What do the animals eat? Where do they travel? How do they carry out the larger patterns of their lives, such as reproduction, growth, maturity, and death? I had no hope that we would learn all these things about the spinners in depth, but I did think we could sketch out their outlines. The greatest problem we met in our quest was the undulating sea surface itself. Dolphins live almost wholly beneath it, and we above it. Even though dolphins often swim close along inhabited coasts, where people may see their fins and backs nearly every day, the controlling dimensions of their lives are hidden, played out by fast-swimming animals suspended in the passing swells, the lenses of the sea surface playing bright, intersecting patterns across their backs as they court, nurture, quarrel, and dive into the dark sea to find their food.

Slowly, slowly, bit by hard-won bit, the life of the spinner dolphin did begin to unfold before us. We learned to know about two hundred dolphins as individuals, telling them apart by the unique scarring on their backs or fins. My field leaders, Dr. Bernd Würsig and doctoral candidate Randy Wells, were already masters of the high-speed, telephoto photography needed to document these usually slight marks. From the boxes and boxes of catalogued slides photographed all along the Hawaiian shore, there began to emerge the patterns of spinner dolphin movement, who associated with whom.

Bernd's wife, Mel, ran the theodolite station where we recorded the tracks of the dolphin schools that entered the bay, using a precision surveyor's instrument. This station was located on a tiny lava shelf that clung precariously to a shoulder of the black cliff, high above the bay. Mostly it was either Mel or Chris Johnson, our student behaviorist, who climbed there in the early morning, pulling herself up by means of tree branches through hundreds of new-made spider webs built every night across the so-called trail.

Much of our insight into spinner social patterns came from watching the dolphins from our ungainly underwater-viewing vessel. The *Maka Ala* was an old Boston whaler skiff, with her bow replaced by a sloping clear-plastic box. It was possible to lie on one's belly on a mattress, head thrust into the plastic box, and to see the dolphins underwater. All the recording gear required to record dolphin voices occupied a shelf above the observer and constantly threatened to cascade down, should the boat roll too far. A few trips in the *Maka Ala* and we consigned her solely for use on calm days, deep in the bay.

We focused our attention first on understanding the details of the social interaction that we could observe in the bay. This meant probing into the meaning of *hana nai'a*. By repeatedly measuring the hormone levels in a small school of captive spinners held at Sea Life Park Oceanarium, Randy had found that females came into full receptivity and fertility for very brief periods—less than a week or so each season. Only then could mating produce a pregnancy. The ability of males to reproduce proved seasonal, too—their testes were hugely enlarged in spring and summer, then shrank to a fraction of that size in winter. But we knew that the caressing went on all year. What sense did that make?

The answer, as we eventually came to understand it, was that *hana nai'a* was a form of social communication mostly not concerned with reproduction at all. *Hana nai'a* simply represented the co-option of sexual patterns into running a dolphin society in its larger sense. Only one pattern of caressing—beak-genital propulsion—seemed restricted to the time when a female dolphin could conceive. This curious behavior consisted of one dolphin placing its beak in the genital slit of the other and propelling the recipient slowly along. Chris Johnson thought she could hear a faint echolocation train as one animal propelled the other. Perhaps they were stimulating each other or tasting reproductive readiness.

We played out ideas such as these around the dinner table with a wondrous collection of young scholars, both team members and visitors who brought new ideas, attitudes, and vigor to our quest, and who pitched a tent on the lawn if there was no bed available.

It was heady stuff to realize that we were the first humans to make a connection between a dolphin society living in the open sea and our own species. Before we were through, half a dozen similar efforts with other cetaceans were underway. At the end, my colleagues and I knew we had just begun.[2]

Only along the shores of certain warm-water islands, such as Hawaii, do spinner dolphins come near land. The species ranges clear around the earth, and most of their number live their long lives wholly in the open sea. I knew that if we were ever to understand these dolphins, to discover where in their lives this mind of theirs fits, we would have to go to sea with them and there find a way of staying up with their wild schools for a long enough to peek in and spin the naturalist's wheel. This seawork we accomplished mostly from the little cabin cruiser *Nai'a*.

One afternoon, Bernd, Randy, and I affixed a tiny radio on the fin of one of the dolphins and followed its school in the *Nai'a*. The dolphin led us out into the black night, where only the distant lights of the Kona shore were useful for our orientation. We had no idea where we were headed, a very creepy circumstance for people used to navigating carefully at sea. Bernd plotted radio signals picked up by our radio-direction finder to draw out the track of our instrumented dolphin and its school. Randy, steering, watched the dimly lit compass and followed the radio's directional signal. Sometimes the splashing forms of dolphins could be seen encased in the glow of plankton light, plunging around our bow.

The lights along the Kona shore began to dim and sink. Ten miles farther out, the island's lee disappeared altogether, merging into the open, trade-wind sea of giant swells, cascading breakers and whitecaps. I felt a lift of relief when the dolphin school turned in the blackness and began to swim parallel to the flanks of the huge, half-submerged volcano, keeping to water 6,000 feet deep or less.

Along that hidden contour, the dolphins moved, diving over and over, *en masse*, for the remainder of the night. Their prey were small, deep-water fishes, many with rows of biological lights along their sides, lacquer-red, deep-sea shrimps, or, where the school's traverses crossed submerged lava flows, curious little bottom-hugging squids almost unknown to science. We figured the dolphins might sometimes be diving as much as 600 feet straight down!

The dolphins were taking advantage of the "island effect." Deep ocean currents originating in the Antarctic Ocean, half of a globe away, piled constantly against the submerged base of our mountain, thus concentrating their load of deep-water creatures into a rich band. The slowly moving water of the deflected current crowded these organisms against the hidden mountain slope, then up to where the dolphins could reach them. We bobbed in the dark on the sea surface above, totally dependent upon the dolphins to tell us where to head next.

With dawn still three hours ahead, the dolphins turned for shore, zigzagging their way in. Their landfall seemed to be a matter of chance, of where the last zig left them. That more or less random landfall determined which rest cove the nearest dolphins would enter. This explained why a given dolphin changed its rest cove from day to day, week to week.

I was surprised at some of what Hana Nai'a began to uncover as we followed more schools of dolphins out to sea. So much had been said of dolphin minds that I was half-prepared to find an exotic lord in a world of dullards. Instead, we found schools of dolphins that did nearly the same rather mundane things, day after day, year after year.

Spinner dolphins slept during the daytime, deep in one of a string of acceptable coves or over shallow, sandy reef flats along the open island coast. An acceptable cove seemed to be one with a patch of white-sand bottom and nearby access to deep water. The dolphins, while sleeping, swam back and forth quietly, largely without touching each other. After their rest, the dolphins ventured offshore; then, all night long, they patrolled the coast, periodically diving deep to feed.

In the morning, the dolphins raced toward the shore where one of the rest coves awaited. We could see them coming from our cliff, first as tiny blips of white, then resolving into a broad rank of animals plunging along across the gunmetal sea, leaping and spinning. Usually, twenty to forty dolphins sought out Kealake'akua. They swam deep into our cove, almost to the glowering cliff. There the school slowed and began to mill over that patch of white-sand bottom. Then they slipped into their daytime rest pattern, zigzagging slowly back and forth, always staying over the sand and surfacing almost surreptitiously, to take quiet little breaths.

Most of the thousand animals that nightly traversed offshore sought coves other than Kealake'akua for rest. The Big Island spinners seemed to be composed of an almost completely fluid society, and every morning parts of it made landfalls elsewhere along the Kona shore. Yet within all this fluidity of association, we also detected that some dolphins clearly had friends. These "habitual associates," as we called them, now and then swam together for a day or so. A curious society indeed. Animal behaviorists have seen this kind of social arrangement before and have named it a "fusion-fission society." This pattern appears in social animals that live in large groups, such as troops of baboons. I played with the notion that savannas and the open sea have things in common, especially because there are so few places to hide.

That, in broadest outline, was what these dolphins did. We began to think that they behaved more like animals with a tenuous toehold in the ocean rather than as the new regents of a sea kingdom. Yet these dolphins had clearly won some part of the adaptive war, and for a long time we were not sure how they had done it. Simply said, they had managed to persist at sea even though they produced relatively few offspring during their very long lives. Forty-year-old dolphins are known, and over about twenty of those years spinner females give birth to perhaps a dozen young, one at a time. The spinner dolphin life span is about the same as that of an aboriginal human, with about the same number of young.

Somehow, suspended for this long life in the open three-dimensional ocean, they had managed to fend off the predators that were always near—especially the sharks, which we frequently saw swimming at the margins of cetacean schools and which not uncommonly left awesome scars on the sides of these same dolphins. Perhaps more threatening were the predatory marine mammals of the Kona coast. Huge (to 20 feet) false killer whales, an overall lead gray in color and thus almost invisible underwater at a rather short distance away, seemed to be dolphin predators. Adult false killers can swim with great speed, considerably faster than dolphins can, and they possess a mouth as full of formidable interlocking white teeth as the true killer whale. Once, on the tropical tuna grounds, a false killer was seen leaping with a dolphin crosswise in its jaws.[3] When these whales came near the spinners, we saw agitation among the dolphins, and we didn't wonder. The swift schools of false killers are commonly seen along the Kona coast foraging along the trash lines. The trash was mostly bagasse, cut-up and pressed stalks of sugar cane from the mills ashore. It floated in long, wavering lines offshore and was notable for the fish it attracted. Want to catch a mahi mahi? Go fish along the trash line.

Rounding out the list of spinner dolphin predators are pygmy killer whales, which also possess a formidable mouthful of teeth, and pilot whales, which have been reported to capture and swallow baby dolphins. Both are common off Kealake'akua. My conclusion: it's no picnic out there off the Kona Coast, and the spinner's central problem is clearly simple survival.

One day, deep in Kealake'akua Bay, Chris Johnson and I cruised above the resting dolphins in the *Maka Ala*. Chris lay flat on a mattress spread on the bottom of the boat, looking downward through the plastic bow at the dolphins swimming below. I sat in the stern, steering the *Maka Ala* back and forth at Chris's command. The dolphins swam twenty or thirty feet down, just above the pale sand, moving quietly in a slow dance, each just beyond the touch of its neighbor's fin tip. They were almost silent. That white sand, we concluded, served to silhouette any sharks that might venture near at a time when the dolphins had almost shut down their echolocation and when they seemed to find their way mostly by eyesight. We could see the protective cadres of males, serious about their business of interposing themselves between the dolphin school and us. We could see the nurture of mother dolphins as they shepherded their sometimes obstreperous young through their early lives.

"They're waking up," Chris called up to me. The dolphins had begun to make several distinct sounds: low banjo twangs, whistles, clicks, and little barks like a yappy dog. Sure enough, the dolphins then left the sand patch, diving shallowly now, traveling a little faster than before. Two slapped their heads against the water, one leapt partway out of the water, and the school moved ever faster. New dolphin voices chimed in, like an orchestra tuning up. Ten minutes later, a dolphin leapt high out of the water in a tight vibrant spin. The school, alert now, began its long, in-and-out dance toward the open sea.

We could see graduate student Shannon Brownlee readying the listening equipment aboard the *Nai'a*. She had taken up the daunting task of unraveling spinner dolphin sounds for her graduate study. I came to treasure my days at sea with this multidimensional, ebullient, sassy young student. There seemed nothing out of Shannon's range, be it art, cooking, close and accurate observation, high-powered statistics, or performing the ancient hula amid the piles of data sheets and catalogued stacks of 35 mm slides.

I changed boats. Shannon and I prepared to follow the dolphins out to sea, to observe their transition from rest to the vibrancy of the nighttime feeding school. We would listen and record their voices all the way out, just so long as we could keep track of them in the fading light. Shannon's hope was that she could somehow extract meaning from the sounds we recorded. Even though I had suggested the problem to her, I thought about the task involved. It was a bit like listening through the wall of the telephone company's switching building and then making sense of all the clicks and squeaks that one heard.

We cruised a hundred yards ahead of the dolphin school and stopped. Shannon slipped the hydrophone (our underwater listening device, or "pickle") into the water, lowering it to about thirty feet—good listening depth. I turned on the big, high-speed recorder. Earphones on her head, Shannon commented, "I can hear them coming toward us." As the dolphins approached, swimming briskly now, their school emitted a cascade of echolocation clicks. We could hear whistles and a bark or two.

A few minutes after they had passed us, we quietly slipped the *Nai'a* into gear, swung way off to the school's side to make our way carefully past it and to lower the hydrophone again, ahead of them. "They've stopped," said Shannon. The school then reversed its course and began making its way slowly back toward the sand patch. We listened again. The dolphins were emitting only quiet little bursts of echolocation clicks now. Soon the school stopped again, three-quarters of the way back to the resting grounds, and began to mill.

Ten minutes later, the school turned outward, moving toward the open sea again, swimming a little faster and a little farther than before. Bursts of sounds filled the water, as if one of them had switched on the "play" button. In and out, in and out, voices turned up and then fell nearly quiet, voices coming on again—in this strange way, the dolphin school ratcheted itself out to sea.

By the time the dolphins were about to leave the bay, the orchestra was on full. Whistles wove in great tangled choruses, clicks came in cascades, dolphins barked and twanged. The dolphins were swimming fast now, little trails of white water streaming from their dorsal fins as they raced along. With each outward turn of the school, the sounds grew louder, more complex, more rhythmic as chorus after chorus ululated into the darkening sea.

It took the dolphins more than an hour to clear the headlands. Just at dusk and well beyond the bay's southern cusp, dark forms of dolphins suddenly, abruptly, spilled from the sea in beautiful leaping cascades, headed right toward the yellow disc of the sinking sun. We could, in that instant, see the elegant, previously hidden coherence of our dolphin school. They were surely all together in whatever it was they were doing.[4] At dusk, we lost them. They disappeared as leaping silhouettes against the red-streaked sky, cascading over the black swells.

It took a long time to understand what happened during this zigzag behavior, which was repeated day after day. I came to believe that, in the largest frame, the behavior represents a dolphin school making up its "mind"—getting its collective act together for a major transition from one major behavioral state to another. While swimming zigzag, the members of a school were shucking off the patterns of sleep and getting ready for a night's foray among both predators and food in a dark world mostly mediated by sound. But more than this, the dolphins were engaging in group decision-making—democracy at its most tedious.

There seemed to be no stable unitary leadership in these spinner dolphin schools. There was no single sergeant shouting out orders. Instead, we came to think, there were probably many points of leadership in this deeply cooperative society, and that, considering the obvious suppression of aggressive behavior, consensus among dolphins was easy to reach. Remember, we are dealing here with a pickup society in which membership changes from night to night.

Top-down, unitary leadership, in any case, would be much too slow to work in an emergency, such as a shark attack. There can be no waiting for orders from on high. I once saw the almost instantaneous group behavior that occurs at such a point of attack. Right off my bow, as I passed over a rather shallow reef flat, a school of spinners burst from the water in a perfect rosette, animals arcing away from a center of disturbance, leaping in all compass directions. The action was so sudden, so unanimous that the dolphins were apparently fleeing from something fearful; I imagined rather than saw an attacking predator in the center of that circle of leaping animals.

In more relaxed times, the decision-making of spinners seems to give way to a consensus of experienced animals, both males and females. It is clear that a hierarchy of age is a strong element in dolphin schools, but how the elders sort out this group leadership was never evident to us. In my scheme, the older dolphins emerged as instructors of group knowledge, as guides-through-life. The young had to wait to take part in leadership. Only over time would they become new nuclei of guidance in the dance.

Our little captive school revealed how the collective leadership of elders might work. Changes in school direction seemed to be initiated by the older animals throughout the school, who were the first to show intentions to turn. Black beaks bent a few degrees sideways, and others almost instantaneously followed. I'll bet that acoustic cues also mediate such turns as they begin, but we were never able to hear them. In the ocean, the subtle guidance of older dolphins amounts to a rapidly jelling group-consensus, an oscillation of the fluid dolphin school toward an agreed-upon end, not the result of some dictum passed down a single rigid chain of command. The school then flows off like the pseudopod of an amoeba in the somehow-chosen direction.

As Shannon and I continued to observe the zigzag phenomenon of dolphins leaving the bay for nighttime feeding, it became evident that the whole event involved complicated, intersecting rhythms in both space and time. As the animals zigzagged in and out of the bay together, their school expanded and contracted at the same time in a spatio-temporal rhythm, spreading widely when they swam fast and then moving in tight, close together, when the dolphins slowed. And not only that, this rhythmic movement had a direct relationship to the cadence of the dolphins' vocalizations! As the dolphins made their way offshore, their sounds rose and fell and rose again, at the same time as the school itself spread, then contracted, and spread again. The modulating beat governed their speed as the dolphins swam buoyantly and rapidly out to sea for a few minutes, then turned back toward the sand patch at a slow crawl, their collective ebullience seemingly gone. Over and over, the school performed this hesitation waltz—out fast, voices rising; in slow, voices subdued; out faster; in not quite so far, not quite so slow—until the school disappeared into the darkening sea.

The more we looked at the behavior of dolphin schools as rhythmic compositions, the more rhythms in deep counterpoint we could perceive. They ranged from tempos a jazz musician would understand to much slower, minutes-long oscillations of sound that Shannon and I could detect only by looking at the long rolls of paper spit from the printer.

My mind flirted over the larger meanings that seemed hidden in this curious operation of dolphin society. Many aspects of what Shannon and I had seen were features of the dolphin school itself, fed back upon its members, rather than simple extensions of the individual dolphins that comprise it. The dolphin voices rising and growing faint, the school spreading and contracting, speeding and slowing, moving toward the sea and then back toward the shore—these things seemed to be heavily group processes, not just the actions of individuals in a school summed. The school is a phenomenon *sui generis*, we concluded, an entity with duties of its own. An individual dolphin cannot spread apart and come together the way a school does. While a single dolphin's voice may rise and fall, it cannot produce a weaving chorus of intermeshed voices. A single dolphin does not an orchestra make.

For spinner dolphins, much of their lives seemed dictated by the daily requirements of the schools in which they live, not just by their own individual desires. In the deepest sense, they are interactive ciphers in an embracing system. They, I began to think, are creatures both of their own individuality and the faceless consensus of the larger society within which they lived. The dolphins' gentility, their remarkable cooperation, seem clear reflections of lives lived within such a system. Their closely similar appearance, one dolphin to the next, said the same thing. The demands of the conforming life had obviously shaped them both mentally and physically. How much of every mammalian life is shaped this way? I wondered. Don't all of us—humans, elephants, dolphins, mice—exist in private balances such as this? Don't we all find a place between conformity and individuality that reflects the larger needs and opportunities of our species?

Questions like these were on our minds when Shannon and I waited aboard our little vessel, the *Nai'a*, watching a resting school of spinners as it moved deliberately back and forth over the sand patch.

Shannon slipped the hydrophone over the side. She, with earphones on, stood listening to their voices. Starting that day, and on others to follow, we began to piece together a most curious fact about the behavior of these dolphins. Everything they did was as if their school, and every animal in it, was responding to a great piece of music that they themselves were composing on the spot. The ruling theme started out slow, lento, and speeded to allegro by the time the bay mouth was reached. This was no simple rhythm, someone marking time with a drumstick, but a complex rhythm, the beat improvised in both time and space. Nor were the collective sounds a mere accompaniment to the physical movement, but instead an integral part of how the movements were determined.

What we were witnessing, in other words, was the dolphins dancing to their own jazz music! The improvised rhythmic sounds of the dolphin orchestra were the stuff of some kind of negotiation process, the means by which the leaderless school made decisions on the fly about how and where to move during the crucial transition from daytime rest to nighttime feeding. As we slowly came to this understanding, we felt we had chiseled loose an important fragment of knowledge about the life of this wild dolphin.

None of this fully explained how dolphins could survive at sea, however. We might have learned a little about how rhythms and consensus worked in a dolphin school, but much about their lives remained obscure. These dolphins were still little more than a school of oscillating, flowing, phonating animals. Why must they and the blackbirds move in great flowing schools whose form is never the same from minute to minute? Why do anchovies school? Why do gnats swarm and dance? What is it about these fluidly moving animals that lets them live as the dolphins do, out there totally exposed in open space?

Wild Hawaiian spinner dolphins off the Big Island coast, September 1980.

Photo by Randy Wells

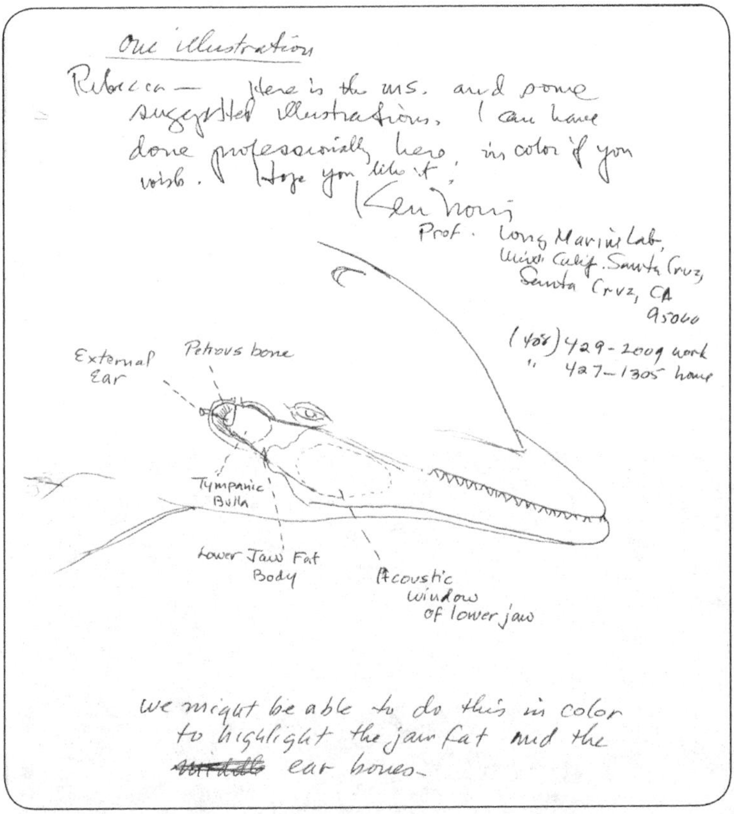

Illustration courtesy of the Norris Collection

Ken Norris's diagram of a dolphin's acoustic system.

Chapter 13:
Of Fighter Pilots, Chorus Lines, and Shark Attacks

My first expectation in studying dolphin communication is that it will prove to have the general characteristic of being primarily about relationship. This premise is in itself perhaps sufficient to account for the sporadic development of large brains among mammals.... All that is needed is to suppose that large-brained creatures were, at some evolutionary stage, unwise enough to get into the game of relationship and that, once the species was caught in this game of interpreting its members' behavior toward one another as relevant to this complex and vital subject, there was survival value for those individuals who could play the game with greater ingenuity or greater wisdom.

Gregory Bateson
Whales, Dolphins and Porpoises[1]

The day edges toward dusk—the dangerous twilight time. Out in the shadowy distance, far beyond the reach of the dolphins' sight, a ten-foot tiger shark moves easily along. Close below the big fish is the deep reef, a dark background of cliffs, boulders the size of houses, and the reaching arms of corals. This is the shark's cover, the backdrop that can hide it from its prey. Having heard the noisy dolphin school passing overhead, that cacophony of sound within which the dolphins constantly travel, the shark almost imperceptibly increases its swimming speed. The shark's head, slicing sideways back and forth through the water, soon picks up the dolphin's vanishingly faint odor trail and follows it, along with the continual sounds the dolphins emit.

The dolphins have already been alerted. Sentries among the forty-animal school—the watch-standers, a dozen animals continuously spraying trains of echolocation clicks into the blue haze beyond the limit of vision—have detected a smattering of echoes from a target that might be moving. A large object seems to be in open water far in front and a hundred feet below. Soon, nearly all the dolphins on that side of their school begin to hear faint, almost imperceptible trains of echoes. Then some begin to detect a slow rhythm in the returned clicks. All know from long experience what that means: the beat of a big fish's tail. The detection soon becomes group knowledge, and many dolphins begin to plot the echoing target. There is no panic, only a routine response to an event that occurs a dozen times a day.

As the shark moves closer, the dolphin school begins to tighten into its defensive formation. Gone now are the bouts of caressing that typified the school minutes before. The dolphins position themselves in close echelon, staggered, almost touching fin tips, so one animal watches the black pectoral fin of its neighbor, the next its pectoral, and so on. A slight movement of a black fin over the white belly beneath will signal an incipient turn, or a dive. The tightened school begins to weave in and out in a curious infolding of animals, a little like twisting the fibers of a rope.

The shark, looming thirty feet away now, appears as a sleek bullet, projecting directly toward the school. Within the now-disciplined dolphin school, a message of imminent attack has flashed in all directions. Perhaps the message involves sound, perhaps it is simply the multiplied message of the school members' movements. Maybe it is both. No scientist yet knows.

The shark sculls closer to the dolphins, changing nothing, and suddenly, in a blur of tail beats almost too fast to discriminate, it attacks. As if hit by a silent shock wave, the dolphin school opens just ahead of the onrushing shark—everywhere a curving wall of dolphins fades away, a foot ahead of the shark's champing jaws. The shark planes down and out of the school, a picture of failure.

The dolphin school closes its ranks and moves on its course. As soon as the shark has slipped a hundred feet astern, the school begins to spread again. Caressing reappears. The clicking sounds have never stopped. The shark will not pursue the attack. Such repeated attack is too costly of carefully sequestered energy in the face of nearly certain failure.

I made up this story, of course. But it matches what I know about both predators and schools of prey. It contains some of the ways I think both senses and schools work. That magic melting-away within inches of an onrushing predator is crucial. The advantages that let the dolphins escape during these extremely brief moments are slight, and they leave little room for error. Yet they are obviously powerful, allowing the noisy dolphins to live very long lives in a danger-filled sea.

In 1984, it was still a mystery to me how dolphins evaded attacks. Having learned something about dolphin communication and social behavior, I was left puzzling how their magic shield could work. I suggested to my colleague Carl Schilt that we explore together how fish and dolphin schools could possibly protect their members in the open space of the sea. Carl shares my fascination with schools, flocks, and herds. At that time, he was exploring the effects of sound upon anchovy schools for his graduate thesis.

First, Carl and I reviewed what we already knew. "Those click trains that allow a dolphin school to locate a shark—they're obviously a fine early-warning system," I commented. A dolphin school, I knew, can certainly detect a shark a hundred yards away, or more. Carl had no trouble with that conclusion. "Then there's the time dimension," I continued. "If the dolphins are ready, the shark hardly ever wins. The actual evasion of an attack seems to take a second or less." In fact, I thought, given the fact that dolphins advertise where their schools are, the very brief moment when the shark fails in its attack seemed to contain most of the story we sought to explain. Carl noted that, just before that moment, a school always tightened. Why did this occur?

Weeks later, Carl and I proposed a relationship, which we called the "group distance." We defined the group distance as that rather precise between-animal distance toward which all the members of a school, flock, or herd seem to close when under threat. We hoped that this construct would focus our thoughts, and then we might begin to explain that tiny time advantage the dolphin school seemed to possess.

We said that when the unmoving eye of one animal—dolphin, fish, bird, or antelope—is fully filled with the image of its neighbor, it has reached the group distance.[2] When under attack, we said, the eyes of the prey school members probably could not afford to move. That, we suggested, is probably too slow. Once all animals arrived at the group distance and held their eyes still, the slightest nuance of movement of one animal should instantly register in minds of its neighbors on both sides. If a spinner dolphin at group distance rolled its body even slightly, its neighbors would know instantly because it would be sweeping the sharply defined zones of its dark cape, pearl flanks, and white belly across its neighbor's visual field. If those neighbors made the same movement, it would be replicated across the school. Before such an evasive movement is well underway, the neighboring animals are already beginning to move in response, with the result that the dolphins flow away from the shark in unbroken ranks, as if by magic, leaving the shark opening and closing its jaws in defeat.

It seemed to us that we had part of the puzzle, but far from all of it. "Carl," I asked, "what can we learn about the reactions of predator and prey during an attack?" I wanted us to understand, if we could, what each animal experienced in this primeval event. Carl, a master at unearthing facts from the vast libraries of the world, swung into action, while I went trolling for understanding among my friends over in the psychology department at UC Santa Cruz, especially with experimental psychologist Bruce Bridgeman. Bruce loaded me up with scientific papers to read, including a magnificent piece of work by a remarkable man named George Armitage Miller, who later became known as the "Father of Cognitive Psychology."

Miller had been using information theory as a lens through which to understand the results of experiments in the processing of sensory stimuli by humans. He began his paper with the cryptic statement: "My problem is that I have been persecuted by an integer."[3] This integer—the number seven or its near approximation—kept appearing for Miller as a measure of what seemed to be an inherent limit in the amount of sensory information that the human nervous system could receive and process. The typical person, for example, could recall immediately about seven digits or keep in his field of attention about seven objects.

Miller observed that this limit forced a trade-off: to process either a great deal of information rather crudely or less information more accurately. Comparing data across different experiments, Miller concluded that humans tended to resolve the conflict in favor of crude awareness of many variables. Like a true visionary, he saw the implication of this idea for vertebrate evolution. "We might argue," he wrote, "that in the course of evolution those organisms were most successful that were responsive to the widest range of stimulus energies in their environment. In order to survive in a constantly fluctuating world, it was better to have a little information about a lot of things than to have a lot of information about a small segment of the environment."

I realized that Miller was giving us an insight into shark perception that might be a key part of our puzzle. A shark attempting to single out for attack one particular dolphin from among the flowing, interweaving throng of dolphins, and then to locate and track that dolphin in three-dimensional space, had to process a tremendous amount of sensory information. If the perceptual equipment of sharks was anything like ours, Miller seemed to be saying, then the attacking shark was bumping up against a physiological wall and had to give up accuracy in favor of processing all the perceptual variables. Its knowledge of the prey's location at any one instant was only a gross approximation, because its apparatus of perception—the sense organs and the mind that interprets them—did not work fast enough to produce a precise picture. Like a man groping for a light switch, it only approximately knew the location of the dolphin it sought to catch. Given just a few fractions of a second more time, the shark could refine its approximations until it knew the exact location of the dolphin it was targeting. But by then it was too late—the shark had lost the cat-and-mouse game, and the dolphins had faded away in their group anonymity.

Bruce also told me of another crucial relationship that factored in the variable of motion. During the first fractions of a second after the shark chose a particular dolphin to attack, its visual system was no more than a simple motion predictor. It recorded the prey's position, went almost sightless for an extremely brief period of time, came into consciousness again after the prey had moved a little, and then recorded another position. By doing this over and over during those first fuzzy blinks of time, the predator's visual apparatus plotted a predicted course for the prey. In effect, the prey's track consisted of dots—points of consciousness separated by extremely short, but very crucial stretches of near oblivion.[4]

Light bulbs lit up over Carl's and my heads! If a dolphin or an anchovy was alone with an attacker, it was very likely dead meat. The rather imprecise predictions of the predator's eye and mind, dotting out the prey's course, would still be good enough to lead a shark to a single fleeing dolphin or fish. The imprecision of vision and consciousness would not matter much, as long as the predator was somewhat faster than the prey. But if during the attack the prey was just one in a mass of twisting, flowing animals, all swimming close together and all looking alike to the approximating shark, the shark could be easily fooled. As the shark's vision shut on and off, it could easily lose track of its prey, embedded in the moving tapestry of very similar dolphins flooding away in front of it. Its imprecise eyes and mind would keep waking up on the wrong dolphin. And then when the shark opened its mouth to bite, these actions slowed the big fish enough to prevent further useful tracking of any of the fast-moving dolphins.

Like bird dogs picking up a scent, Carl and I raced on. This quest of ours was getting interesting! Carl continued to flood my desk with papers that might be relevant to our search for understanding. One day he pushed a little gem onto my desk, a work by Laurie Landau and John Terborgh of Princeton University, which described a sharply pointed, little experiment that squared Miller's pioneering story with our quest.[5]

These two naturalists had confronted a single fish predator (a pickerel) with various numbers of prey, starting with just a single fish. With just one prey fish present, the pickerel caught its lunch every time. Faced with two prey, it hesitated but quickly succeeded nonetheless. The uncertainty of the predator grew with each successive fish in the prey group. Five prey fish and the predator was having real trouble. When faced with about seven prey fish, failure of the predator became an all-but-foregone conclusion. The predator rushed at such a school, which melted miraculously in front of it, leaving the attacker fanning its fins in apparent frustration. We were intrigued that the number of prey fish it took to thoroughly confuse the pickerel—seven—was the same as the number that had haunted Miller in his research. Like Miller, we weren't sure if we were dealing with some deep relationship or a simple coincidence.

I recalled for Carl that the smallest spinner dolphin school my Kealake'akua mates and I had ever recorded was composed of five animals. They were extremely skittish—and now I knew why. They were pushing against the lower limit of what constituted a protective school! Five dolphins were hardly enough, not just because one of them might be tracked by a skillful predator during an attack, but also because there were scarcely enough of them to carry out the fixed duties of their school. They would have to trust in only one or two sentries. A larger school, in contrast, would have sentries peppered throughout the swimming mass of mammals, making the school not only more sensitive, but also more accurate.

Piece by piece, Carl and I knew we were beginning to put together a much larger story. We perceived that what we were missing was a better understanding of how timing and relationship enabled the remarkable communication that allowed a dolphin school to act as a single coordinated entity. One experiment began to crack open the door. Melba Caldwell, a psychologist, and her cetologist husband, David, had recorded the sounds of a small captive school of common dolphins. From these sound exchanges, they had teased out the some of details of interdolphin communication. If a dominant dolphin, an old adult, made a sound, one that seemed to have the animal's "social position" somehow stamped on it, and a subordinate dolphin responded right away—within a second or two—a communications channel, a party line, was opened across the school between the two animals, and it carried with it the implication of status.[6] Such an initialized, precisely timed series of sounds could allow communication between the two animals, even through the din of a traveling dolphin school, and the message would carry with it the implications of rank.

For Carl and me, the dimension of time, the rhythmic beat of life, kept appearing. Carl had located another gem, this time the work of W. K. Potts, who described what he called "the chorus line effect" in his studies of flocks of shorebirds.[7] Potts apparently conceived his central idea while watching the dancers' line at the Radio City Music Hall in New York. The high leg kick of the row of dancers flashed like magic along their line—2.5 times faster, he calculated, than it could if it was relying on the maximum speed of normal nerve transmission and subsequent muscle action in a human. The dancers accomplished this feat, Potts realized, simply by watching to the side, down the line of dancers, for the approaching kick. This allowed them to mobilize their muscles for the kick in advance, well before the wave of legs actually arrived, shaving off about half the time required for the total act. I remembered that both bird flocks and dolphin schools traveled in echelon formation, stacked up and back, allowing maximum visibility between even distant members in all possible directions! I thought: they must be dancers, too!

Carl and I kept searching. From a neurophysiologist friend, I learned of another effect that may well be involved in school function. It is called "aerial or probability summation," and it relates to the *precision* of reception and reaction, not its speed. If one tests the sensitivity to change of just one of the thousands upon thousands of temperature-sensing nerve endings in the skin of the back of a human hand, the minimum detectable change is about 1/100°C. If the whole back of the hand is tested, with all its myriad of receptors, the result may be ten times more precise—a 1/1000°C difference may produce a response. So dolphins gathering in schools may achieve a sensitivity simply unavailable to a single dolphin. The lone attacking shark emerges as a clod in the presence of an exquisitely sensitive school. How might that advantage be played out? I wondered.

If only humans could fly, would we form into bird flocks? Well, Carl and I thought, we *can* fly, can't we? And so we were led into the history of formation-flying of war planes. There, we found a graphic and remarkable parallel to the arrangements found in other animal groups that travel in open space. What exhilarating fun this detective search of ours was becoming!

During both world wars, pilots of fighter planes and bombers reported on what they had encountered when they engaged the enemy. Out of grim necessity, new strategies arose from these debriefings, evolving into schemes of protection from their enemy counterparts up there in the vacant sky. Early on, everybody agreed that a plane alone was shorn of any protection but the single pilot's reactions. But if planes flew together in such a way that all sectors of the sky were under constant surveillance by many eyes, they could hope to see the enemy far off and thereby concentrate their group firepower on the incoming attacker. Then they had a much better chance of coming home. Thus was born flying in formation.

The pilots found they must learn to watch each other. In particular, they had to learn to watch the planes farthest away from them for hints of intent to dive or climb. It was out there at the edges that first contact would be made. Then they could maneuver so fast that a single attacker had trouble following. (Aha! The chorus line effect!) To look for such signals, and to look clear across the formation without their vision being impeded by the plane next to them, they learned to stack their planes in Vs, or echelon formation, the arrangement we often saw among the schools of dolphins and flocks of birds.

Because things happened so fast, and because the enemy learned to attack out of the sun, the design of planes was changed so that crewmen equipped with machine guns could scan all sectors of the sky. Pilots learned to use clouds, and even the ground, to inhibit the enemy. If a damaged plane flew close to the ground, it severely reduced the maneuverability of an enemy attacker. The attacking pilot had to think both about attack and about crashing into the ground on a dive. We knew that shorebird flocks under attack from hawks did this same thing, and that the sea surface was a reverse barrier against which predators pinned their prey from below. A fish or a dolphin leaping alone would fall back from a leap out of formation and thus for a few moments become vulnerable.

Racial barriers that often seem so important among people at peace frequently almost disappeared among pilots. It didn't seem to matter if one's skin was black, tan, or white, or if one spoke with a patois that instantly identified one's roots. What mattered most was alertness and skill, and whether one knew and followed the rules of survival. I thought of dolphins and that remarkable cooperative temperament of theirs. The deep camaraderie of pilots, in fact, had become legendary, and not just in the imaginations of Hollywood screenwriters. Every pilot came to understand that his survival rested on the alertness and skill of his buddies. I wondered if a kind of sweetness, like that of the dolphins, tended to emerge among pilots, a giving to each other, perhaps beyond the level of mere personal survival. I wondered if this might have affected the way they came to regard the society they tried so valiantly to protect.

Carl added one last crumb to our pile. He had learned of a phenomenon called "looming." If the side of a fish tank is made into a transparent projection screen and a moving picture of a predator abruptly looming in attack is projected against it, prey fish—as you can imagine—flee. If these prey fish are of a species that typically lives on the ocean bottom and doesn't school, they will flee for the first few times an attack is projected, and then gradually they will cease their flight. They will learn the attack is not real. But if the same looming stimulus is presented to open-water-schooling fish, such as anchovies, they will never learn.[8] Project the looming predator a thousand times to an anchovy school, and it will open as if by magic every time. There is no room for error, no time for judgment out there in open water, and the mind of the anchovy has been shaped accordingly. The connection between looming stimulus and flight must be hard-wired. For dolphins, we reasoned, cooperation—the *sine qua non* of dolphin-predator evasion—must be similarly embedded in the structure and function of the brain.

Carl and I finally put all these fragmentary observations together and proposed that schools, flocks, and herds can be understood as information-processing systems constructed in such a way as to defeat the attacks of any single predator. We envisioned each group member as sensing, integrating, and relaying information about what was going on both outside the group and within it—the approach of a distant predator, the location of food, or a life's worth of sociality. Together, the members made up a coordinated, quick-responding system, a kind of higher-order brain. We named this construct the "sensory integration system (SIS)" of group-dwelling animals.[9]

We reasoned that the nature of a herd, school, or flock operating as an SIS should change depending upon the primary sense being used. In daytime, vision should usually predominate in organizing such groups, and because vision is a moderate-distance sense, the group should work close together. (This should be particularly true of the protective dolphin or fish school, because in water the distance at which vision is operative is even more restricted.) At night, and in very murky water, hearing should become the dominant organizing sense, because it is a long-distance sense and because vision has been all but negated; hence the group could take a different, more spread-out form.

Dawn Goley, another of my students, opened another vista to us, providing a clue about how the SIS might actually work in a dolphin school. Through a magnificent example of spinning of the wheel, she watched and watched a little school of captive white-sided dolphins (an open-water species) over two years' time. Gradually, gradually, she learned that when her little school of wild dolphins slowed into sleep, they closed only one eye at a time. This state of affairs was almost impossible to see at first. Only fleetingly when they faced her through the port could she see both eyes. To everyone's surprise, including mine, the open eye of a sleeping dolphin did not scan the environment for predators—that task is left to the watch-standing echolocators of a dolphin school—but was directed inside, to look into the school where the instructions about survival were being given. Then, she learned that after four hours or so a sleeping dolphin moved across the center of the school, opened the closed eye, closed the previously opened eye, and settled into another four hours of quiet, restful, one-eyed sleep for the other side of its optic brain.

Dolphin eyes, she learned, move separately, like those of a chameleon, one at a time, and most of the time they move in different directions. This remarkable state of affairs can happen, she learned, because the optic brain of a dolphin is decussate. Unlike ours, it is divided into almost separate halves. Signals from the eyes don't have be sent across the dolphin brain and integrated with messages from the other half. That is too slow to avoid the rush of the shark, too slow to allow the school to fade away fractions of a second ahead of any attack. Instead, each eye and each brain-half work together as a quick-response system.

The SIS concept helped us understand what had always been the larger question in our research: why did dolphins have such large brains? What purpose did their large brains serve? The dolphin brain began to appear as the necessary tool of an animal that relied on the individual members of the school being tied together in relationship, coordination, and cooperation. The large dolphin brain makes it possible for the school to function as a sophisticated information-processing system that far transcends the capability of any individual dolphin alone, an entity very much like a super-organism.

We saw that the school had a meaning and role in spinner dolphin society that we humans, despite our own sociality, could understand only dimly. The school is the place where dolphins spend their entire lives, and that constancy is a major shaping force. The school is where an individual dolphin learns, takes part in the social concourse of life, uses the considerable capabilities of its large brain, and where, in the end, it dies, never having left the confines of the school's moving envelope. Such an animal's life has been the epitome of a constant, pervasive kind of sociality. In such a society, one gives as well as receives on a constant basis, and this very cohesion and cooperation has shaped the minds and bodies of the animals involved. Dolphins are incomplete animals by themselves, and true dolphinhood can only be realized within a school.[10]

The spinner dolphin gives up much of its individuality in being part of the protective school. It becomes the cooperator of all cooperators. No wonder a kind of sweetness is often exuded by these animals. No wonder they usually wait for instructions from the larger group, or that their human trainer becomes the surrogate for the larger school. They never take off on their own recognizance.

Not all dolphins are like the spinners. The bottlenose dolphin usually lives in nearshore waters, where there are things to hide behind, where the nearby bottom narrows both their world and that of their predators. Sometimes these dolphins wander off alone, but probably always they remain in touch with their schoolmates by sound. Such a pattern may actually be a very loose school in their terms, and even then, in the narrowed environment of shallow water, they can learn about and track such sharks as might be there. As a result, bottlenose dolphins are much more like us than spinners. They and we, who once trod the savannas and forest edges in our groups, are edge animals. Perhaps that's why they have become the mainstay of dolphin exhibits the world over. We have subliminally understood their needs, because we are much like them and have designed our relationships with them accordingly. I know that our success with them did not result because we truly understood these things.

In the end, Carl and I knew that we had just begun to penetrate the true fabric of the open-space society of the spinner dolphin. All those banjo twangs, screams, chuckles, and donkey brays of spinners were the marks of a fluid society whose inner sociality we hardly understood at all. We never came to understand the deeper structure of their societies, and that is where the frontier for the dolphin naturalist now lies.

Thinking back on the parallels between us and them, I came to realize that we are far from exempt from the life of relationships that Gregory Bateson predicted should so profoundly influence evolution. If we come to understand the mixture of individual and group that lies within us, just as it exists in the dolphins, then I expect vital things will come clear.

Part III • Windows to the World

Gamboa Point (in the distance) and Whale Point (closer in) as viewed from Dolan Ridge at the Landels-Hill Big Creek Reserve, on the high and rugged Big Sur coast of California.

Present-day geothermal pools, such as this one at Wai-O-Tapu, Roturua, on New Zealand's North Island, mimic conditions believed to have been present on Earth during the time when life began.

Chapter 14:
Creation Myth

The deepest of life's mysteries—its origin on the earth—was on my mind as I walked across the tarmac of the frigid, windswept airport at Nuuk, the capital of the gigantic island of Greenland. I had finished the research for an article I was writing on arctic beluga whales for *National Geographic*,[1] but because of my curiosity about the beginning of life, I had one last mission to fulfill before boarding the plane for home: collect some of Nuuk's rocks to stuff in my luggage. Nuuk's snow-dusted airport, you see, is carved into the side of a truly ancient mountain made of rocks estimated to be 3.76 billion years old. Rocks dating back to that unimaginably ancient time when life was still relatively new are exceedingly rare. Such inexorable forces as erosion, mountain building, and subduction have, in the interim, left very little of the earth's crust untouched.

Scientists understand very little about the appearance of life. They do know with some certainty that the sedimentary rocks of that time were laid down without the corrosive effects of free oxygen, under a primeval atmosphere composed of gasses such as methane, ammonia, carbon dioxide, molecular hydrogen, and water. Just about everything else is conjecture, scenarios pieced together around the scant available evidence.

Perched now on the shelf in my office, the rocks from Nuuk inspire me to draw my own scenario of life's beginning—that long-ago event being, after all, the necessary prelude to Mountain Time. It's a picture of dark and shallow seas, of swirling mist and an ocean jelled with the products of light, water, and lightning. The pieces of the story come mostly from the pronouncements of biochemists and physicists, but I've arranged those pieces to fashion my own creation myth, an origin story for naturalists.

Before the beginning of life, time as we know it did not exist—there was no one there to take note of the progression of things. A gathering cloud circled the sun, drawing to itself the dust of the sun's creation. The particles, large and small, clung together in the grip of a mysterious force beyond my understanding. The force grew stronger as the particles piled deeper, since the force was somehow intrinsic in them. This force, gravity, drew in a stream of particles from limitless space, in a bombardment of incredible intensity. A sphere began to take shape, and it circled the distant sun where before only a cloud of particles had impeded the out-rushing rays of light.

Within the growing sphere, the particles jostled and layered themselves according to their densities. Like the heart of a golf ball, this new earth's center became filled with the dense particles, iron and lead and uranium and all the others. On the surface, a crystalline froth accumulated; farther out from the core, gasses and water vapor swirled under a corona of ionized gas.

The gasses seethed and roiled around the spinning globe in unimaginable storms. The constant rubbing of their particles spawned jagged lightning, which tunneled long wandering tubes of nothing through the murk. The lightning flashed and the tunnel-tendrils collapsed and boomed in thunder. The brilliant electrical barbs slammed into the now-solid surface of the earth and flashed back again, up the vacuum trails into the clouds.

The very ferocity of these streaks of electrical light charged the gasses surrounding the transitory lightning tubes, welding together molecules made powerful by this energy. Amongst these, nitrogen joined with other atoms to form ammonia. Carbon played its chemical games, too: it combined with itself to form chains and rings, and it also reacted with water, hydrogen, and nitrogen to create amino acids. The products of these reactions were the latent stuff of life, their locked lightning able to charge a simple wave into life. Thus the acrid sky of the early earth, long before oxygen sweetened it for the likes of us, was a swirling gaseous pool within which many of the molecules of life were present.

The remarkable experiments of S. M. Miller[2] lend credence to this scenario. In his laboratory, Miller simulated an ancient pre-life atmosphere, using a mixture of gasses without free oxygen. When he discharged sparks of electricity through this gaseous mixture, a rain of the various amino acids resulted. If he added hydrogen sulfide gas, sulfur-containing amino acids also rained down. These were pieces of the future life. Given the pieces, energy was able to do much of the rest.

As the new earth cooled and the sky began to calm a little, water gathered on the surface, partly condensed from the cooling gasses, partly born from the recrystallization of minerals, and partly squeezed out of the rocks as the earth and its gravity grew. Eventually the earth was covered with vast seas and lakes, and into these reservoirs rained the carbon and nitrogen compounds formed in the atmosphere, creating a chemical soup.

These early seas were life's incubator, not merely because of what they contained, but because of their watery essence. This commonplace matter—water—was and still is the central material of life. Only in water can life exist, or so it appears. The chemical processes of life require the rapid, but measured pace of change that can happen only a liquid environment. They also require a medium that can dissolve and carry chemicals the way a car carries its passengers, allowing the assembling of the troves of ions, atoms, and molecules from which life draws its substance without holding those constituents too strongly.

And not just any solvating liquid would have sufficed. It was necessary for life's medium to remain liquid under a wide range of temperatures and, when chilled to its freezing point, to congeal as a material less dense than the liquid form. If ice did not float on water, the oceans would have frozen from the bottom up and life may have never come to exist. So it seems that only in that narrow, liquid state of water could life possibly have found a place. Only there could its processes have moved fast enough to stay ahead of the final death. No wonder that deep in our beings we are attracted to water with a love that seems beyond explanation.

From the mountains and valleys above the ancient sea came other constituents of life, particularly mineral ions. The venting of volcanoes provided some, and others eroded from rock heaved up from below. These, too, were washed into the sea, forming a mild brine with a concentration only about a third that of today's ocean. Remarkably enough, the cells of most modern, living vertebrate animals—latter-day creatures in this story, by any measure—contain about the same concentration of salts as that primordial sea, as if ancient life patterns had somehow remained locked inside them. How could that be, when so much life that behaves so differently has intervened between the first cells and these modern ones? This remains a mystery that I cannot penetrate. Maybe ancient instructions remained in the first cells, and somehow came to be used much later, after long lying fallow.

Along the shore of the primeval sea were calm pools, perturbed now and then by wavelets spilling over the barrier rocks. Sometimes, the sun beat down, and, in the shallower places, the water was often feverish with heat. The sea had been gathering for a very, very long time, becoming a sink of chemicals from the land and sky, like the acrid water in one of those desert lakes with dried salt around its edge.

In these quiet places at the margins of the sea, something new appeared. Wavering intermeshing strands of an inorganic gel developed, locking some of the water of the pool in a loose embrace. This gel held its chemicals quiet, often atomically close to each other, just as they are now held inside living cells.

There were metal atoms in the gel, too. They became the nursemaids, the catalysts, for the intermittent chemical reactions that began to occur, speeders of events that otherwise would have been almost immeasurably slow.

The temperature rose in the seaside pools, and self-sustaining reactions began to wink on here and there throughout the syncytial gel, like a hundred gardeners starting their lawn mowers across a greensward. In between the pathways of jelled sea, a watery soup ebbed and flowed, bringing in new chemicals and washing away the detritus of these newly begun reactions.

I doubt that a human walking the edge of that primordial seashore pool would have seen anything at all. A finger dipped in the gel might have detected that the pool had become warmer than before and that this new warmth seemed to propagate in a slow wave up the wavering tendrils. It wouldn't have seemed like much. Nonetheless, metabolic life had begun.

Now, calling this metabolically active gel *alive* is a matter of some controversy. Most early-life theorists have suggested that the assembly of intricate DNA molecules came first and that life followed its template. I hew to the contrary view of Freeman Dyson, who argues that something far simpler had to precede the appearance of DNA—namely, a self-sustaining, energy-releasing process among chemicals, capable of growth. In a word: metabolism. This rudimentary living matter could metabolize if there was a reliable source of materials (food) for its growth to occur, and if the temperature of the environment allowed water to remain liquid.

To me, the insistence that DNA was present at the origin of life smacks of scientists confronting a vast and intriguing new discovery—this replicatable molecule that can direct development with the greatest precision—and then, quite naturally, building a theory of the beginning of life around it. More likely, as Dyson says, the first life wasn't that good, that precise. It had to get over a barrier of messiness to exist at all. That's the way things are at the start of nearly any process you can mention. It takes time and tinkering before something can become precise and smooth-running.

The first life, messy and fragile as it was, possessed a key ability. It could work against entropy, the normal tendency for things to become more disordered. It was, in its small and tentative way, like a kid cleaning up his room, lining up socks in drawers, hanging up clothes, putting toys away. Scientists call such a force *negentropic*. Life, in this sense, is a blip of negentropy in a decidedly entropic universe.

But metabolizing gel couldn't remain life's standard-bearer forever. It was too fragile, too likely to be mixed up by ocean waves, too dependent on chance meetings of reactants. With time, the conditions were ripe for a spontaneous innovation to occur that would give metabolism a much more dependable foundation.

Metabolic reactions had built up chains of mostly carbon and hydrogen, oily molecules insoluble in water. And so over much of the pool there stretched an oily-looking film, as if someone had washed his frying pans in it. Over near the rocky reef, waves spilled into the pond, breaking the film into thousands of little patches. These wrapped around themselves, enclosing tiny droplets of water solution and metabolizing gel. Time and again, the film was beaten into clouds of oily droplets until there arose some droplets with just the right chemical components to be self-sustaining. Just like that, the first proto-cells were born, and with them came internal stability. Inside, the stuff of life was held still, kept together in close proximity, able to arrange itself advantageously.

The primordial membranes were dirty with impurities of various sorts—they were not complete walls—so food could find its way in and the dross of life's process could make its way out, to be wafted away into the surrounding water. It is unlikely that the protection they afforded the cells was complete or even very good. Ahead lay long corridors of time during which these crude barriers would be shaped into the complex electrochemical walls that now stand watch on what is allowed to enter and leave the immediate precinct of life.

The encapsulation of life brought with it the statistics of birth and death. The early cells, in their crude way, could reproduce. When they grew too big, they simply broke apart into smaller pieces, each containing, with luck, the requisite parts of life's machinery. Because of this simple fissioning process, any one individual proto-cell was expendable. It could be pinched out without threatening the stream of life. Thus when there was a population of reproducing proto-cells, death became a statistical event, never consuming all of life at once, even though it claimed each member in the end.

These first cells had many vulnerabilities. They could only succeed where the nutrient molecules were thick; their metabolic reactions were unordered and sporadic, their reproduction imprecise, random, and subject to all sorts of environmental vagaries. At some point, however, polynucleotides appeared, changing the game completely.

These remarkable molecules—simple forms of the RNA and DNA that serve as every modern cell's essential planning documents—contained, in their structure, precise instructions for the construction of other molecules, and they could replicate themselves. Perhaps short strands of RNA or DNA formed spontaneously inside the early proto-cells; maybe they entered as molecular parasites, as Dyson has suggested. At any rate, somehow, sometime, the molecule took over the regulation and reproduction of the cell that surrounded it, and then was able to copy itself, and then to add new instructions, one at a time. It "told" the cell where this and that piece could go, and, as important, when.

Dyson has—very appropriately, I think—compared the RNA–DNA complex to software, and the cell's metabolic machinery to hardware. The hardware came first, as it always must, and only later did it come under the strict regulation of the software. Together, they were unstoppable. The software was precise in its commands, but it was also mutable. It could—and did—change, causing things to happen that could not have been imagined at first. In time, it began to allow instructions about instructions, steering life's stream along paths of mind-boggling complexity.

In terms of geologic time, what may have happened next could have taken place in a flash. The world's first "overfishing" event began. The supply of molecular raw materials surrounding the tiny cells grew more and more dilute as life expanded and raced ahead of its resources, and as fewer organic molecules rained down from the sky. Increasingly, the rich packets of chemical resources assembled within cells were the only adequate sources of sustenance, and life began to exploit other life.

The age of ecology had burst upon the world. The proto-cells of life no longer simply jostled against each other in an unlimited molecular soup from which each could draw. Instead, they began to compete for the dwindling supply of free-floating nutrients, to eat each other, and to scavenge molecules from those that perished. They became enmeshed in a network of relationships. These events must have started very early; there seems to be no way of knowing when.

In this new world, death took on a new significance. Confronting limits for the first time, life had to fit itself to a finite earth, and the death of cells consumed by other cells and starved by the dwindling of the primordial soup was the necessary means. It was the first instantiation of a basic principle: because the earth can't pony up new space and resources for every new wave of life that comes along, life cannot go on expanding forever. It must, through death, give back the materials lent it by the earth.

The onset of ecological relationships was also the beginning of Mountain Time, in all of its many manifestations. As the early cells vied for their places in the ancient shallow seas, natural selection—the survival of the fittest—emerged as a clean shaping force. Working on the gradually lengthening, software code molecules, this selective process proved able to guide the invention of incredibly complex structures and processes.

One of these processes was photosynthesis, the harnessing of the sun's energy to construct organic molecules from simpler, readily available raw materials. This innovation was an elegant solution to the problem of obtaining food. Once photosynthesis had taken hold, life had the two fundamental modes that characterize it to this day—autotrophy and heterotrophy—and could once again expand its reach.

Then, over another long stretch of time, an incidental waste product of photosynthesis began to exert its far-reaching effects. The coming of an oxygen-rich atmosphere, released by the explosion of photosynthetic cells, seems to have taken place long after the beginning of life, some 2 billion years ago. Traces of the ancient cyanobacteria that released this molecular oxygen exist today as fossils, their concentric colonial shells frozen into stony cabbages. I have found them in the oldest rocks of the Mojave Desert. Some of their descendents, probably little changed, still live in a few special corners of the world.

In time, this simple emission of gas profoundly altered the land, the waters, and the atmosphere—and nearly all life along with it. The time before this event is well marked in the earth's stratigraphic history by deposits of ancient reduced iron, a material that could only have been laid down in an oxygen-free atmosphere. One of the largest of these deposits occurs in the "far outback" mountains of Australia, while others are scattered around the earth. In the post-photosynthetic world, in contrast, iron simply rusted because of the newly abundant oxygen.

Once life had a map, an atmosphere rich in oxygen, and both producers (autotrophs) and consumers (heterotrophs), the processes of Mountain Time began to hum along at a more rapid tempo. In the face of a changing world, the DNA strands altered, bit by bit. The lifestream was nudged and jiggled. Certain kinds of cells, driven by the inexorable force of natural selection, achieved a new level of complexity when they moved from living communally in colonies to joining together as coordinated, multi-celled individuals. With its specialization of function, multicellularity made possible the evolution of tissues and organs—and opened up an immense new vista of possible body plans and life strategies.

As many-celled worms, jellies, bryozoans, mollusks, and arthropods began to diversify and fill the oceans, life grew ready to claim the other parts of that thin shell over the earth's surface that we now call the biosphere. When it eventually happened, the invasion of land was a monumental step. Profoundly dependent on water, life had to take with it little measures of the precious liquid as it moved away from its primordial home in the sea. Inside impervious skins, inside the eggs that have come to connect one generation of life with another, have gone little vital pools of water.

I have perceived terrestrial life's deep dependence on water best in the desert. There, the availability of water sharply defines everything that is alive. Kangaroo rats gather seeds and take them into burrows below ground, urinate in the chambers where they leave the seeds, thereby humidifying the air. Vapor is then imbibed by the seeds, which are then eaten by the rat, which thus conserves its precious, precious, and very tiny store of liquid water.[3]

The desert moss, somehow persisting on a boulder receiving the full force of the summer sun, is black and crisp, a cinder. It seems impossible that this black mound is actually a moss, or that it is alive. Yet the moss is poised to start its internal machinery, to accelerate in moments when a supply of free water becomes available. The light touch of a passing shower, for example, might be enough. I have many times skirted the fringes of this profound puzzle with water from my canteen, spilling a half a teacup-full onto the blackened plant. In less than fifteen seconds it returns across the boundary between quasi-death and life. It miraculously unfolds and becomes a lush, dark-green carpet, once again ready to accept light.

In time, life invaded all the available spaces of the earth, ramifying its forms and arrangements. Along the way, life crowded upon life as never before. The motes elbowed in against each other. Sometimes they drew lines in the sand, whose effect was to exclude other life. Sometimes they took places in each other's protection; sometimes they took on the job of cleaning up the biosphere. Nothing was wasted; the strands in the webs of interdependence multiplied. Rivers began to run clear, and in spring, the dragonflies emerged, sun-shafts glinting from their iridescent wings. The space–time mosaic of Mountain Time had come into full flower.

Apparently alone among all animal minds, ours seem able to look back on this whole process of life, to reconstruct and contemplate our possible past and these curious chemical arrangements of things. Of what use is such an ability?

This is no idle question; indeed it may be the central question of our times. We would do well to use our minds to better understand, through stories such as this, just who we are. Our bodies and minds have been billions of years in the making, and the processes that have landed us here connect us to the earth and to every microbe, cricket, jellyfish, and spider that has ever existed and will exist. Is this realization not the fundamental source of ethics?

I will speak for myself: now that I understand better who I am, the almost unimaginably diverse living things of Earth are not foreigners anymore. I know in my bones that we are all of this home of ours: crickets, columbines, jellyfish, redwood trees, frogs, lichens, desert moss, spiders, and all the rest. We are relatives. And my kinship with all the earth's biota, even the simplest flatworm, does not degrade me. Instead, it makes me, and you, miraculous. I know this because I walk in the midst of beauty and love and a perfection of stones, sand, water, and life. My sense of these perfections has been built into me by evolution, right along with the magical arrangements of my body.

Banana slugs (Ariolimax columbianus) *discovered near Pico Blanco, Big Sur, California, March 2008.*

Chapter 15:
Yin and Yang

In that Yin/Yang figure from China, in the dark fish, or whatever you want to call it, there is a light spot. And in the light one there is a dark spot. That's how the two can relate. You couldn't relate at all to something in which you did not somehow participate. That's why the idea of God as the Absolute Other is a ridiculous idea. There could be no relationship to the Absolute Other.

Joseph Campbell
The Power of Myth [1]

If you would have asked me twenty years ago what I thought of the yin and yang symbol, the black and white fish curled around each other, I might have replied that it was another of those faddish sorts of things that you find on New Age T-shirts. Since then I've come to understand a little of its symbolism. Chinese philosophers speak of two polar energies, yin and yang, that by their fluctuation and interaction are the cause of the universe. I still struggle with that statement, but closer to us I now see that yin and yang are remarkable descriptors of the relation between man and woman, and of larger patterns of Mountain Time into which we fit.

The Chinese wisdom traditions had formulated this conception by the third century BC, when the School of Yin-Yang flourished.[2] The diagram they evolved remains the most elegant encapsulation of the apparent dualities that pervade the living world: right–wrong, man–woman, life–death. A bounding circle—the outer unity—embraces the duality. Some call it the boundary between knowable and unknowable, the boundary to the ineffable. Some say it represents the boundary between us and God.

I think of it as the outline of the earth on which we play out our oscillatory games, our human games of duality. The earth, for me, is our immediate rule giver. Yet, beyond the earth, I can perceive dualities that in fact continue into the physical world of the larger universe. For instance, the orbits of all celestial objects are gripped in interactions with the gravity that exists between them.

Inside the diagram are those two parts of yin and yang, the curved figures embracing each other. To me, the curved boundary between the two parts suggests that each is in oscillation with the other. To me, that boundary looks suspiciously like a sine wave. I wonder if, somehow, those ancient Chinese knew about the sine wave, the perfect oscillation. I wouldn't put it past them.

In each figure, there is a dot of the opposite hue, black in white, and white in black. These not only say, as Joseph Campbell perceived, that in every duality there is some of the opposite member, but that without this admixture, the duality itself cannot exist. Altruism does not exist without selfishness to play against.

To put this idea of duality in homely terms, think of the thermostat that shuts your room heater on and off. You choose room temperature by adjusting the little red arrow to 70°F. What you've actually done is to select the midpoint of an oscillation, a duality. No heating element, alone, can hold a room at 70°F, but with this magic thermostat you have told the heater to turn on at 68°F, sending heat into the room until it reaches 72°F, and then to shut off again until the room drops to 68°F, whereupon it comes on again. The room then oscillates in its duality, back and forth around your chosen 70°F.

The thermostat utilizes a little double strip of two different kinds of metal soldered together. The two metals were chosen because each expands or contracts at a different rate with temperature change. Bound together, they respond to temperature change by bending, almost uncomfortably like those little, curved, black and white, yin and yang fish must.

At the limit of one excursion, the bending metal touches a contact, turning the heater on; at the limit of the other excursion, it touches another contact, defining the oscillation through which the room is allowed to swing. It is, at its heart, a lovely little bimetallic yin and yang.

The early Chinese already seem to have had the idea of a thermostat in mind, centuries before they had heaters or electricity to shut on and off. They also apparently grasped that bending of the yin and yang duality operates at one level of organization, the room, and its response at another. Dualities within dualities, nested like dishes in a stack.

Here I want to stick to the man–woman duality, at least for awhile. That relationship is an oscillation produced by two different beings who must clasp, but who each take a different half of life as their own—two different agendas, two different metals—but nonetheless the necessary two parts of the human species.

Like the two metal strips of the thermostat, we embrace each other, because without our oscillations together, our species will cease to exist. We frequently forget that neither of us, man or woman, is an autonomous being. Alone neither of us is complete. We are each half a deck, so we must clasp.

Alone, each of us is assailed by profound wordless loneliness. We have trouble defining ourselves, yet each of us, male or female, knows that in our clasping we vibrate from the differences between us. Therefore, we fall into each other's arms with an intensity and inevitability that defines the human species, and much of the rest of the living world.

This clasping is no simple embrace. The two partners may spin and whirl, touch and stick, and sometimes come to define each other. Or they may fly apart, and then each half returns into its incompleteness, marking time again.

I well remember a time in my mid-twenties when I came upon a young woman and, in my growing loneliness, literally fell into her orbit. Like a mindless moth spiraling around a lamp, I circled inward, and one dark night I found myself tramping in the ice plant below her close-shuttered window. I cared not at all where I scrambled in the blackness, nor if I might fall. Had she opened her window, we would have flown together, and my and her inward spirals would have ended.

Through it all, my reasoning mind fought against this almost overwhelming force, knowing that she, a child of the city, could not go where I knew I must go.

I somehow pushed back the sweet dizzying grip that held me, and in a pool of confusion made my way back to my car. Then followed a dazed week, when I tried to recoup the parts of my being. As the grasp of this nearly overwhelming force began to subside, I could look outside again. The sweet tight feeling in my chest subsided and my head cleared.

I've thought that the experience was as if someone had injected a great jolt of some powerful chemical into me that took away all will and, at the same time, reinforced its grasp by the overpowering pleasure it induced. I still marvel at the strength of this coming together of yin and yang. Even though it tears at the romance, at the endless songs we have written about love, I cannot help but note that neurophysiologists now reaffirm that a chemical jolt is, in fact, involved—a flood of a molecule called oxytocin.[3]

Sometimes, when I see young lovers looking shyly outward as they hold hands, I think of that experience. The necessity to embrace, the distant look in their eyes, as if there was no one else in the world—no need for more than just two. Two such people are deep in the thrall of this state called love, which is also the first coming together of yin and yang, the culmination and cause of their duality.

That experience long ago was the beginning of the realization that much of what we do, beyond love even, is reinforced by systems operating within us that shape our behavior. Love is only one of these.

The dark tadpole in the yin-yang diagram is the yin, the feminine. It is said to represent the receptive, the dark, the soft. The light, the yang, the male, is said to correspond to the creative, the bright, the hard. Somehow, for me, a naturalist, these words merely graze the essences of these two roles; the words represent mere facets of the two crystals. They are just attributes. It is better, I think, to define the yin and yang of our species in functional terms. I verbalize the feminine as the keeper of the flame, and the masculine as keeper of the outer bound.

These two must have been the clear halves of life back when we lived in nomadic societies, wresting our sustenance and our security from the wild land. Then, male and female may have had such cleanly defined roles that we could clasp as an understood part of our dual lives. The feminine world was more than figuratively at the center, while the male half flowed far out, guarding the space and resources needed for life.

I don't mean that, in aboriginal times, the clasping of yin and yang was easy or, in modern terms, necessarily fair. I doubt both those things. I expect that the two roles were allocations of the realities of life as humans then faced them. However harsh the theater in which they were played, I expect that because such roles had arisen from ancient roots of human sociality they would have been deeply invested with the emotional validation of clear parts well-played, filled with something like joy and a harsh, uncompromising beauty. Today it is our uncertainty that blurs these fundamental things, that produces our unease and disconnection.

I sense that I would have fit right into such an ancient society. I would have risen in the early morning dark, pulled on my skin clothes, looked back in protectiveness at the women and children sleeping, and gone out on the hunt with half a dozen other men. We were a meritocracy, fit together by long testing. We each knew what to expect from the others without the necessity of many words. We were, we felt, damn good.

When one of us found a line of moccasin prints headed toward our encampment, in moments we faded into the woods, treading among the dew-softened leaves in well-practiced near-silence. A wary laconic communication followed about strategies, predictions from the signs we saw—data—and assessments of validity. How many intruders? Who? Going which way? Intent? Our beings would have become charged with controlled excitement and, if need be, implacable will.

I know myself, at least that far. I might have constructed a scheme, a likelihood, for intercepting and observing "them," and I would have felt a lift of excitement in the contest. Each of us would have known what to do, and each of us would have known what to expect from the others. We had become organized that way.

You might ask, "Isn't this the way wars start?" I would reply, "Yes, exactly."

We ancient men were builders, too, and the functional tools we created possessed an elegance that merged into and defined what we now call art.

Yin is so different. It is the nest within which life is brought forth and nurtured, and then let to fly on its own, like folding and pushing a paper airplane into the wind. Yin creates and constantly gauges nuance in the indirectly negotiated meshwork of sociality, nurtures and guides the evolution of self. Yin is the part that sees into other beings, it is the observer, the sharer, the healer of ills. On one side, it is love, the antithesis of pain; on the other, fiercest defense of its own. Yin has its own art no less than yang does, and, like the art of yang, it expresses the metaphors of its own being.

The scientist, in his stiff way, talks of the one-fifth dimorphism between men and women (men are, on average, that much bigger, more muscular than women); he talks of the dominance relations that stem from this difference, all within the hunter-gatherer world, in the face of the fluctuating resources that drove the wandering by season and throughout life.

Yet, not all nature is like this. Many species that lack difference between the sexes—such as the gibbon, a primate able to swing through treetops with amazing ease and athleticism, and which eats abundantly available leaves—live a settled monogamous life within fixed boundaries, there being no need to struggle for transient food.

Other species, such as elephant seals, push the differences between males and females to their limits. Modest-sized females slide in between their gigantic contesting males, literally keeping their heads down lest they be taken for a male. These males and females live nearly separate lives, except at pairing.

So, we humans are in-between: mostly we are of each other, but part is different. And it shows. We are capable of love and steadiness, which takes two, yet the pull of difference may take us on long hegiras away from each other. Our males play their male games—contests such as football games that lock them to their TV sets. Earlier in the day, it was female time, and some of them watch the dramas of relationship—the soaps—with equal avidity until there is a dreadful growl indicating that the Super Bowl is about to begin on another channel. A wise man once said, "To still the oscillation of yin and yang, there should be two TV sets."

Why is this difference there? Part of the answer, I think, is that ever since life took up the strategy of hiding variation and keeping it at the ready by having chromosome pairs lined with genes of different strengths of expression (dominance–recessiveness), there has been the necessity of sexual difference. Such stored variation can only be saved or uncovered by us coming together in our difference. Only in this way can the vital products of mutation—variability—be stored or tested for use. Without this storing, we would long ago have lost the struggle between us and the microbes.

The other half of the answer is that the two roles are in some ways mutually exclusive. The bearing and nurturing of children is far more a sedentary nucleus than defense or the running down of prey.

Male and female is another of those ancient things I keep finding. It had its genesis a very long time ago in Earth terms, probably not long after the origination of life itself. So the binary sexual difference is almost ubiquitous in the larger forms of life. If one traces its occurrence back through the various phyla, nearly every possible experiment with this duality has occurred.

On land, plants early experimented with swimming cells, little haploid, single-celled organisms that could meet others and fuse into a duality. Then, later, plants came to utilize pollen, flowers, and seeds, separating their lives into two parts—the one, the plant, fixed in place by its roots, and the other, the seed or pollen, charged with the tasks of movement and of coming together.

Among the vertebrates, some seem to use remarkably simple methods to continue the yin-yang relationship. The female of the giant ocean sunfish, or mola, is said to dribble eggs, and the male, sperm, and only because they both keep to certain water masses does such profligacy work.

From there it gets more complicated. Females of certain frogs climb trees to lay eggs in frothy nests that they whip up from the mucus of their bodies, out on branches that hang over a pond below. The eggs are fertilized by males who have climbed up the same tree. The tadpoles take form in the froth-suspended eggs, grow for a while, then secrete a compound that dissolves the bubble nest. Then they fall, to plop into the water below and swim away.

In most animals, the males have less energetic commitment to the process of reproduction than females—it usually takes a lot less energy to produce a sperm and get it in place than to produce an egg, mate, nurture an embryo, give birth, and then, following that, to nurture the young. But stored energy—fat—and the carrying of children are impediments to running, and so the female usually becomes the more sedentary one.

This difference, it seems, sometimes allows males to spend their surplus evolutionary capital on displays to impress and lure females. But, often enough such display is turned around on the males, used by the females for assessment of the male's virility and strength—indications of what he may pass on to her offspring if she lets him mate with her. The oscillation of yin and yang again.

And thus coyness was born. The female sage grouse may circle the almost grotesque dances of males, who perform on special dancing grounds, and there pick a mate in the strange process called lekking.

With mammals like us, there is still another twist. The carrying of young internally—pregnancy—allows much greater protection of young during early life than if young are simply hatched from an egg. The developing embryo grows inside its guardian. Perhaps as important, such a parent can move without being locked by incubation to a nest—the better to find food, to live in a traveling society, or take young away from danger. The arrangement allowed the hunter-gatherer way of life to develop.

These variable ramifications of sex are commonplace, and one could easily spin out the complexities far beyond those I have mentioned here. But it is important for us to know about them. It helps us understand what remains essential about the sexual process.

My point lies a little beyond these things. It is also simple. It is simply that we mammals are one small part of a very long stream of experimentation with the complexities of sex, of the ramifications of duality, if you will. We are in no way separate from that very ancient event when life took its great jog and produced a way to build complex beings who could face the very tiny bacteria and viruses, those who because of their very minuteness and simplicity could perpetuate their stream of life merely by growing a little and splitting in two.

Oftentimes, the oscillations of yin and yang can oppress, obscure, push away the commonalities among us, prevent our looking together for the shared essences of our communal being.

So the monk finds that, by being celibate, he can extend his love to all who enter the monastery. He seeks to avoid the divisive grasp of sexuality, of yin and yang, by pushing aside their inevitable, built-in tensions in favor of a neutral state where both unconditional love and acceptance are possible for all.

One of my favorite authors, Kathleen Norris, puts it well in her elegant book, *The Cloister Walk*.[4] "With someone who is practicing celibacy well, we may sense that we're being listened to in a refreshingly deep way," she writes. "And this is the purpose of celibacy, not to sustain some impossibly cerebral goal, mistakenly conceived as 'holiness,' but to make oneself available to others body and soul."

The Mountain Time world takes another tack. In every wild canyon, the collective arrangements of yin and yang mediate and fit life to the land. The locust breeds, then its progeny spend nearly all their lives underground as larvae. Eventually, prodded by a remarkable time-keeper in their cells, they emerge all at once, some after fourteen years, some after ten, some after twelve years from the time they first disappeared underground. The predator never knows when the emergence will come, and cannot wait. So the adults flood the upstairs world; so many that no predator can eat them all. Their excess comes to strip leaves with impunity, until the leaves are gone (and thus to limit themselves in another way), then to breed, to go below again, their normal controls having been tricked a little.

Each animal and plant has its strategy, its place-and-time; each beats the odds in its own fashion. In the canyon, the different species jiggle and sink in together, finding their place in ecological space, like stones-through-time, forming a mosaic on a stream bottom. Mountain Time.

Plants especially, but not exclusively, have frequently found ways of circumventing the difficult processes of sex, which cost every sexual species a large fraction of its adaptive substance. It takes two to tango, and that's two tickets at the door, instead of one, for the same result.

The flowers of some plants may not open, but their stamens may still drop pollen on their own stigmas inside the closed flower, fertilizing themselves internally. Thus, these plants proliferate, but they also tend toward the uniform. They become nearly identical life spread over the land and, at the same time, lose a little of their adaptive fit into Mountain Time. My guess is the new wrinkle will be costly in the long run, unless the plant reserves the opportunity to revert to sexuality now and then. A pure "selfing" plant will have gone stagnant in the eyes of natural selection. In the normal jiggle of adaptive change, they alone will have been still, and in time they will have to seek out that part of the mountain that still remains old.

So the earth is clothed mostly with polar opposites, each storing and expressing a part of the story, the partners oscillating together within the inclusive boundary of the earth. Take-home message: Sex, troublesome as it is, is an integral part of the central engine of change among the larger living things. It's what lets us fit our species to a changing earth, to find and keep our place in Mountain Time. Get used to it.

"White Fang" peak in the Granite Cove area of the NRS's Granite Mountains Reserve, during Field Quarter 1990.

Chapter 16:
Uncharted Territory

There isn't time left for us to fake ourselves out any longer. While our own numbers continue to escalate, the atmosphere shivers toward disequilibrium, the land threatens to feed us no longer, and our energy sources pinch down. It is patently obvious that the human species is the cause of the world's environmental crisis, yet almost exclusively we talk, not about us, but about pollution, environmental decay, the collapse of fisheries, and extinction.

Even as we begin to realize dimly that we are locked on the surface of a small planet with the products of our destruction arrayed all around us, all we seem to do is to chafe uncomfortably, rather than turning the magnifying glass on ourselves. We must stop avoiding introspection, I say, if we are ever to come to grips with the decay of the earth. In the last analysis, we will have to deal with humans and what they do as a first order of business.

Yes, I know—it's not particularly popular nowadays to talk about the seriousness of our situation and our own role in creating it. Our culture constantly reinforces the values and sensibilities that keep us rushing toward the environmental precipice in a state of complete denial. We want to be selfish, and to hear nothing of how it might be our undoing. When people like me talk about humans and really try to understand our own species, both our warts and our magical minds, you can almost hear the buzz of tension and the groans of discomfort.

Challenging the blithe ignorance of my fellow humans, I've noticed, is sometimes best accomplished indirectly. My tool of choice in this is irony. And so it was the other day when I dreamed up an essay contest on the subject of the environment. Why not, I thought, award prizes for the essays demonstrating the *least* environmental sensitivity? The prizes could each represent a kernel of the present human condition and, in this way, perhaps spotlight our distorted values.

Grand prize, I thought, might be a week's cruise on one of those huge ocean liners. This would symbolize our love of excess—plowing the ocean, expense and fuel be damned, amid all the delights of a Byzantine court. Second prize could be a case of Easy Cheese™. This product—sprayable soft cheese in a stout metal can—symbolizes our command to disregard the larger world. For a tiny bit of highly processed cheese, we must also buy the heavy metal cylinder and then discard it, forgetting that we have extracted the ore for that cylinder from the earth, built and transported it with great expenditure of energy, and that when discarded in some landfill the cylinder most likely will never be recovered again.[1]

The third-prize winner could receive a gasoline-powered, 1/4-horse leaf-blower. Leaves in fall drift down to form a carpet of color, but the damn things also cover up driveways and walks, so for the majority of us who must have concrete under our steps, this little beauty is the ticket. It doesn't stack up the leaves in piles or anything like that, but it will rearrange them nicely or blow them onto the neighbor's lawn. Powered by an inefficient, pollutant-emitting, two-cycle engine, it and its kind contribute a remarkable percentage of all engine exhaust fumes to our atmosphere, in addition to a sizeable bit of suburban noise. The blower epitomizes the deification of unnecessary things. It also represents a special kind of waste. The leaves will be back, but that's not the point.

Fourth prize: a six-foot, live-in, fiberglass Canada Goose decoy. This imaginative creation is a little hard for the average hunter to haul around, but given a little help, and a full camouflage suit, he can pop up from inside and nail a few of our remaining migratory waterfowl. Humorist Dave Barry (the man whose writings first brought the goose to my notice) notes that the goose could have many additional uses, such as girl-watching on public beaches. The goose validates using all our weapons against the other life on Earth, even though clearly the contest is already won and the rest of life lies supine before us.

It makes me a little itchy to realize that I might well sign on for an ocean cruise, spray Easy Cheese™ on my processed meat sandwich, enjoy the tumbling leaves as they hurry away from my blower, or come to treasure time in the goose on some busy beach. Such is the stupidifying power of our culture.

But enough of this talk of culture as it is currently expressed in our human society. What I am really interested in is culture understood evolutionarily—culture as a biological attribute of the human species. It is culture in this sense that's the underlying cause of our environmental crisis, what got us into this mess. It's also what we desperately need to understand most about ourselves.

In the evolutionary sense, culture started a very long time ago. By "very long," I mean well before the human species first thrust itself on the scene. We are not the sole custodians of culture, even now, contrary to the ruling assumption of the anthropocentrists among us. Cultural animals are all over the place among the mammals, and, in more cryptic, stereotyped fashion, culture appears to be present in many bird species. We have merely unfolded the possibilities of culture further than the rest.

The founding precept of culture is present when an animal is able to understand the gist of this message: "You no longer need to listen solely to that long genetic strand of yours. Your conscious perception now lets you learn from the world around you, it lets you teach these things to others of your kind, without the need to be guided directly by the DNA strand. You are, in a limited sense, freed—freed into the next order of abstraction above the genes. Now let's see if you can figure out how to drive."

In other words, when the rules of the world could be taught, culture had emerged. When young gathered around an adult ape fishing for termites with a grass stem, watching, trying it themselves, culture was in operation. Or when a group of macaques of Japan learned to wash their food by watching others, and the washing practice soon passed from one to another—that was the spread of culture.

When an animal teaches its young to use a stem as a tool, or a technologist invents a new memory chip, a tradition is founded, and the precise messages for that behavior pattern will probably never be encoded in the DNA strand. To be sure, the predilection for such behavior is probably so encoded, the physical capability that allows it to be performed is also encoded, and the emotional substrate that sustains it is already there. But the behavior itself springs significantly or completely from the minds and memories of the animals involved, not directly from their genes.

The key thing about culture is that once this evolutionary jump has been taken, natural selection must work in the abstract. It is pushed back, away from the individual or the population and its genes. Selection can no longer easily pinpoint the perpetrator of an unfit act and remove the responsible gene. What and whom does Nature have to grab hold of when someone invents Easy Cheese? Furthermore, cultural things come and go like the wind. They are not easy targets for natural selection to hit, because they change before your eyes or are gone before you know it. The natural selection of genes is much too ponderous a process to control such elusive violators of its rules.

Only later, indirectly, and according to the pace of natural selection of genes is a behavior pattern passed on by culture brought into court. Only then will Nature judge whether or not the use of the pattern advances the species. And even when Nature sits in judgment, it doesn't judge the value of a specific behavior pattern, but whether or not the whole species remains fit and competitive in relation to other living things.

The effect of culture on the operation of natural selection is particularly pronounced in the case of the human species. This is because of that wonderful thing called language. This newly developed communications system lets us figure things out and then store up what we find, for all to see, use, and think about. When our ancestors began to use utterances with agreed-upon meaning to tell creation stories, our minds started to become all hooked together, and this gave us enormous power. This power allowed us to preempt anything, use anything, discard anything. It's why we are the ones, among all the many species possessing culture, who are responsible for bringing on the current environmental crisis.

Our language so speeds human communication, and has given us such advantage over the other living things with which we share the Earth, that we have been able get away with murder, literally and figuratively, as well as with Easy Cheese and leaf-blowers. But our immunity may not last forever. When we humans devised chlorofluorocarbons, for example, we reaped the short-term gains of refrigeration; only slowly, over time, will Nature tell us through natural selection that it was a bad idea, because the chlorofluorocarbons leaked into the atmosphere and let in excess ultraviolet light. From an evolutionary perspective, we are in that delicious, but precarious and frightening, transitional period when we find ourselves with plenty of capital to spend before our advantages over the others in Mountain Time are used up.

We humans are cultural animals *par excellence*—and yet, much of who we are is cast in genetic stone and changes only slowly, just as it always has. Modern humans are probably almost indistinguishable from Cro-Magnon man, who emerged tens of thousands of years ago. Yet, in an equal period of time, our culture has taken a thousand wandering courses, built the idea-strands of religious faiths, tested and reshaped them, and released the newest floods of the scientific and information ages.

So, even though we humans have escaped from the rigors of Mountain Time, the battles we fought there linger on deep within all of us. Although nearly every other living thing (save the microorganisms, who love us best when we claim victory and multiply our numbers) lies prostrate at our feet, we still play out the games that got us here. We still covet space and resources, consider only ourselves, ignore the future, prodigiously multiply our numbers, and lash out with violence. It takes us too much time to put down our weapons and take up the causes of our neighbors. We still push against our boundaries, sweeping other life before us, destroying at will.

The hard-wired, DNA-coded legacies of our ancient struggles in Mountain Time are, I am convinced, the source of the avarice that often becomes so overwhelming a force among us. They are what compel the billionaire to grasp with both arms and, even though he has enough for 10,000 people, to continue raking the tokens of wealth toward him and to hold on so tight. But the proclivities we've inherited from our pre-cultural ancestors haven't by themselves built the world of ocean cruises, Easy Cheese, and leaf blowers. It's been necessary also for us to turn our backs on the canyon, on Mountain Time, face inward at ourselves, clang closed the great gate of our citadel, and come to believe that we are all there is, that it all was made just for us.

The folly of this self-centeredness is something we should have by now learned and incorporated into our cultural heritage as a counter to our inherent animal nature. We should be acutely aware of both the tremendous freedoms and the terrible responsibilities that have come with life outside the canyon of Mountain Time. We should know that the burden of judging the environmental consequences of our activities is ours alone, that we must now drive the Ark of Nature ourselves. Culture has indeed made us special, but it hasn't made us separate.

I hold out some hope that there is still time for humans to learn this lesson. For all our turning inward, down deep we still worship the mountain through which the clear river runs, where the shining globes of dew still hang on spider webs, where the black swifts still build their nests behind the waterfall. We ever more fervently cluster icons of wild animals and plants around us, even though in life many of them are now just fragments, or even extinct. We abstract their beauty in our art, and we hardly know why.

Kenneth S. Norris

Photo by Norden H. (Dan) Cheatham

Ken Norris contemplating Mountain Time during a Natural History Field Quarter trip to the Granite Mountains, April 1983.

Chapter 17:
The Salmon's Run

At the mouth of the river, dense flashing schools of silvery fish have gathered after their long swim in from the distant sea. They mill just beyond the sandy river mouth bar, assembling in the freshwater breath of the river. These fish are preparing themselves for the ascent back to the clean spawning bed from whose gravels they issued a handful of years earlier.

As little fingerlings, these same fish descended the river backwards, facing upstream, but sliding downstream in the river's current. They crossed the river's bar where the spring freshet had broken through, then made their way out into the dangerous but food-filled sea, to grow prodigiously. Some wandered very far out—2,000 miles or more—into the stormy seas of the North Pacific, near the Aleutian Island chain. At some point, their schools turned and began the long swim back, to mobilize again, precisely off their home river mouth, among the several they could have chosen.

It has been determined that these fish locate their home river mostly by smell. Even a blind fish can find its way home. The major cue to home seems to be a precise chemical odor, perhaps derived from the aquatic vegetation of their natal stream. The guidepost is so evident to them that they can swim right through the effluents of pulp mills and industrial plants, "following their molecules."[1]

The new arrivals at the river mouth are near the end of their last swim. Inside their gill covers, little cells appear whose job it is to pump excess water from a salmon's body. Without these tiny bilge pumps, the freshwater of the river would filter through the exposed blood vessels of the gills and kill the salmon in short order.

The school of milling fish, ready now with the blocking sandbar broken through, rushes into the river, a pulsatile gout of half a million individuals. You can hear them come as the water rushes over their moving bodies, a vast dark pod of fish riffling the surface with their backs, fins, and tails. There is much about such an event that transcends the individual—a gathered group of a million bits of will that somehow carries with it the primordial wisdom of the salmon species.

These fish cease feeding as they ascend the river. Instead, their bodies rapidly descend through the stages of aging toward their inevitable death. A flood of corticosteroid hormones reorganizes the physiology of each fish. The fish consume first their bodily reserves and then the very substance of their own bodies, until, at the end, at the spawning grounds from which they came, the salmon have aged to become all but unrecognizable as salmon.

This death's imperative does not affect a fish's precious cargo—the shining eggs or the milt. Just before the final act of spawning, tattered males and females gather over their natal gravel to swish out a depression. Then, head to tail in a final paroxysm, a cloud of creamlike milt is jetted into the clear water, and it wafts over the handfuls of ruby eggs that the female has extruded among the gravel grains.

The two fish swish their tails upstream of the egg-filled depression, blowing gravel up into the current to settle over the now-fertilized eggs. At last, the exhausted fish scull into the shallows and die, joining a windrow of carcasses floating flaccid at the lapping stream edge. If the gravel in which they have spawned is clean, with crystal faces shining and cold, clean water filtering up through it, the eggs will be aerated and hatch. If not, the whole exercise will have been for naught.

The central nature of reproduction and death is outlined here, combined, in the Pacific salmon's case, into a single event. Like the salmon, nearly every multicellular species, including our own, lives within a defined span, the terminus of which is preprogrammed death.

The salmon are semelparous, which means they reproduce only once and then die. There are quite a few other semelparous life forms. The adults of many insects don't feed at all. Their job as adults is for male and female to find each other and to mate and lay eggs. This is done by the almost-magic of specific chemicals the females produce, pheromones, which are wafted on the air and lead male to female.

Some plants fit the definition of semelparous, too. The yucca plant lives for a long time in some rocky draw, growing, storing sugars in the bole of its central rosette of spiky leaves. Then, in a rush of growth that you can almost see, it sends a stalk eight feet in the air, calls in its pollinators with an odor bled into the passing air from a spire of white flowers, and dies, its life trace carried forward in thousands of seeds.

It would seem that the odds have to be darned good for a species to depend upon a single shot the way the salmon does. Having a proven spawning bed helps. But success depends upon the stream, which must stay clean through the years, waiting to be found again and again. And, of course, some such streams will fail.

This pattern works for the salmon because it isn't really a single shot. The salmon's strand of life depends upon a filigree of many spawning streams, and not upon the fates of individuals alone, but upon a population of fish that goes to hundreds of different spawning beds. The individual salmon, like each of us, is a cipher in a statistical game.

Here once again, just as we saw with dolphin schools, many of the salmon's life arrangements are made above the level of the individual. There is a kind of life to a school, just as the fishes' life thread is dependent upon many schools and many spawning streams. That is Nature hedging its bets. Beyond the many schools, the life of each species is always in flux, as the earth, the rivers, the air, the soil change. Today the coming of the human species is the greatest challenge.

In the salmon's story, we can see that the life of the individual consists of a protective capsule—the body and its manifestations—around a reproductive core. Together capsule and core move as an individual along a lifestream in the face of wear and tear upon bodies, finally ending in death for the carrier of life, as its program runs out.

I have wondered if there is an organization of death. Is it a single event without form, just the end of life? No, I must conclude—far from it! For a species, the fitting of the stream of life into an ecology takes place in three major stages, consisting of two bottlenecks and a cap, and all three are mediated by death. Let me explain what I mean.

The first bout of selective death, the first bottleneck, intervenes just after the time of reproduction. Such death may come internally, within a mother, as eggs or embryos are being formed, usually because the process of development has somehow gone awry. Or such selective death may come just afterward, when the newly hatched or the newborns first go off on their own into the outer world.

We humans call this bottleneck infant mortality, and we fight it back for all we are worth. But we are far from alone in our struggles. Such selective death seems to assail all multicellular organisms in some form. In some years, in some species, it may wipe out almost every new life. It is, in the last analysis, a strategy that fits new life into the ecology from which it will seek to wrest enough resources to grow and then to reproduce itself, thus to perpetuate this particular stream of life one step further.

There is much that is economical about having this first bottleneck occur so early in life. Energetically, tiny eggs "cost" little compared to growing the often huge, complex body of an adult. There are only so many resources for life available in any particular place, and for vertebrates most of these provisions will be taken up in growing and maintaining a body, which is the carrier of life through the world.

It is most economical to do the weeding out—the fitting of a species to available space and food—early. So larvae, or early embryos, are life's Kleenex. For many species, they are scattered across the landscape without a backward look. For others, care and nurture is lavished on the new lives, so that a particular lineage may not pinch out.

Every species that I can think of, including us, contends with the first bottleneck. I will describe how it affects the lifestream of just two, one a fish and the other human. The stories come to the same end, even though a fish during its reproductive life may lay a million eggs or more, while a human female may produce a mere three hundred. The difference is that the human mother carefully tends many of the new lives she helps to start, while fish broadcast theirs into the sea and swim away.

For a time, I headed a laboratory where we attempted to bring the life cycles of wild fish into hatchery control, so we could hope to raise them for food. Over and over, I was struck by the deepest delicacy of some newly hatched fish. Tiny hatchling mullet, for example, would die *en masse* if they so much as touched a surface and thereby scratched their vital mucus coat. Breaking this coat, which covers the entire outer surface of a fish's body, allowed the entry of the ever-present bacteria or molds, and soon the larva was gone. The scientists working with me finally succeeded in raising mullet larvae in a specially constructed spawning tank, provided with a spinning current that pushed the tiny larvae away from the lethal walls.

During that time in my career, I came to know a quite magical seer-of-a-scientist, Reuben Lasker. Lasker worked with the California anchovy—a silvery schooling fish—wondering why the species had both very good and dismally bad years, even though anchovies spawned every year, laying huge numbers of eggs. If most of the resultant larvae survived, then the sea would seethe with fish from that particular year-class. From many other years, very few made it to adulthood. Why? Lasker's question was far from trivial. Anchovies, and other fish much like them, occur around the world, and many of the world's major fisheries are dependent on them.

I should explain that Lasker could "read" the age of an anchovy—in other words, tell the year from which it came—by examining the tiny circular ridges on the surfaces of its scales. A "good anchovy year," he found, was likely to have contributed an important fraction of all the anchovies of a region at a given time.

Lasker puzzled over this pattern. He concluded that the success of anchovy year-classes seemed to be related to the weather. If the weather had been bad around spawning time, with winds or storms, few anchovies would result from that year. If the weather had remained calm, there might follow one of those good years, with numberless fish dimpling the sea's surface.

Lasker knew that, in calm times, the water near the sea surface would arrange itself in a series of layers according to temperature; the warmer water layers, being slightly lighter, would stack atop the colder layers, forming a series of micro–thermoclines. I saw such a layer once—or rather its boundary with another layer—while scuba diving off California's Santa Catalina Island. Twenty feet down, I was sculling slowly through the brown columns of a kelp forest, amber light slanting down. I looked up to see a wavering, just-visible, translucent sheet, spreading away among the kelp columns. In the slightly moving water, the layer glinted in a rolling silver wave. I slowed and hung in the water. I could just make out specks of tiny life floating on the sheet, like kids on an underwater trampoline.

Lasker developed a means of collecting the tiny anchovy larvae from such layers. His apparatus allowed a diver to suck in samples from a layer, providing him with a given amount of micro-thermocline water, including eggs, anchovies, and their food.

Then Reuben went the genius's extra step. He proposed that if the anchovy larvae remained suspended on such a boundary when they first began to feed, there was likely to be a good year-class. Such a potential for success, he theorized, existed because the silvery layer would not only collect larvae, but also their food, stuff tinier than I was able to see.

Under a microscope, he and his assistants could count how many anchovy larvae there were on a given area of the sheet and how many food items there were. A tiny larval fish, Lasker said, could only swim so far to reach food or it must die.

When an anchovy hatches from its egg, it has not developed enough to have an open mouth. But it does carry a food-filled yolk sac protruding from its abdomen. This sac supplies food for the newly hatched larva for a matter of days, while it continues to develop. By the time the yolk sac is expended, the anchovy's mouth has "broken through"—developed into a functional set of jaws—and then the tiny fish begins to feed for the first time, if there is food predictably and constantly near.

This is the point at which the anchovy enters the first bottleneck—the crucial few days that determine the fate of a year-class of anchovies or, in other analogous ways, the survival of nearly every other living thing. The tiny fish, its lunch bag empty, but its mouth newly workable, must quickly find and capture sufficient food or die. This is all by design, I say. It is Nature's testing time, the time for serious weeding-out among the profligate products of reproduction. It is the time of fitting life to the realities of the larger world, of jumping into the next dimension.

Lasker kept going, seeking the larger and larger surrounds for his work. He calculated the regular relationship between how far a larva has to swim to catch food and whether or not it survives. If food is dense enough on the trampoline to allow frequent capture, there might be a good year-class—but only if the weather continues calm. If storms come at this crucial time, the micro-thermoclines are scrambled and few new anchovies enter the schools. Nature's cross hairs have to be right on target if the sea a year hence is to swarm with young fishes.

When good weather holds on during spawning time, anchovies can become unimaginably abundant. Fishermen talk of "black spots," huge shoals of anchovies swimming just below the surface. The fishermen set their nets around them, yielding tons and tons of fish at a single encirclement, great milling, flashing masses of fish, in such abundance that they are pumped from the net into the fishing vessel's hold in a curving stream of silver, thicker than your leg.

Even so, anchovies aren't everywhere. At places just beyond the "good anchovy grounds," something in this delicate strand of events has failed. Like the blessed frogs of Hidden Spring, larval death has been an important part of defining the anchovy's limit.

The human species is also regulated by the first bottleneck. For the aboriginal woman, the many births she endured became commonplaces. Birth often was invested with a deep-seated fatalism, wrought by the overwhelming likelihood of early death for the newborn. The mother, except for her nursing, had no alternative but to release her new child into the world of diseases, without names and almost endless in number, mothering it as best she could, but also knowing that, likely, she would fail. A measure of her fatalism is that at first the mother may give no name to her newborn, pushing back the conferral of personhood until "it" traversed the first bottleneck.

In even the most elemental cultures of today, the mother will have heard about disease, but she may still match this view against the older idea that magical, evil forces are at work, ones that swirl around the village and that can be grappled with only by the shaman or curandero. In one sense, the two views, our world and hers, remain much the same. Both acknowledge that the time of birth is a time of supreme testing.

If we stand back farther than such mothers are ever able to do, climb the mountain, and look down upon Mountain Time's canyon for a while, then infant mortality, the first bottleneck, reveals itself as a strategy that fits life to the mountain—a necessary testing if a species, human or otherwise, is to find its place with the rest of life in the world at large. Thus reproduction is, in an important sense, an economic event. Kleenex or no, larvae have a cost for those who produce the eggs and spawn. So, even though spawning may involve huge numbers of eggs, that activity is likely, in aggregate, to be limited by a female's ability to produce and carry them.

There always remain limits. If "all systems are go," the young may flourish until all usual space in the Mountain Time mosaic is filled. Out at the edges of the core area occupied by a species, success may decline to 50:50. Farther out still, only now and then can a species occupy that piece of habitat. At the edge, anchovy schools may be small and transitory; just beyond, none at all will be found.

This tells me that this relationship of life and death is not just one-sided. It is not just a species spreading to its possible limits. It is also a species clawing for space in Mountain Time. Like every other such relationship, it is a duality, the teetering this way and that upon the knife-edge of an equilibrium. We must understand that to understand Nature.

There is one more truism that can be drawn from these two first-bottleneck stories. It is one we humans badly need to understand. The reproductive process is profligate, launching an excess of life into an uncertain world. Death, on the other hand, is the selective partner, paring the lifestream by a thousand different means, shaping life to the vicissitudes of ecological space and time.

Our passion for life is therefore matched against Earth's finite space. Because lately we have won this struggle much more often than we have lost it, human life has flooded the planet to such an extent that we test new Earth limits, ones that have remained hidden until now.

The second bottleneck comes with the end of the female's contribution to the lifestream. In humans, we often note the time by the arrival of menopause. This cessation of menstruation and, more importantly, of ovulation usually occurs in the fourth or the early fifth decade of life.[2] The egg primordia of the human female, present in her developing ovaries from the start of her life, have been developed and paid out throughout adulthood, some to be fertilized, most not, and now they are gone.

You may wonder why the second bottleneck, defined as the end of feminine reproductive life, engages both males and females in the profound changes it carries with it. The answer seems clear to me. The genetics of yin and yang tell us that the sexes are far from separate at the genetic level. The black dot in the white fish and the white dot in the black fish are real enough in the genes that build males and females. We are much of each other.

This time of life was once a limit of great force. We tend to forget that, during most of human history, both male and female lives were short compared to ours. For all but a few, the second bottleneck was the end of life—it and life's cap were telescoped into one, as it is with the salmon. Today the second bottleneck seems an almost toothless dragon. It is a time for appointments with various specialists, not death.

Compare a typical life of the present with that of Alexander the Great, who led his first army and won his first battle at the age of sixteen. In 339 BCE, as he was succumbing to a fever and as his whole army trooped through his tent in requiem, he had reached his thirty-third year. He had also conquered much of the known world. His life span and that of present-day gang members in our inner cities are about the same.

Today we note the second bottleneck's arrival when we begin to hold books at arms' length to read them. "Time for you to get glasses," the wife says. Or time for the dentist to make a bridge to substitute for decayed teeth.

Decayed or worn-down teeth were once no trivial thing. I recall holding a skull taken from a California Indian burial and noting that the teeth of this approximately thirty-year-old individual were worn down flush with the jaws. This condition had resulted from a life-long diet of food ground in stone implements, which had cast a continual stream of sharp little crystals into the food. How completely different a life than mine! The remaining teeth, most with inner structure exposed, must have been a constant source of pain and probably infection. Teeth seem to be designed for a life span that more or less matches the timing of menopause, not our present old age.

As we watch TV, we marvel at the professional football player still zinging passes at forty-two, or note with kinship the decline of the world-class sprinter who can't quite release the glorious burst of speed that once carried her to win after win. That is the second bottleneck in action.

Women feel this second bottleneck far more than men, since their bodies readjust hormonal state once menstruation no longer marks the monthly cycle. Psychologies take a hit when birth and nurture is no longer an option, but with a little care and some help from outside, a postmenopausal woman may perpetuate the illusion of fecundity for years. The pattern of menstruation followed by menopause occurs, remarkably, throughout the primates, even in two obscure branches, the flying lemurs and the batlike flying foxes that we might not think to include in our group.[3]

In hunter-gatherer societies, the events of the second bottleneck must frequently have marked the approach of death, that time when the old one might choose to remain behind, to sit alone under the thorn tree, as the tribe files off, with no one looking back. The insurmountable problem had become simply to keep up, to follow the wandering tribe for endless miles in the heat.

A battle with parasites commonly sealed off such a life. By the time of chosen death, the parasites' movement could sometimes be felt beneath the skin of the old one. For their part, these parasites had already reproduced many times over, and their localized death along with that of the old host was of no consequence to their species. They had already secured their place in Mountain Time.

Until relatively recently in human history, food-getting, shelter-building, birth, nurture, puberty, and the shaping of new social beings defined people's existence—that was most of what there was. Death was frequently quick, often violent, but it was always a presence, a reality not to be hidden away.

The coming of agriculture, and of trading centers, called off the implacable finality of keeping up. For the first time, there could be a permanent home and the predictability of stored food. The inevitable physical debilities of age did not matter so much. So, for the elders, the equation of the second bottleneck changed, and, even if they were unfit for the trail, a valid place in society might still be found for them.

Humans are among the few species with the biological potential for postponing death until well after the second bottleneck. Semelparous we are not. Thus, having developed the technological means for keeping many of the ancient threats to life at bay, many of us can expect to live many decades after the second bottleneck, sliding slowly into old age—what I call "life's cap."

It intrigues me that while the second bottleneck centers around the final expenditure of eggs by the female, the defining element of the final cap of life switches back to the other sex. It is the time when the male begins to lose his virility. The male, because he builds brand-new sperm from scratch throughout most of his life, retains his fertility in slowly declining form for much longer time than the female. But male humans, by their seventies, are about to become ciphers in the reproductive equation.

Once the final cap is approached, both males and females all but cease to matter to their species, except as fading repositories of culture and aging hierarchs within their families. Both males and females can see it coming. It is not uncommon for a male approaching sixty to have a last fling, to sire child after child. Sometimes, he manages this by choosing a woman far below his age, often one in the bloom of post-pubescent youth and certainly one with her fertility intact.

Then, beyond that, for the first time it may be possible for male and female to look at each other and say: "Is that you over there? Give me your hand. It doesn't matter much about male and female anymore, does it? Let's just talk while I put my arm around your shoulders."

No victory, no victory at all—except for preserving fading storehouses of culture—lies in defeating the cap of life. In attacking it, we rail against the very thing that has sustained the life-force on a finite earth in the first place—old life being replaced by new.

As I write, we humans have pressed our life span into the cap, and we are now the longest-lived human society in history. And we continue to press against the phantom limits with every resource at our command.

A full press is on to "defeat" the manifold diseases of old age. A major and increasing percentage of the medical effort in developed countries goes to deal with problems of the aged. Go into any modern clinic and watch the clientele hobble by. Most are the old to the very old. By any assessment, a very high percentage of these are the dependents of society; clearly they can no longer serve any viable biological function.

Forty percent of those over 80 will have some degree of mental decline; for many, full-scale dementia. At best, the ancients whose minds remain clear live in their families as loved connections to the past. Many others become overwhelming burdens to themselves and to our society. There is deep, formless cruelty in this pressing of life beyond its designed limits.

For the old people themselves, it is frequently a fearful time of life. We know that we are down to rather few years, and most of us accept that with simple calm. But above all else, above any pain that we might face, there is this specter of socially imposed decay, of bit by bit falling away, and most of us do not want to be burdens on our families or to our society. Those possibilities streak dread across our time.

The diseases of the old are largely the result of living well past the time when a person, male or female, has any reproductive role. If the life force is negentropic—lining up socks in the drawer, keeping the machinery of life orderly and working—then in striving to move beyond the point at which this is possible, we have begun to exceed the plan of our species. By this, I do mean that the diseases of old age are preeminently ones of disorder. That is significantly what cancer is: a disease of proliferation of uncontrolled cells opposed by a weakening plan for repair. That, in fact, is how the cap works. We must, somehow learn to accept this and limit ourselves in the spirit of the Kalahari aboriginal. Somehow contrive to make ourselves comfortable, not immortal.[4]

In our intercession into life process, we are at once faced with reassembling a thousand falling pieces into simulacra of humanity. It's like the One-Hoss Shay falling apart, with the owner frantically putting back piece after piece while the rest continues to decay. This is being done under the simple assumption that to defeat death is good; no deeper does the ruling thought seem to go. It ignores the sink into which the aged are being cast—one of declining vitality, dependency, and often great pain. It also ignores the vast cost to society. (I am reminded of a recent set-to in the national legislature in which it was suggested that, by making the eligibility for Medicare one year older, they could go a long way toward balancing the federal budget.)

In taking up the task of pushing against the limits of the human life span, we assume that we have the wisdom to succeed, we who hardly understand the systemic nature of the body, let alone the Earth. Consider that each time we beat back the force of a bottleneck, we multiple our numbers by some large factor. Defeat infant mortality, and the world's human population takes a jump. Push back the second bottleneck, and it takes another surge. Press against the cap, and the world floods over with people.[5] Little outposts of humanity appear and spread everywhere across the map, like little measles.

For the first time on Earth, we must consciously do this supremely difficult thing of controlling our numbers ourselves, even though through our entire history we have used our numbers as a weapon to take space, to co-opt resources, to push back the others on the mountain.

The whole saga looks a bit like the dilemma Great Britain faced when it found that its navy could no longer rule the world's seas. The cost was simply too great for a modest little island to afford. And so they shrank back to their island and declined into obscurity as a world force. That's about where the developed world is today, relative to our aging population.

Ken Norris baits his hook on a fishing trip to Mt. Lassen.

Photo courtesy of the Norris Collection

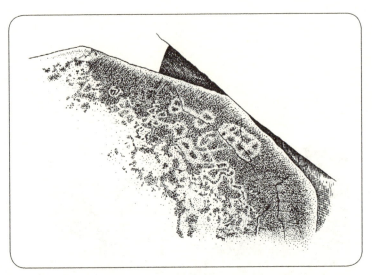
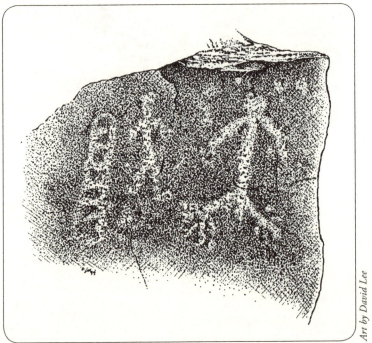

Rock art images left by early hunter-gatherer inhabitants of the Granite Mountains in the Eastern Mojave Desert of California.

Art by David Lee

Chapter 18:
A Natural History of Gods

The descent of the Occidental sciences from the heavens to the earth (from seventeenth-century astronomy to nineteenth-century biology), and their concentration today, at last, on man himself (in twentieth-century anthropology and psychology), mark the path of a prodigious transfer of the focal point of human wonder. Not the animal world, not the plant world, not the miracle of the spheres, but man himself is now the crucial mystery. Man is that alien presence with whom the forces of egoism must come to terms, through whom the ego is to be crucified and resurrected, and in whose image society is to be reformed.

Joseph Campbell
The Hero with a Thousand Faces[1]

We pulled into the gravel parking lot of the local Baptist church. My host, a resident of the Midwestern town, graciously introduced me to the minister. He was a big, enveloping bear of a man, prayerful, welcoming, gentle. I watched as, figuratively, he took his congregation in those great arms of his. The word *flock* fit wonderfully. They swirled in happy clots around him, while he loomed above.

A beautiful dark-haired child of nine zipped by using a walker. She had been born with a debility that affected her walking, but it hardly seemed to matter. In that cloister, she was at home, laughing, seeking out her friends. A tiny reedy old lady took my elbow and told me about the preparations she was making for a church celebration. I extracted from her that she lived alone, a widow, and it was obvious that this church was her life, the balance point around which she swung.

As for me, I was welcomed without a questioning look. Once introduced, no question of dogma, or baptism, or personal views ever arose. I was simply among them and they closed around me gently, accepting me. The organ sent its deep commands through us all, we turned to a hymn and in homely unison sang out the simple verses, and then the sermon started.

There were formal prayers drawn from the ancient scriptures, and the murmur and cadence of voices saying well-remembered lines that told of supplications and allegiances to their loving God. These were things that drew the congregation together into a webwork of unity. Nothing was said in this sermon about the wrathful side of this God, and I wondered for a moment how such opposites were so easily subsumed under the love they spoke of. I thought for a while and concluded that all rule-givers must be like that, otherwise there is no discipline, no map to follow. Every leader must be such a duality. I listened on. I soon realized that the sermon was a series of instructions to the congregation about living together, specifically about the rules governing human cooperation and altruism.

This naturalist sat there in one of those jolting moments of understanding. I'd not had much use for organized religion during my life, but here was a mainstream religious institution espousing what I, as a biologist, had already come to believe—that caring for others occupied a central place within the cultural concourse of our species. I had arrived at this conviction after much swimming against the current within my own discipline. The prevailing view of evolutionists—that the ultimate business of all life was to maximize its reproductive fitness—meant that human behavior had to be selfish, that we cannot give to another outside our immediate genetic family if there is significant cost to the giver involved.

After retiring from active university work, I took up the question of what role the great systems of faith play in human society. I did this with all the dispassion I could muster, trying to understand the origins of religion in evolutionary terms, to see if it was possible to rebut the claim, made by more than a few evolutionists, that churches today are anachronisms flying in the face of the inevitable biologic commands of our species.

I now understand that churches, temples, and the rest are conduits of culture through which rules for living can be shaped and taught in a contemporary world. They are, in fact, natural extensions of us, vital constructs by which we fit ourselves to the larger world. And as the keepers and shapers of ethics, I believe these ubiquitous sacred institutions of ours may help us come to care for the Earth in a deep enough fashion to save ourselves.

Flowing like a single deep river through all the faiths and religious belief systems of humankind, I believe, is a fundamental human need to contemplate the forces larger than us, to see beyond our individual limits, to grapple with the ineffable. Such a need, I think, has been at the genesis of every religion the world has ever known. Wherever we have found ourselves, we seem to have wondered about spheres of things beyond our ability to see. We have understood that we are very small and that these larger things control us.

Where did this essential aspect of human-ness come from? While I think it probable that we humans alone ponder where we came from and where we are going, and we alone imagine a god or gods carrying out the business of the larger sphere, our sense of the ineffable is made mostly of old parts, evolutionarily speaking, some very ancient indeed.

It may be that the reach toward the ineffable started with the wanderers of long ago, the groups of social mammals that constantly moved from place to place to satisfy the hunger of the pack, like present-day wolves. Wandering required that the pack reach consensus for many of its choices, thus lifting "decision" to a new plane above that set by their genes. These animals carried their world with them, and so each decision was likely to reflect a mixture of the social arrangements of their vagrant culture and of exquisite assessments of dangers and possibilities in the world just beyond. This all required abstract thought. The ability to think in abstractions arrived in this way in many different species at many different places on earth and over a great span of time.

Abstract thought, of course, could arise only in group-living animals. The group is the larger abstraction, the surrounding context within which the individual life is played out and against which thoughts are formed. Group creatures understand that they are parts of larger systems—families, clans, packs, herds—all layers of abstraction beyond the individual. All the events and consequences that spring from the social relationships of the group, all that one does to create oneself in relation to the outer world, is done without ever dipping down into the guiding structure of the genes. This condition is what I have called culture, and it goes hand in hand with abstract thought and a large, facile brain.

The appearance of the capacity for abstract thought in group-living animals was, I think, a major turning point in the history of life. Down the path thus opened lay the teaching of young, politics (the game of relationships), and then, much later in the primate line, religion and its related concerns—ethics, faith, and the long search for meaning in life.

Already present in the group-living primates of long ago was another necessary precondition for the emergence of a spiritual sensibility. This was the ability to experience a thousand different shades of emotion. Evolved and elaborated in beings for which social interaction and relationship were paramount, this emotional foundation of behavior became, over time, the capacity to feel guilt, compassion, and a deep, wordless love for other beings and perhaps the Earth itself.

Once our wandering Hominid ancestors could conceive of worlds beyond the reach of their immediate senses, contemplate the finitude of their lives, and feel deep emotional bonds and hurts, systems of faith could be born simply from these beings existing in a natural world full of mysterious forces and patterns. The vast powers of the earth wholly beyond their comprehension—the capricious storms, the floods they could bring, the restless moving earth that could be rent like window glass, and conversely, the beneficence of rain, the beams of the sun inviting one to curl up and purr for a while like a kitten—these all evoked a sense of wonder, demanded explanation, and assumed such emotional freight that it was as if one could carry on concourse with the Earth. The shadowy realms just at the edges of perception became places where our early ancestors felt, more than saw, forces larger than themselves and came to understand that they were constantly at work all around them. Then, it was only natural that the invisible forces of the Earth be given faces and names, be made sense of by the creation of cosmological systems.

The primates in the human lineage probably reached this threshold over which they could look into and think about the larger world, and beyond that, about the stars and their own creation, well before they evolved into anatomically modern humans. We can only speculate about their cosmological outlooks and belief systems. What is practiced today in our churches, temples, and mosques no doubt bears little resemblance.

Not long ago, however, our ancestors were wanderers too, not very different from the first god-inventing humans in the way they lived. They were hunter-gatherers who obtained their sustenance wholly from the wild land and relied solely on an oral tradition to pass along their culture. The constraints upon their lives were the same as those of the animals and plants they sought. Since they were clear participants in Mountain Time, I can imagine their religious belief systems and practices to have been similar, at least in overall outline, to those of our proto-human ancestors.

Around the world, a number of hunter-gatherer cultures survived into the twentieth century, intact enough for some of the details of their beliefs and practices to be recorded by anthropologists. One such group of people, the Chemehuevi[2] of California's Mojave Desert, have particular significance for me because their world included the Granite Mountains, where I have spent many of the most enchanting days of my life.

The landscape around the Granite Cabin binds me to this Earth like no other place. It always serves to remind me of the roots of our ancient wonder and our love. When I arrive there after an absence, the sparkle of sun from the crystals on the familiar boulders tells me I am home. I see as a gift of love the bright yellow nodding water mimulus, the glinted light from the trickling spring, the pinyon branches heavy with cones about to open and spill sweet seeds among the needles below. These and infinite other bits of beauty leaven my life and draw me hard and insistently to this piece of Earth. I have no doubt that the Chemehuevi felt the same way.

Around the Granite Cabin, signs of the Chemehuevi's presence are common. Black volcanic grinding stones poke up above the pale granite gravel. Rhyolite and chalcedony arrowheads still surface on the sandy flats. Down below the cabin there is a flat area where artisans once sat, flaking blanks of pink, marbeled rhyolite into knives, scrapers and arrow points. Just to the north, at the edge of the nearby wash, an almost flat granite slab emerges from the gravel. It is pockmarked with bedrock mortars, glassy smooth cups in the rock, where women sat in the shade of another gigantic boulder to grind their gatherings into meal, and to talk out the webwork of their lives.

Up on the rocky roof of the cave behind the cabin, where you have to crawl on hands and knees, are painted rusty-red pictographs of hematite powder, perhaps made into a kind of paint with cactus juice. What looks like a sun, or a tortoise with too many legs, is about to fall away as the rock itself spalls off.

I tell my students of a black cleft among the boulders a little farther up the wash, where I once found a bare whitened branch, a witching stick, propped at the entrance. Such sticks marked caves for the Indians as ones that held stored food. Sure enough, back in its depths, at shoulder height on a cornice of the granite wall, I found a storage olla, slumped and broken. In its neck was a carved wooden plug, sealed tight with what seemed like ancient beeswax. Inside the olla there once had been a cache of food, perhaps piñon nuts, perhaps meal from gleaned seeds.

The spring behind the cabin holds an almost mystical significance for me. The Chemehuevi people must have known of it, and I suspect they described its location and significance in a sacred song. Songs were the Chemehuevi's oral history, defined the terrain that sustained them, and dictated how and when their little bands should travel. In recounting the long wander from mountain to mountain, the springs that sustained the file of people walking out their lives, the caches they left, and the seasonal sources of food they could find, the songs bound together the realms of the sacred and the practical.[3]

There were several interlacing Chemehuevi songs describing different paths through the desert—the Mountain Sheep Song, the Deer Song, the Salt Song, the Quail Song. For hundreds of years or more, the Mountain Sheep Song led the Chemehuevi past the Granite Mountains on their way to the lofty San Bernardino Mountains and back. Their lives were one long trek as they pieced together their passage from such events as the seed-setting time of the chia, the ripening of the piñon cones, and the movements of sheep and deer toward the springs. There were many springs mentioned in the Mountain Sheep Song, and I like to think the Granite Cabin spring was one of them.

My suspicion hangs mostly on a story geographer Dick Logan told me. Dick and I were once colleagues on the staff at UCLA, and I knew of his work on the weather patterns of the East Mojave Desert. In the late 1930s, he was tending one of his weather shelters up the bouldery slope of the Granite Mountains when he noticed an old touring car stopped on the gravel road below. Standing around it was a handful of men, and another was looking under the hood. Dick climbed down the mountain to see if he could help.

The men were Chemehuevis who had been hunting desert sheep on the mountain behind. Such hunting remained their right under the settlement with the federal government, which also gave them reservation lands near the river. The one who spoke was an old weather-beaten man, obviously their leader. Learning their plight, Dick offered his help. In those days, before most paved highways, this could mean a day's commitment or more since the nearest garage was many rough miles away at Essex Station. At any rate, Dick did take the leader to Essex, where they obtained the needed part, returned, and were able to fix the car.

The old man addressed Dick in thanks, saying something like this: "Not many white people would have helped us the way you did, and we are grateful. But we are also poor and have little to give. There is, however, one treasure that we can share with you. Follow me, if you wish. It is just a short way."

With that, the old man led them up through the boulders, up the mountain a little, to a place where a gigantic slab of granite leaned against a vertical face of the mountain. "It is narrow, so crowd on top of one another," said the old man. He took a few steps into the cleft, lay down, and began digging in the gravelly floor with his hands. Soon water flowed out into the little pool—sweet, cool, and clear. The old man drank, and then each of the rest followed. "You will always find good water here," the old man said. Then they filed down to the car and were gone.

It seems probable to me that the spring Dick was "given" is the same one I later discovered and where we built our cabin. The arrangement of rocks is right, and it is on the correct face of the mountain. This possibility brings me closer to the mountain and to that long-gone Mountain Time world of the Chemehuevis.

The Mountain Sheep Song is in fragments now, effectively dead, since no real owner of it remains alive and very few speakers of pure Chemehuevi remain. For me, this carries with it an irreparable sense of loss. No one now can "know" the desert the way those wandering people once did.

Wherever Chemehuevis wandered, the stern hand of forces beyond understanding showed each person to be a cipher in a larger scheme. The People talked and wondered about that fact, and then accepted its rule into their myth. In various fashions it remains that way for all of us. At the westernmost limit of their world, the Chemehuevi climbed rocky promontories that reached above the trees. There they could look out over the California coastal plain below to the limitless mirror of the sea. For them, that shining sea was a manifestation of Ocean Woman, or Hutsipamamau'u, the prime creator and the principle supernatural being among the many other beings, spirits, and demons that animated their world.

The songs and sacred stories of the Chemehuevi may have been based on actual events, but over the thousands of years that the songs were sung and the myths told, the precise events of the past slipped into myth. In fact, for all of us, past events become distorted by the imprecision of memory. Irrelevant events drop out of our stories, and our songs grow and change like living things. Time, that elastic dimension, trickles away, loses meaning. Yet within Chemehuevi myth, there still remain recognizable hints of their more northern past, long before they settled in the austere western deserts.

Today, on their reservation lands, the Chemehuevis seek some semblance of inner peace in reconciling their ancient society with the heedless one that has swept over them. Since I am not one of them, I feel a strong sense of reticence in writing about this living people and their history. I feel a fragile, one-sided bond to them. For all the rigors of a hunter-gatherer's life, they were of this desert where I write this, and I am not. I only drink of its essence when I come, in the distorted reality of the new visitor overwhelmed by the beauty and perfection of this difficult land. I can only brush with my fingertips what their lives must have been like. It is the same with the desert itself.

I imagine a scene that took place several thousand years ago. The people on the north hill gather near their ancient midden, its rich black soil built by innumerable campfires like the one that flickers now. Mussels, brought up from the intertidal band below by the "shellfish men," steam in their shells, and wild melons roast. A trickle of clear water issues from the hillside, bending around the toe of the midden and flowing toward the river below. The people sit out of the sea wind behind the brow of the hill, eating, casting the shells of mussels and the waste of melons onto the soft soil.

A woman has many times noted little plants pushing through this soil—those with the succulent paired first leaves have proved to be melons. She picks ten seeds from the cast-off rinds and thumbs them in a line into the moist midden soil, each one about a foot from the first. A few days later, they push through the soil, all in that same line. She is sure now. She gathers and plants more seeds away from where the people now sit, and soon the outer midden is a tangle of vines, and then the melons appear and swell.

In ways such as this, hunter-gatherer peoples began gradually to cultivate the plants and care for the animals that provided them with food. While some societies added this new form of food-getting to their existing subsistence activities, others developed its potential to such an extent that it largely replaced hunting, fishing, and plant gathering. Agriculture—that long, slow co-evolution between humans and domesticated species—had begun.

With such agriculture, however primitive, a way was shown to co-opt the space of other species and to turn it to our needs. Just clear the competitors away, fight them off, and tend a garden. A steady food supply was thus secured. With this came an end of wandering. Food assured, they made permanent settlements and found that the controls on human numbers had been loosened. Without asking why, our species struck out in a thousand directions, co-opting canyon after canyon in the new human scheme. The new salient, however, remained cast in terms of a species still locked in Mountain Time, still struggling for space and resources against neighbors and still taking all it could. Soon we all but forgot our Mountain Time roots.

Agriculture changed human society in myriad ways, and the changes it wrought in our dealings with the ineffable were as profound as any. Reflecting on the nature of our present-day religious institutions, I can see that much of what I find objectionable or unhelpful in religion arose after human societies became more settled, after we turned our backs on Mountain Time.

First, there is the matter of doctrine. The Chemehuevi's way of expressing their cosmology in myth and song was symbolic and psychological. Although the broad outline of a myth was relatively fixed, its specifics were not. When an elder told a myth, he was expected to embroider it with improvised details. The rules and ideas of institutionalized religions, in contrast, tend to become frozen in place as the final word of this or that God.

As a naturalist, it is difficult for me to accept descriptions and explanations of the world that come from dogma. I find that people of faith can easily assign causes to events that have no basis in actual experience or observation of the world. They care little for proof. A religious person easily concludes: "There are things I am unable to explain by rational means. I will accept my God's word about them, no matter how strange they seem to me. Perhaps it is not for me to understand at all." This might be a reasonable approach for the largest questions about existence and the cosmos, but I know one thing for sure—even the most difficult puzzles here on Earth can be enlightened by the naturalist's methods, which clearly distinguish theory and fact and include strict rules for how one goes about making the former into the latter.

My ideas about ethical behavior don't square with the ruling assumptions of the faiths, either. Most of the world's great religions employ the ideas of sin and of judgment or reward in the hereafter as a way of coercing upright behavior. If such external carrots and sticks are necessary for ensuring the moral conformance of the faithful, why is it that I, a non-believer in sin and judgment, have lived my life as one devoted to helping those around me? I have not been passive; I still care deeply about what happens to the Earth in our hands. For me, these commitments come from within; they are part of who I am, how I am built. Isn't it so for most of us? Aren't we all living evolutionary dualities, exhibiting the potential for both selfish and altruistic behavior in the same skin?

Finally, there are few, if any, faith systems on Earth that can be held blameless for a great deal of violence and human suffering. Throughout human history, churches have not infrequently been co-opted into the political schemes of men, and, given the absolute power they could command, terrible excesses have sometimes resulted. Absolute power from any source can do that, whether in a church or in the court of Ivan the Terrible. The inquisitions, the many wars of religion, the various waves of religious persecution, the forced conversions of "heathens," and so on may have arisen from the very human pronouncements of those who came to lead the church or those who wished to use a religion for the political needs of the time, but the fact remains that untold millions have died and suffered in the names of the various faiths.

I mention these pitfalls of faith not to condemn religion, but to put it in perspective. As I noted above, there is much about religion that is positive and even essential. For example, it is difficult to imagine society without the instructional parts of its faith systems, the parts that provide a moral code and rules for living together in harmony. Such rules have usually been practical instructions designed for various times and places, both for those who quest for such answers and for people of no pretenses at all, who simply want to be enveloped in arms stronger than theirs and to be borne along.

We need religion also because not everybody thinks like a scientist. Many react strongly against the very thought of rationality, taking refuge in things of the heart or the spirit, that emotional substrate that lies so close beneath the surface of all of us. Thank goodness. It's important that this key duality of the human skein continue to exist. For those who put more credence in a sermon than a monograph, religion is what provides discipline and ethical guidance.

Religion may be necessary, too, because in the face of the increasingly dire warnings Earth is sending us, science won't be enough. Science is by design a value-free system and won't be much good for compelling us to exercise discipline and do the right thing when we confront the dilemmas just ahead. In typical human fashion, we must be pushed over this or that brink before Science gets our attention. With its ability to so powerfully motivate human behavior, religion may be the force that finally gets the human species to act responsibly toward the Earth—to listen to the alarms raised by Science—before we rush headlong over the ecological brink.

I'm not naïve enough to think that religious institutions, as they currently exist, are up to the task. If religion is going to help us avert the coming catastrophe, it must change and re-orient its priorities. But I look around me and I see the signs of this beginning to happen. Perhaps in this regard, I *am* naïve, but I see us moving nervously closer to bridging that huge gap between Science and Faith, bringing them closer, in a kind of modern-day yin and yang, to forge a new social team.

Many will claim that religious institutions are ossified behemoths, as resistant to change as anything in society. This is only partly true. Faiths are part doctrine and part the society around them. They will change. It's only a matter of time.

Even though we may be dismissing, and even condemning, in our impatience over how slowly the citadels of faith seem to change, we should understand that they are always being remade. If one crowds up too close to history, such change may not be evident. In the Dark and Middle Ages of Europe, little might have seemed different from year to year, given the baseline of a single human life from which to judge and the monolithic stabilizing grip of the church that once held unchallenged sway. But to examine the entire history of faiths is to learn that much has, in fact, changed, and—in terms of Earth Time—very quickly. The Egyptian gods were magical; Greek gods were like the cast of a soap opera, there for the watching while you figuratively munched on your popcorn; the Hebrew deity was prophetic; the Christian God originated as one, but fractionated through time into three forms, assisted by cadres and cadres of angels with various tasks to fulfill.

If the world's faiths are indeed changing, or capable of changing, toward what are they moving? I think it is the very concept of God that is evolving—from a personified being, in whose image we were created, to a more impersonal, but no less powerful, embodiment of nature and the universe. We are beginning to understand that the Earth is the rule-giver—the loving and sometimes wrathful rule-giver, the one to whom prayers and petitions have been subliminally directed, the all-encompassing one whose manifestations are, in fact, the very definitional essence of beauty. The Earth is the silent one whose silence has been heretofore been taken as affirmation, but which might better be regarded as providing mere slack in our tether. Although looking ahead is far more chancy than looking backward in time, I have come to believe that this evolution is happening. I think that is what the present ferment among us is about.

As the giver of rules transitions from God to the Earth, a new ethical system emerges. The new ethic insists that we forgo a measure of our ancient self-centeredness. It encourages us to embrace our altruistic sides, to give ourselves to the needs of the larger system—the community, the human species, all other life, the Earth. If this ethic is based in faith as well as in scientific understanding, it will be that much more powerful. Harnessing the inborn human capacities for love and wonder and channeling them into altruism, is, after all, one of the strengths of religious faith.

The shadowy dicta of older gods now seem to me like first approximations, crafted when our understanding of the Earth was just unfolding—back in times when the outer boundaries of the known world edged into the forest and sea, back when very few could read the written word so the words of preachers held special power, back when time was still elastic, back when we could not see our Earth as a small spherical planet on every TV weather report. Within about ten lifetimes such as yours and mine—blindingly swift, in Earth terms—the godhead has shifted and changed, like a slide coming into focus. The flights of angels have been grounded. The devil with his bubbling cauldron of burning sulfur has been revealed as simply part of the tensions within and between us, the many and complex oscillations of human polarities. No longer do we have to imagine a God as the face of the forces larger than us. We may never fully understand the grand workings of Nature, but now we can see them as what they really are.

Remember the Chemehuevi, so much closer to the Earth than we. They lived in a world of spirits that animated their days, the many voices of a larger god. They understood Earth to be a giver of life, the one who caused the streamlet to tinkle from the desert rock in the springtime world overflowing with gifts.

I imagine a Chemehuevi woman representing her people's relationship to the rule-giving Earth. I see her rounding a stream bend to find a bank of chia in full seed, to be swept into her gathering basket until the tiny black prizes were finger deep, and she knowing that she had the Earth or its godly manifestations to thank. I imagine her watching the men bring the mountain sheep into camp when the dusk began to color the sky, seeing the game as a gift from the Earth, a gift of nourishment for her and the infant she had carried across the vast desert on her back. A love more powerful than we can now know, a pervading sense of the beauty of that known land of her people, must have welled up in her in such moments of peace. Yet she knew well the wrathful side of the Earth's nature. When the rising sun stilled the foreboding voices of the owls, the giver could turn implacable, bringing a withering heat. Unless the ollas were full, there would be little for the summer, and even the jackrabbits might gnaw at the bark of cholla for the bound moisture it carried. There was no mistaking, ever, what the rule-giver said.

Today Earth still speaks to us in the same way, in both love and wrath. We pour the gasses of our society into the Earth's very finite atmosphere, and the Earth speaks back by locking heat inside this narrow envelope. A terrible slow blow is even now being struck, one that has willed the seas to rise and inundate the works of the overflooding human species.

Although we have moved far from being able to understand the Earth's stern and loving commands, they are coming clear again. We must now make the rivers run clear again. We must find a new equilibrium on Earth, tend its land and seas with heartfelt tenderness and not take what we cannot soon return. We must make space for those creatures who ride along with us. We are just one passenger. We cannot take it all and forget them. We must find our place in this new equilibrium of life. We must come to understand, in our very bones, that we are children living by the commands of a finite Earth.

"Ken & Phyllis Norris Experimental Gopher Ranch" — established 1987.

Ken Norris leading his flock across the pasture at his home in the Santa Cruz Mountains.

Chapter 19: A Bowl Full of Earth

I look out my window, here a few miles north of Santa Cruz, California, to the forest of oaks and redwoods, and then to the fields spreading over the bluff top. I wonder: how did my love for this part of the Earth come to be?

My family and I settled here just two and a half decades ago. We traveled up a dirt farm road one foggy morning just at dawn and stopped amid a canyon-edge oak grove, shaggy with trailing poison oak vines. A battered old house trailer had been set in place where we would live while our house was being built. Our entourage included four children, three dogs, a parrot, and two cats. The smallest dog was pregnant and would soon give birth under my cot. The trailer leaked in the torrential rains of that year. Bracket fungus grew inside the trailer's door frame. Intimate is one way to say it. Primitive is another.

I can't say that I loved this land in those early days. To be sure, I marveled at the redwoods that thrust far above the rest of the forest, but a gloominess seemed to pervade the steep canyon. Everywhere through the forest, I could see the stumps of the original redwoods, many wider across than I am tall. The charred remains of the logger's slash was littered everywhere. They'd been at it for a long time. The first felling had been done by double-bitted axe and bucksaw. Pits, in which springboards had been pounded, could be seen on most stumps. There, lumberjacks had stood as they cut through the huge trees six feet up, avoiding the spreading buttresses where the trees clasped the ground.

Such gloom has since been replaced by deep attachment, born of the passage of time and a sense of the resilience of wild things. I now can see that the place is still alive, and that ten thousand stories are still being played out in ancient patterns all up and down the canyon and over the meadows. Without requiring words, the big and little things of this land have crept into my understanding, just as they would have for a little child growing up here. The canyons and the meadows are all of a piece now. Above me, the fleeing storm clouds move by, driven by winds that flail the wide-reaching redwood limbs around in great arcs. Down beneath the felled logs, I now know, are the egg clusters of salamanders, and, if I went there and pulled at the moist, rooting wood, I would also find tiny blind shrew moles, long-nosed, with fur a lush gray plush.

What I could not know at first was that the ancient Mountain Time pattern of the forest still persists after a half-dozen assaults since the coming of Europeans. Only when I followed deer trails down to the creek and then climbed back up, my naturalist's eyes open, could I see that the species of the forest have arranged themselves in a series of horizontal bands winding along the canyon slopes.

At the edge of the stream, poised among the ferns and lush gardens of coltsfoot, alder trees still reached high for light. In a tier just above them were the big-leaf maples, which scale their golden salvers onto the slow-flowing water in the fall. Above the maples, I passed through a broad band of young tanoak trees. This species had once been ravaged all along the West Coast to supply tanneries with its sienna-colored bark. Midway up the slope, I found what some call a rarity—a thin band of youngish California nutmegs amidst the other forest trees. Nutmeg wood is white as paper and for a time supplied local furniture makers, until all the big trees were cut.

All the way up the slope, I climbed past rings of second-growth redwood trees, each ring growing around the spreading root base of an ancient cut-off stump. Many of these trees were now more than one hundred feet tall. They were scattered everywhere through this forest, probably because they can catch the fog. When fog wells up the canyon, it is caught and rains down from the tree's sharp needle tips, soaking the duff below. Finally, at the top of the canyon, I walked among the oaks and the red-barked madrones margining the meadows.

This re-emergent forest is in our hands now, protected by a fragile agreement that affirms that we, and other settlers like us, will not damage it. But it is not enough to simply live beside it. We settlers must know at least a little about the banded canyon in order to care. Otherwise, the agreement is just paper.

My outer frame of understanding, for this and every other bit of land I have come to know, is Earth process. The mountains, the terraces, and the embayments are the direct result of the dynamics of the Earth, in whose balance we, individually, count for nothing at all.

Down the road below my house, there is a promontory, four hundred feet above the sea, the edge of an ancient, uplifted sea terrace. One day I stood there watching the sky. Cirrus clouds hurried by. They, the highest of clouds at the upper edge of the breathable atmosphere, were perhaps five miles above me—about half the road miles to nearby Santa Cruz. What a thin blanket of air we live in, I thought.

I looked out over the sea toward Japan, the reach of my vision extending a few dozen miles to the west, still short of where Guide and Pioneer Sea Mounts rise up from the sea floor and where the continent steps down into the abyss. That is the continental slope, and it margins all the continents. The abyssal ocean, I knew, averages between two and three miles deep and stretches for 7,500 miles unbroken to Japan. Well, two-thirds of the way out, Mellis Sea Mount and the Empire Sea Mount Chain must be crossed, but they are just blips in the long traverse.

I imagined that the Earth was a one-mile-diameter sphere. At that size, the ocean was a sheet about as thick as the water in a wading pool—about one and a half feet—and just above it, the usable air was about the same thickness. How thin is this domain that seems to us so grand, as we gaze up from within! We take this viewpoint of ours as the one that matters, and we point to the insects who can't even see the horizon from down in the grass. But mostly we just look down in the things we do, when we build, when we clear land, when we plant, when we figure our income tax. This viewpoint carries with it a false sense of superiority that seems to confer upon us the right to do what we wish to the Earth, without asking.

On another day, under a solid cloud deck, I swung my binoculars along the horizon to the north. I could almost see Año Nuevo Island, just into San Mateo County. By swinging around to the west and then southward across to the mouth of Monterey Bay, I could just see the top of a little detached peak of land off the Santa Lucia Mountain coast, atop which stands the Point Sur Lighthouse. That, I knew, was a little isolated lump of volcanic rock, brought up from the far south along the boundary fault.

I continued scanning east along the Pacific Grove coast, and, because of the cloud layer above and crystal clear air below, I could see the building tops of the Hopkins Marine Station through my glasses, more than thirty miles away. I panned on east past Monterey, where its houses and hotels stepped up on the pine-clothed hills, and then up the deep bay to the Pacific Gas & Electric stacks and Elkhorn Slough. The almost-flat Salinas Valley was invisible behind, below the curve of the sea. I ended my sweep of the horizon north of Rio Del Mar, where beach bluffs rise and the bay slips out of view beneath the bordering hills. I figured I was able to see about 180 degrees of horizon in this single scan. So much human history was in that panorama; so many singular natural environments were there amid the crowding things of today's world.

Then I noticed something that sent a shiver of awe through me. Throughout that whole scan, I could perceive the edge of the Earth! Between me and Monterey, and all around the Monterey Bay and west and north, the horizon was a single, precise, unbroken line. A circle really, the inside rim of an upside-down salad bowl put on our part of the Earth. And I was in fact standing at the center of this upside-down bowl. If I moved in any direction, a new bowl's worth would be there. How many such moves before I had seen everywhere? Beyond the bowl's edge, about twenty-three miles away, the Earth curved down and out of sight. Only twenty-three miles to see over the curve of the Earth, even from my rather high vantage point. The infinite Earth of my imagining slipped away, and in its place was a very finite globe, spinning in space, far, far smaller than I had ever imagined.

Suddenly a sense of the proportion of things swept over me. It came as a shock to perceive how small our Earth is and how thin the blankets of sea and air are. A sense of the Earth's fragility in our collective hands swept over me. I thought of the battered forest in the canyon. It came clear in those moments that it was easily within our collective powers to wreak irreparable havoc to this Earth. I had somehow remained insulated from such an understanding because I knew I couldn't do such a thing. I had forgotten for a time both the flood of our numbers and the inter-threading mycelia of our social arrangements that had crept almost everywhere throughout Mountain Time.

The Santa Lucia Mountains, visiable in the distance across Monterey Bay, as seen from Back Ranch Road below the Norris homestead in the Santa Cruz Mountains.

UC Santa Cruz Natural History Field Quarter students in the White Mountains, looking westward toward the snow-clad Sierra Nevada.

Chapter 20:
Embracing the Mountain

Old Blue was loaded with hardly a word from the three of us instructors. Supplies and dunnage moved in assembly-line style and were strapped down with practiced efficiency. "Triads" was called, and everybody was already aboard. This was our last wander in the wilds and everyone knew it; voices were a low murmur, but we were all wired tight with unresolved thoughts.

For most students, this was a final exploration within the protective cocoon of the university. At its end, they would scatter into society, taking with them a miscellaneous trove of facts, as well as attitudes and concerns that would shape many of their lives, and that would even nudge the world a little. They knew it, too. The quiet voices said it eloquently and also expressed a collective need. To be sure, like little boys finding a frog, they would quickly abandon all other thoughts when Steve would point out the fragile *Lewisia* flower set against the soil at treeline or when I would explain the probable origin of the layered rocks, but most of all in these waning, precious days, our comrades wanted to explore themselves and their place in this world. That was the serious work that remained to be concluded.

Our "resource person" was Yaakov Garb, a brilliant young man who had designed his own doctoral program in bioethics at the University of California at Berkeley. He was to hold all of us spellbound more than once with his probing mental explorations of today's dilemmas. Because there is always a flip side to such serious contemplations, we knew we must dance together over the same dusty mountain one more time, in affirmation of our miraculous bonds of trust. We wanted to read the doggerel we had written to each other because there was no one in Old Blue who would laugh and say nay.

We were, as I have said, all together, and our instructors' need was almost as great as theirs.

Frank Murphy was our new student instructor, drawn from an earlier class. It's hard to fool steady, smart Frank and he has a great collection of red neck and hurtin'-cheatin' songs for the campfire. He was driving when we spotted Dr. Vandenburg on a bicycle. Frank steered the bus around a corner after the good doctor, who turned toward us, revealing a great flowing white beard and a goofy smile. His faded blue denims and tan work shirt gave us conflicting signals.

Our route took us across the great San Joaquin Valley, up the west flank of the Sierra Nevada Mountains, and into the canyon of the Merced and Yosemite National Park. Out of experience, we bypassed the ravaged jewel of Yosemite Valley, so crowded with people, busses, and stores that its magnificent cliffs seem trivialized by all the hubbub below. It was simply too painful to see this during an exploration of Nature such as ours.

Instead, Old Blue climbed up toward the spine of the Sierra Nevada, and we watched from our windows as the forest changed character—mixed fir and pine forest giving way to stands of the magnificent dark-barked red fir, and then to slim lodgepole pines with bark like corn flakes. At 9,900 feet, we reached treeline. There, at its margin, were gnarled whitebark and limber pines, with needle tufts like poodles' tails, and branches so flexible they could be tied in knots. In winter, these trees must deal with ice storms that etch and scour above the snow blanket. We could almost see the sleet-filled wind beating against the windward side of these pines, whipping the branches and scaling away bark until the trees were pink, like skin switched after a sauna.

Then, suddenly, we were over the Tioga crest and racing down the vast eastward-facing glacial chasm of Lee Vining Canyon, where only 9,000 years ago ran a river of ice. "What power do we have over any of this?" I thought, "and what is 9,000 years in the life of the Earth?" We could easily envision that absent glacier. Spalled-off cliffs were still picked clean by the now-vanished ice. Hanging valleys had been left far up rock faces where threads of silvery water now leapt free and fell into vapor.

I remembered my father telling me about the first road to scale this side of Tioga; in places it was just a shelf of timbers laid on a frame of steel rods that had been rammed into the cliff, just air and scree below, and old Model-Ts picking their way up and over, while passengers looked inward toward the rock face.

Steve stopped Old Blue at a gravely turnoff to cool the brakes. Down below, we could see the shining disc of Mono Lake, a lake set in a volcanic ash-filled bowl of the Great Basin desert. The bowl has no outlet and so the lake is saline and alkaline. To swim there is to float high like a cork and to emerge coated with white salts.

We camped above the lake in a narrow aspen grove defined by a tumbling crystal rill, one of the last free-flowing streams to reach the lake, the others having long ago been purchased away to supply water to the greater Los Angeles area, three hundred miles to the south. "From here," I told them, "the water of these mountains must pass through two lawyers, a politician, and a certified public accountant before it reaches the sea."

Clouds swept in platoons off the Sierra crest, moving eastward. In afternoon's light, trails of rain could be seen, reaching down toward the gun-metal lake. Decked in slickers now, we gathered around a smoky fire amid the aspens to listen to Yaakov. He probed and quested among us for the elusive answers to how the human species should regard Nature in the coming world. Uncompromising about the truths we often hide from ourselves, he thrust and parried.

Steve and Frank and I were just three in a company of peers as we explored with these so-called students. Passionate minds, diverse minds were there, at least the equals of those who led them, made eloquent by the urgency of the task they took up as theirs. There were incipient poets, teachers of the young, doctors, midwives, scientists, runners of the gears and engines of society, and there were those deeply engaged in probing the basis of human ethics. Still-forming minds, yes, but less encumbered with the past than we, their ostensible leaders. That past was what we were most useful for. Steve and

I tempered the discussion with the dimension of time, while Frank was our bridge to the others.

Bread was passed around and no one left to cook dinner. We all sat still around the smoky fire, water dripping from the bills of our caps. Dinner would come later, and since the food group of this trip was dominated by vegans, the fare was to be sparse indeed—just cabbage and paprika soup and, thankfully, that bread.

Next morning I met Steve on the street of the hamlet of Lee Vining, he having brought the bus in for gas and I to talk to the Mono Lake Committee in preparation for our arrival next day. Almost silently, we made our way across the highway to a hole-in-the-wall cafe, ordered up plates of bacon and scrambled eggs and hash brown potatoes glistening with cooking oil. These transitions of diet, I thought, proclaimed largely for ethical reasons, cannot be made with a stroke of a pen. There is a lot of physiology involved. I routinely carried a salami in my sleeping bag, inside a zip-lock bag, to stay the pangs, but this breakfast was better. Stroking our tummies in satisfaction, we made our way back to camp.

That night, the wind swept down from the Sierra crest and almost blew us off the mountain. We tentmates, Tye and I, thought we were about to go airborne at one point as cottonwood branches snapped with rifle-shot sounds above us in the swirling black.

In next morning's calm, we packed up and drove south to the headquarters of the Mono Lake Committee, a scruffy old converted house pervaded by the spirit of David Gaines, an environmental activist killed in an automobile accident some years back. He and a small cluster of friends dared to think of saving Mono Lake from the imperious forces of the huge City of Los Angeles. David and Goliath. The committee had gathered around them a collection of young environmental soldiers, some from our earlier Field Quarters, and these young people lived in and worked from the old house.

Their efforts were spurred when the lake level dropped lower than ever, connecting Negit Island to the shore. Wholly vulnerable, a large proportion of the world's California Gull population nested on this little volcanic cone, and for a time coyotes and other predators could walk across dry land into the colony. But the lake level rose again in time for the birds to maintain their population. The thinnest of survival margins!

Given such ammunition, the efforts of the activists worked. Mono Lake and its life still remain. They still worked from the old house, not trusting that they had won. Their simple message was and is: "No, this unique lake and its life must not disappear because of the machinations of humans. The time for such retreats has passed. The time for shaping our affairs into the future world has come."

In the camp ahead, we would continue to debate the complex issues posed when such human patterns are set against the patterns of Nature. How can we say which will prevail—or, harder still, which should prevail?

We drove south along the east face of the Sierra Nevada, a nervous land of craters and volcanic ash, where geologists keep careful tabs on a magma body—live lava—gnawing at its rock roof and rising in its chamber, mere kilometers below the surface. Earthquakes are so common here that some shopkeepers in nearby Mammoth Village despair about keeping goods on shelves.

We skirted placid Lake Crowley, a magnet for fishermen. It lies in the center of what geologists call the Long Valley Caldera, the remnant bowl of hills around the site of a past and quite colossal volcanic eruption. The lake is the modern representation of an ancient lake that has occupied the caldera back into Ice Age times. "See those hills south of the lake?" I announced. "They form the southern rim of the caldera. Can you see that they curve right across the valley, more or less at right angles to the major north/south-trending mountains? Those hills were formed in a single, almost unimaginably massive volcanic event that happened 730,000 years ago."

We topped the crest of the hills and drove down the long grade toward the town of Bishop. I pointed to the pale peach-colored rocks called the Bishop Tuff that made up the long damlike slope and read an excerpt from my brother Bob's book, *Geology of California*:[1]

> The rock is considered a welded tuff (ignimbrite), the product of incandescent gaseous clouds of ash and pumice that showered the countryside, ultimately producing pasty flows of glowing material that moved quickly downslope into the Owens Valley as well as northward into a large area south of Mono Lake.... This eruption was an event of cataclysmic proportions and incredible violence. Nothing on such a scale has been observed anywhere in the world during historic time.

I read on: "The eruption of the Bishop Tuff was very abrupt, lasting days or weeks at most, and 144 cubic miles of superheated ash and steam were erupted, some of which has been detected as far east as Kansas and Nebraska, while about 5,000 feet of ash from the event fills the caldera of today."

"Nothing to fool around with," we concluded trivially, as Old Blue approached the bottom of the great rocky volcanic dam. But we did not wonder that today most people living in the long trough of Owens Valley have laid out their escape routes and hang on the latest pronouncements of the U.S. Geologic Survey seismic teams that monitor the rising magma body.

We rumbled into the town of Bishop, there to roust out an old and treasured colleague, Phil Pister, who for a few moments put down his day-to-day chores at the California Department of Fish and Game to walk to the local park with us and to challenge us with his example—which was that a single individual, regardless of station or position, *could* matter in the struggle to shape the coming world. His has been a career spent within a governmental agency, and all the while he has been a constant ethical force far beyond his office. Some years ago, for example, he managed to catch the last remaining individuals of an endangered species, a tiny pupfish, place them in buckets and then plant the fish in a secret spring, while a lawless group of fishermen sought to remove this last impediment to their sport by planting predatory bass in what they supposed was the pupfish's last habitat.

He told us of a movement to dam tiny creeks throughout the west for household water power, which he was opposing, and wondered aloud who should prevail—the fish who spawned in those streams or the human species. "Each of you can matter, if you just will," he told us, and then he walked back into his workaday world.

On south we went. The east wall of the deep valley was now a looming, huddled 14,246-foot massif—White Mountain—disappearing upward into roiling clouds. We wondered aloud if Old Blue could make it to our proposed high-altitude camp, or would late season snow banks block the road before we got there.

At the hamlet of Big Pine, we turned east up the Westgard Pass road. This steep, narrow road crosses the southern toe of White Mountain, and from its highest divide we would turn north up the spine of the Whites to our camp. In just a few, relentlessly up miles, we would climb from about 4,000 feet at the valley floor to 8,900 feet at our hoped-for camp. On the way up, we would travel from the desert margin into a dense piñon forest near treeline.

The hills of the pass were bright with flowers—a perfect time for the plant geeks to test their new naming skills. As the bus groaned its way up the steep grade at twenty miles an hour, Steve began to call out some names. "Brittlebush," he said brightly, "*Encelia farinosa.*" Eyes turned to low yellow-flowered domes dotting the dry hills. "Indigo bush," I said, pointing to shrubs in the dry streambed covered with flowers of deepest blue, not remembering the Latin name.

"See if you can call out the plant family, too," said Steve over the speaker.

A voice from the seats called out: "Prince's plume, Brassicaceae." We scanned the slopes and soon located an elegant, six-foot spike clothed in yellow flowers, leaning from the hillside. Soon the hills were dense with them.

Steve pulled off at a grove of cottonwoods, where a little stream of water gurgled and disappeared into the gravelly wash. "Batchelder Spring," I announced. "We'll give Old Blue a fifteen-minute breather here." Moments later, the cry went up: "Rattlesnake!" I rushed toward a wide circle of students to find a feisty two-and-a-half foot Panamint rattlesnake in the center, reared up in a striking coil, head waving back and forth.

I moved into the cautious routine I performed only once a spring; that is, to catch a rattlesnake, just as Doc Cowles had done for me many years before. The bite of this particular snake, I knew, was no picnic. Its venom is hemorrhagic, causing the tissues around a bite to hemorrhage and swell enormously and to turn black and blue. Sometimes people lose fingers to such bites. A healthy adult human is not apt to die from it, but neither is happiness to be sought this way.

I selected firm ground, maneuvered the snake over it, pressed its head down with my walking stick, which I had fashioned for this purpose, making sure the snake was pinioned securely. Then I slid my fingers behind the snake's swollen jaws, and quickly grasped the snake's tail with the other hand. I had him clean and lifted him up immobilized. I pressed my fingers hard behind its jaws, which then opened under the pressure, erecting the snake's two curved, glassy-sharp fangs.

Students gathered around me and peered warily at the snake, as two drops of amber venom appeared at the fang tips. I brought their attention to two pits on the snake's upper lip—the loreal pits—and told them what Cowles had taught me, that by using these heat-sensing pits, this snake could track the warm body of a jumping mouse and then strike it in mid-air. I lofted the snake gently into the brush, and it slithered away.

I sensed, more than heard, a hum of discord from some of the students during this demonstration, and later asked Frank about it. He told me that, yes, a number of the students didn't like to see the snake handled in such a rough fashion. I mused to myself that humanity's ethical frontier advances like the wind and that the fermenting vat of change is to be found especially among new-minted adults, such as these students of ours. Almost miraculously, under their minds and hands, a new worldview was beginning to form that said, "Treat snakes with consideration, just as you would the rest of Nature."

Many times in our springs together, I had felt such little jogs suggesting I should change my ways, reshape myself a little, and here was another one. Such changes are always a little irritating, never comfortable. If one becomes swathed in certitude, I thought, or comes to sit on too high a pedestal, or lives too long with the old patterns without any change at all, these jogs may become steps too painful to take.

Are such new imperatives always right? Should one always try to change? Not at all, I came to think. The cry for social change is usually a simple, almost mindless bludgeon, a probe into the unknown. Always, I think, it is driven by emotion, not some carefully crafted intellectual position. This I knew: the process of social change in us happens most powerfully in our questing years and is made possible by the alienation from old values, the escape from the nest that marks this age. Miraculous waves of consensus appear. This year, everybody should wear tie-dye or turn their baseball caps backward. "Our little band of comrades is right in the middle of this life stage," I thought. "This being so, why should they listen to me at all? It must be that I represent neutral ground outside their families, a wisdom base from the past that can be tapped before society moves on past either of us."

In the case of the snake, I felt that a truth had been said. When I began my explorations as a young biologist, rattlers were killed without remorse. That was a leftover from the time when men were invaders in a threatening land. They hacked open room for themselves in the wilderness, in search of some semblance of safety. There were snakes without limit out there, part of a long list of enemies. But now, as the human race floods the wild land, it is Nature that needs protecting. This need has become a shout of anguish.

The idea that Nature is sacred, that Nature is somehow what sustains us, was obviously seeping into our youthful society, taking form. In the case of my handling of the rattlesnake, on one side of me, I felt a sense of escape. I knew that sooner or later one was going to get me. On the other side, I felt that ache of personal reshaping. And so I cast aside my live demonstration. Later I would scan the roads for dead rattlers hit by automobiles, a truer symbol of our times anyway.

The first shaggy juniper tree was called out. Scarlet splotches of Indian paintbrush appeared and then took over the banks of the wash, growing up amid buckwheats. The forest began to thicken, and a new little buckwheat, pale grayish green and saffron, made its appearance. It formed mounds that looked like little frisbees scaled onto the forest floor.

Steve downshifted the bus as the road pitched up. We slowed to five miles an hour. Steve danced on the pedals like the rawhide farmer that he once was, searching for the place where the gears would mesh. We slowed and slowed. I thought we might not make it. Finally the gears slipped together as the engine roared, and we began to creep forward again. A little cheer went up from the seats, and I could see Steve flicker a smile. The engine drew down to a mahogany-deep bass.

Purple penstemons appeared and were called out. I thought about how we'd just drawn a plant transect up the mountain. Everyone who was awake had now actually seen, not just been told about, the bands of living things that are arranged by climate and altitude around every such wild mountain as this.

We reached the deceptively flat summit, and Steve turned up the road that roughly traced the ridgeline. "Grandview Camp," Frank called out a few miles later, and we turned in among the piñons to find an elegant camping place, a nearly vacant camp with tables, a fire pit, a double outhouse downslope, and plenty of flat places for our tents on the springy duff beneath the trees. We'd made it! But just barely: snowbanks criss-crossed the road 500 feet above camp.

This camp was the terminus of our springtime journey. For a week, we would explore the mountain and the adjacent valleys, then huddle around the campfire each night to talk and sing our songs until the last embers turned gray and everyone straggled off into the icy night to bed down.

On our last full day on the mountain, in the sharp light of the alpine morning, we gathered for the hike up to Schulman Grove, a ragged and wind-shaped patch of bristlecone pines clinging to marble ridges far above us, above the limits of most other trees. The way to them wound up the spine of the White Mountains. We stopped for a few moments near the highest ice-burned piñon. The deep Owens Valley and the Sierra Nevada lay before us to the west. A single Clark's nutcracker floated far out in vacant space above the chasm, calling.

Up and up we climbed until we entered a sparse grove of ancient and blasted trees—the bristlecone forest. What defines these trees most is exposed cinnamon-colored wood of such fine grain that it flutes and etches like a sculptor's marble. It hardly seems to rot. The living trees are often just winding bands of cambium and bark twisting up the lee sides of wood sculptures, leaving the dead tree heart exposed as a rampart against wind-blown ice. Living branches are long tassels, growing at the ever-so-slow pace of twenty years to the inch. Mostly, these trees persist, set wide apart on the steep mountain slopes, because they can subsist on limestone soil, which defeats most other trees.

The cones engaged my imagination the most. Beneath each tree, they lay in deep windrows. It seemed that these trees spend much of their life force, most everything they can extract from the impoverished soil, assuring that their seeds can play out their statistical game. Ten thousand seeds cast, and only one might find a crevice where the squirrels cannot reach. In the long sweep of tree-time, that expenditure might define a tree's life commitment.

Impossibly unlikely events may rule the fate of a bristlecone forest. Because of the sheer numbers of seeds, rare events become likely, and then nearly inevitable, as over and over for 5,000 years, the trees reseed their austere patch of marble. By single-chance events too tenuous to be reconstructed, the trees may even move from mountain to mountain. That's much of what reproduction and all its manifold strategies is about for them: turning the unlikely into the inevitable and thereby spreading a life force as far as it can go, just like the blessed frogs of Hidden Spring.

Beyond this spreading force, what limits a bristlecone will be defined by the tree's design of life, its basic blueprint. Out at the margins of the tree's range, where that plan no longer works very well, other trees with other plans will press in. It's out there that the battle of limits is won and lost.

These trees have often been called the oldest living things on the earth. They look it, but the statement springs from the pen of a publicist, not a biologist. There are many other plants—oaks, for example, and even the lowly creosote bush—that seem to represent clones flaunting the whole the idea of a life span, and they are clearly older than the bristlecones. In the creosote's case, year-by-year death consists of the dying of the inner part of a bush while an outer circle lives on. Over 15,000 years' time, the plant becomes a ring, but in fact the bush has never really died.

Around the bases of some still-standing bristlecones are fallen trees, linked into the calendar by their characteristic growth bands, which go back nearly 10,000 years, well into Ice Age time. Somewhere up in that forest grows Methuselah—at 4,600 years, the oldest known tree on White Mountain. Dendrochronologists drilling with long, thin, boring tools have taken out wood cores that let them age this and many other trees. I think I know where Methuselah is; it is a grotesque ruin of a tree, protected by an exposed wall of bedrock from landslides, perhaps the most destructive event that these trees face in their long lives. But I'm not telling. Some people inevitably would pick at its wood, take home branches and carve their initials if they knew, and Methuselah would soon be defaced or even dead.

Thinking about such life spans and then our own, and about these mindless "strategies of life," we glissaded our various ways down the steep mountain, back to camp. By the evening's campfire, Frank announced that he had discovered that today was the fiftieth anniversary of Spam, implying that I had secret cans of the pork product in my sleeping bag, along with my salami, and that for this reason, I would welcome some sort of celebration.

He and his co-conspirators took me by both arms and inserted me into a line of marchers lined up in the shadows. With one of their number on guitar beating out the melody, we marched around the fire chanting "When the Spam comes marching in." Frank was in the lead, holding a frying pan into which he had cut a large-sized Spam into little jiggly cubes.

Frank had earlier confided that he had attended a parochial school where a big bossy nun used to switch him when he was bad. Here on White Mountain, he used those same coercive tactics on all of us, vegans and all. Little glossy cubes of processed meat were skewered on toothpicks and thrust peremptorily at those seated by the fire, as we danced by. The true vegetarians held these offerings with obvious distaste, as if they held a dead mouse by the tail. This was followed by a command performance from the audience: Frank chose "The Dance of the Sugar Spam Faeries."

Then, with no obvious seam, the mood around the fire shifted. Things once difficult to say, fragile things, rose to the surface, the stuff lying just below the silly song and Spam-celebration layer. Steve read a touching springtime salute to our student friends. In a sentence or two each, he touched the essence of each student. Some hardly knew he had been watching.

Undercurrents stirred. We touched and clung at the thought of parting. Ahead were uncertain futures, and there was leaving Old Blue, ending the quest, pouring out of the cocoon of trust as if we had come to the end of the bus line. Faces caught the flickering firelight; the guitar picked up old favorites, those songs nobody had to think about to mouth the words. I contributed a much older example of my "Songs of the Pleistocene." The instrument went around, and then there remained just a murmur of voices from the half a dozen lying close to the fire on the needle duff, backs icy with high night air.

Next morning, our last on White Mountain, I took up a folding camp chair and my notebook and wandered off alone, down through the 200-acre basin of sage and piñon that held our camp, into a deep and lovely defile I call Painted Canyon. It was ablaze with lemon-yellow and red lichens, splotched over rocks from which delicate saxifrages leaned. An impressionist's wild canvas.

I scrambled up the canyon wall and onto the rocky west flank of the mountain to gaze down into the deep vault of Owens Valley and across its hazy depths to the Sierra scarp beyond. That mountain mass stood like a wall above the valley floor, a 10,000-foot rock face riven by canyons and topped by a sawtooth of minarets and cornices, spilled over with snow.

I searched for a warm place out of the wind where I could think and write. Later that day, I wanted to read my thoughts, with all of my colleagues and young friends gathered around me. Then we would start Old Blue and head down the hill. What should I say? What should be my tone? I knew I must not forget that I was a teacher. I must not take the reins like a preacher and go galloping down the emotional slope that was so close to the surface. At the same time, I must not retreat behind a recitation of dry facts; that wasn't what this spring had shown. It was clear that beneath all of our science lay our emotional beings, our hopes, our fears, the human equation of yin and yang, and our eternal search for the rules that told us how to live.

The walking was easier now, so I slanted up toward a cluster of gnarled old piñons that overhung a low rocky wall brilliant with scarlet mound cactus. In the rock's shelter, I hoped I might find a bit of warmth from the chill high mountain air. There, perhaps, I could think what to say.

In that little sunny bowl, the ancient shag-barked tree reaching out above me, I unfolded my chair and set down my pack. The mountain floor was shingled with flat stones that clinked musically when I scuffed them with my boots. Rusty-rose books of them protruded from the soil.

The Poleta Formation, I thought. The shards I had kicked loose were truly ancient in human terms, fragments from a shallow early Cambrian sea, sifted down as mud on the seafloor at very near the time when the first vertebrates appeared in the fossil record, 580 million years ago. That number by itself meant scarcely anything. It was far too long for a human to comprehend. The curious backboned creatures of that time were the primitive jawless fishes, the earliest kin of modern lampreys and hagfish. Perhaps the Poleta's origin was even a little earlier than that, since paleontologists have yet to find vertebrate fossils in its rocks.

I picked up a layered rock. Each layer's surface had once been the seafloor. I held a packet of ancient time. As the Poleta Formation rock had been pressed deeper and deeper by layers laid down above, the rock's time began to lose any meaning. All through the history of vertebrate life, the rock packet had lain buried, essentially unchanged. Now, the mountain had been thrust up and eroded away, revealing the Poleta in our strand of time. In another blink, my rock shard would be gone, dispersed by events in the frenetic living layer that clings like a sheet to the earth's surface, the layer we biologists call "the biosphere." Abraded by the alternation of heat and cold, split by ice, etched by acids from living things, in a single tick of the mountain's metronome, it would separate into its constituent dust. The earlier record would then be obliterated and another beat in a great cadence of the Earth would begin.

To the north-northwest, lying across the Owens Valley, I could see the great lava dam, the southern wall of the Long Valley Caldera, rimmed by morning light. The dam was obvious from where I was, as if the Corps of Engineers, multiplied a thousandfold, had been at work. Almost directly below me, the streets and buildings of Bishop were arrayed in a little cross-hatch, immersed in the hazy blue.

After a while I began to write, as much for me as for the students. At first, I reflected on the overwhelming smallness of humans in the face of the powerful forces and long sweep of time that were evidenced in the view before me. Then I grasped the essential paradox of the human situation and the message I must leave in the students' minds. Though we humans are very little poker chips in life's game, we must realize that together we impact the Earth, and we must act accordingly.

I wrote a few pages, then put down my notebook and sat looking across the airy deep. The chill breeze gusted in a little now. I rose from my seat and lay down on the warm Poleta shards. I looked where my left hand rested—the shard had a pattern on it. On its surface was a little volcano that had been cast up out of the Cambrian seafloor mud by a worm. I was touching the Cambrian seafloor!

I tried to reconstruct that ancient time-slice. The worm had gone down its burrow, ingesting a bit of mud. It must have been after the organic film on the mud's grains, the same food sought by many worm species today. It digested away the film, surfaced, and on the slope of its tiny volcano, it reversed the process of swallowing, depositing a long sausage of cleaned sand on the slope. Again and again, the worm had done this, until the little starlike volcano had been produced.

I put the shard down and spread my arms again over the warm stones. My fingers clung to the vastness of White Mountain and the Earth beneath it. Remarkably, I felt a wordless kinship welling up, born of Poleta shards, the lichens, the pines, the wind, and the majestic bulk of the mountain. I sensed our deep dependence. Held in the ethos of White Mountain was the way we must go. We are not privileged, except by virtue of being, very likely, the first to understand.

I claimed, as a true forebear, that ancient vanished worm over whose house I ran my fingers. I realized that I felt differently about worms than I had before. I liked them a lot. And our many other relatives—the bacteria, the fungi, the plants, and animals—they seemed a wonderful collection, like any family's relatives. Perceiving myself as part of their same stream of life was a profound feeling. It was like tracing one's geneology back and finding that Benjamin Franklin is a sixteenth cousin twice removed. One feels differently about Ben after such a revelation, just as I did about my Cambrian worm friend.

The recognition of my relative insignificance, combined with this sense of kinship with all life, gave me the great comfort of surrender before an unimaginably powerful rule-giver. I perceived that if I surrendered to the Earth's imperatives, I could feel a deep connection to the beauty of the world, use my little armament of inborn skills to assure food and shelter, and reproduce and nurture my kind. Among humans, these are the things most firmly welded together by what I loosely call love.

I recognized that these feelings of mine were probably very similar to those of people who have lived in systems of faith throughout human history. The difference was that their times had not been ripe for perceiving the Earth as rule-giver, while in mine that realization was beginning to unfold before us. I scratched my head at how close the ethical imperatives I felt so strongly there on the Poleta were to rules that have been derived over and over back into dim prehistory. Yet in some of those ancient ethical systems, the Earth had been all but left out.

Was I not also reaching back into human history to our own shaping when I clasped those elegant Poleta shards? Was I not also holding an instruction book that told of the ways we must live, codified in terms of passion, love, and the perception of beauty? Therein lies a frequent omission of science, I thought. Science is constructed to operate without emotion, regarding it as an unreliable impediment to understanding. But emotion, it seemed, is actually the vital stuff that organizes understanding.

I lay back in my warm Poleta bowl in thought, scratching more words into my notebook. Over my shoulder, I faintly heard a swish-swish in the air over the piñon tops. I turned my head to see a raven just as it changed its undulating loose-winged flight into a tight drop toward the rocky outcrop to the side of me. The bird spiraled down, wings cupped in taut downward curves, primary feathers spread like fingers. In the same glance, I saw the object of this maneuver—a black sagebrush lizard splayed on a sunlit rock, half out of a crevice. A flash of black and the lizard vanished into its crack. The raven stalked the Poleta shards for a few steps, then, like an ultralight aircraft, lifted off into the breeze and sliced away over the piñons. I wrote a few more pages, thinking of how the raven and lizard had kindly expressed another piece of what I wanted to include in my recitation.

I realized the morning was coming to an end, and with it my contemplative interlude. I paged through my notebook. I knew that most of what had gone through my mind remained unsaid. I folded my chair and walked back to camp. Old Blue was already loaded. I took my place on a camp table and, with barely a preamble, began to read what I had written.

"I think I know what old folks like me are good for, even though we may no longer count in the reproductive dance. The dimension of time in the world is not easy for any of us to comprehend. But as short as my span has been, it is three times as long as most of yours. I have kept my eyes open. I have thought hard. And so, all through our travels, I have tried to bring us and the mountain together."

"Remember the Bishop Tuff we drove through when we dropped down into Bishop? That formation is a massive dam, the leavings of the cataclysmic eruption of the Long Valley Caldera a mere three-quarters of a million years ago. When the eruption sent boiling black clouds into the stratosphere, flashing with self-induced lightning, the flanks of White Mountain became sifted deep in ash. We saw a remnant of that ash blanket yesterday. Then it was over. The skies cleared and then the bristlecones came. How, no one knows. Maybe they were here before the eruption. Or maybe vaulting from mountain to mountain is easier for a bristlecone than we think. Perhaps they marched across the lowlands when the climate was different. Now, Long Valley Caldera stirs again. Almost certainly, nothing we can do will matter in the least to it. All we can do is monitor its rumblings and flee when our scientists give warning."

"Even though all we humans can do is flee before another eruption of the caldera, we must never doubt that taken together we humans are changing the face of the world. Seemingly insubstantial life has changed the world before. Very early in the history of life, at least six times farther back than Poleta time, the atmosphere was an acrid mixture of gasses largely without oxygen. And then came tiny, single-celled life—we might call them bacteria or archaea or algae. Somehow, in such tiny motes, the intricate chemical process of photosynthesis had been shaped. Able to synthesize their own food from raw chemicals, those motes of life reproduced in unimaginable numbers, spreading everywhere in the sea. The waste gas they released—oxygen—changed the atmosphere and shaped the history of nearly all life after that time. How different is our time? In our numbers, aren't we also changing the world?"

"You may feel insignificant in this flooding, relentless process, but think further. Each of one of you is very special, and not just because we are now friends. Only a tiny fraction of the world's people knows what you know. Few have seen what you have seen. Each of you is a nucleus of the new understanding, and it is through such people as you that the society of humans will be steered."

"We now understand that everything springs from our Earth as it hurries through space, and that she circles in the most delicate equipoise. Clearly, the human race has grappled with its position in the cosmos since travelers first watched stars wheel overhead. In a tumult of change, we are now reshaping our private visions of place, as we come to know more and more about the Earth itself, as we have returned again to enshrine the mountain, and the Earth itself."

"Though we humans are probably the first among the animals to perceive these relationships, such knowledge confers no space for arrogance. Quite the opposite. It says, instead, that we must define and live by a world ethic that will surely be more rigorous than any ever conceived throughout our long history of searching. We must come into balance with the Earth. That seems to me to be the command directed at us."

I paused to recount the story of how the raven had tried to capture the lizard for its lunch. Then I read on: "We humans have spent much of our history attempting to escape the stark equation of raven and lizard. Our houses and cities are the result. They are bulwarks against implacable Nature. But they only incompletely carry with them the things that hold our lives together."

"In our incomplete cities, we long for the wholeness of Nature. Think of how many signs of this deep void one finds there. Why did each of those trees I saw in the city ghetto grow inside a cage, a cheval-de-frise, with bars bent and sharpened at their tips? Those trees are connections to missing nature, and the bars are there to repel rage at disconnected lives lived in a partial world. Think of the animal icons we provide our children—the neighborhood parks, clipped lawns and tamed streams, the gifts of flowers, the dog lying on the hall rug, even the astroturf on our playing fields."

"We escaped from the sometimes-brutal realities of the Mountain Time canyon, but in our relief we nearly excluded the mountain from our thoughts. Along with the mountain went the Earth itself. But quietly the mountain continued to govern, the Earth to rule. If we violate the Earth's trust, evade its imperatives—as, for example, we are doing as we fundamentally alter the Earth's atmosphere—the Earth's 'wrath' could be extreme, and all of us, perhaps, could be obliterated."

"Why aren't our citadel cities enough to protect us? Simple enough. We excluded all the checks and balances of Mountain Time. At Big Creek, we began to understand that a balance is required between all members of the living world for the dimensions of Mountain Time to be expressed. The river will run clear. That's it! The River Will Run Clear. There is, it seems, a magic curve for all life, just as there is another for rivers when they plane down mountains. That means, of course, that a balance must be struck in Nature that involves the wind and the sky, the water and every living thing, in all that it uses, produces, or performs."

"The imperatives of the seafloor worm, or the raven and the lizard, or our own selves, are not only to avoid capture in a split second to live another day or to succeed next time in securing prey. They are to build lizards and ravens that take viable places in the larger world. Those imperatives remain ours, even in our cities. It's as simple as that."

"We must not forget how little we know. This history of ours, and of the life on every mountain, is intricate almost beyond understanding. It has taken the time since life began to assemble and to fit and test. In our simplicity, we think we know, but we don't really. We cannot leave behind the others who have been fitted to the Earth along with us. In their intricate patterns lie the fruits of the Earth's wisdom about us all, and about itself. In these patterns lie the balances that can allow our kind to continue. We must forever return to the Earth to learn and relearn this crucial story."

Quietly, we climbed aboard Old Blue and took our seats. The bus roared into life, and we moved off down the mountain. At the crest of Sonora Pass on the sawtooth of the Sierra, we stopped for a snowball fight, full of vigor and noise and poignance. And then we continued down the western slope toward home.

Another postscript: When we reached the town of Sonora and stopped for gas, Frank and I walked out on the busy sidewalk to take a stretch. Walking three people ahead of us was a bulky figure in faded and patched khakis. I saw a flowing white beard swish from side to side of his body as he moved.

"Frank, Frank," I whispered, "You don't suppose that's Dr. V?"

"Sure looks like him," Frank replied.

Then we noticed a slight figure strolling at his side, her dark dress puffed up at the shoulders, a pencil stuck in her tightly coiled bun.

"That's—," Frank began to say.

I hushed him and whispered, "Kindred spirits."

Back at the bus, we found Miss Preen's locker open and empty.

Miss Preen, Field Quarter librarian.

Phylly Norris, at home in Southern California, 1959, babysitting Congo, an orphaned gorilla infant destined for the Honolulu Zoo.

Afterword 1
By Phyllis Norris

Let me tell you a little bit about Ken Norris, our author. We met at Scripps Institution of Oceanography, where he was a graduate student and I a lab tech with the marine botany department. He lived just over the fence from my small rental apartment in La Jolla, and we met fairly regularly during "coffee breaks" at Scripps. In time, he drove me to Van Nuys to meet his family and, while there, took me on an exploration of the rural areas of the San Fernando Valley. We climbed down a woody bank and made a little bench of rocks. That was where Ken asked me to be his wife. He said that as a biologist, he would probably not make much money, but we would have the "greatest adventures of our lives." To seal our engagement, Ken slipped on my finger a plastic ring from a cereal box that sported a small black plane that flew off when a lever was pushed. I never could wear the ring for fear of losing the plane, but I have cherished it always.

And adventures we had: we camped all over the West; drove across the country with the kids; visited almost every national park; spent much time at the Bunny Club in the Mojave Desert; went on many whale-watching trips in Baja California; explored Peru, Bolivia, Chile, and Tierra del Fuego for six months; and lived for many years in Hawaii, mostly on the windward side of Oahu near Sea Life Park and the Oceanic Institute. I had other kinds of adventures when Ken turned to me for help with his research. Once, for example, I had the challenge of sewing a radio transmitter harness for a rough-tooth dolphin named Pono, who had chased an unfortunate young male trainer out of the tank with much snapping of teeth. Fortunately, Pono liked me.

When Ken was curator of Marineland of the Pacific, we lived just up the hill from his work. Ken was a wonderful father and a favorite of all the neighborhood kids. They would come over and say, "Give us the works!" Ken would respond by putting them up in trees or perhaps painting bull's-eyes on their bare bellies with washable paint that he told them would never come off. Our yard was full of animals fascinating to kids: chickens, a crocodile, alligators, snakes, and lizards. Inside were geckos, horned toads, antelope ground squirrels, and even a young owl named Aristotle, who flew silently across the living room from bookcase to bookcase. (Later Aristotle lived on an outside owl perch, where he feasted on chicken livers and mice. Even after the great world drew him away, he would return at dusk each day for food and follow Ken, the dog, and me on our evening neighborhood walks.) We also sheltered a young sea gull as it learned to fly.

At other homes, we kept many other interesting pets. Three of the most notable animals who shared our lives were a young bobcat, Hopi, a very young gorilla, Congo, who left to grow up in the Honolulu Zoo, and three young possums found clinging to their dead mother by our paper boy. Of course, there were also dogs and cats, and in Hawaii we adopted an African grey parrot, Russ, who now at age 35 has reached middle age. Several minah birds lived with us, and for a while a mongoose was a special friend for one of our kids.

As a scientist, Ken was never afraid to go to scientists from other fields for help with his current research. For instance, Ken asked friends who were chemists and physicists to help him discover what kind of fat was in the jaws of some odontocetes (toothed whales), wondering if the fat could conduct sound back to the solid ear bones. The radio transmitters Ken used, as well as many of the electronic hydrophones and other pieces of equipment, were made by talented friends.

One of Ken's remarkable qualities was an intense curiosity that he combined with patience and a sense of wonder. He was always asking questions, wondering what, how, and why. Ken observed redwing blackbirds sitting on the nearby farm fences. From time to time, they would suddenly take off as a group to fly above the field, turning, diving, and climbing before landing once again. Did they have a leader? How did they manage to turn with such a graceful coordination? Was the behavior helpful to the birds? How do bird schools work, and are they like fish schools or dolphin schools? Ken would puzzle over questions like these, and sometimes the "ah-ha!" button would snap on in his brain—so, that's it! Or ... is there more to it than that? Time would pass, sometimes months or even years, until another ah-ha moment. Ken was never jealous of his ideas and not only shared them freely, but commented that there was more to do than any one person could ever fit into a lifetime. As a scientist, he considered it his duty to keep looking, thinking, asking those questions of the animals (or plants), and sharing his thoughts with others.

One other thing about Ken was his sense of fun and play. He loved a good gathering around the fire with friends or students. He told good stories, and the responses of his audience often guided his thinking. Sometimes new ideas would emerge, and sometimes, as part of the fun, Ken's stories could be rather wild. He told many kids, for example, that if you lick a banana slug, you will gain enough extra energy to run long distances like the Miwok Indians. Field Quarter students were wise to Ken's tall tales, but they did get them thinking. Ken always felt that one's life should be part work and part fun; much to our delight, he worked very hard, but played equally hard.

One of Ken's fun inventions was a new organization called "The Society for Informing Animals of Their Taxonomic Position," an affiliate of the American Miscellaneous Society that poked fun at the human need to divide the natural world into neat little categories. Stationery was printed and a board appointed. Since taxonomists always seemed to be reclassifying and changing the names of familiar animals, members would, in the course of their travels, seek out animals whose names had been changed and call out to them to let them know of their new names.

As I said earlier, adventures were plentiful and good friends abundant. Our kids had a wonderful advantage with Ken's students, many of whom spent lots of time at the house and acted like older brothers and sisters to our four. Many became my cherished friends, almost like an extended family. I have been happy to share their triumphs and marriages and to watch their children grow. Many of Ken's colleagues became good, special friends also. All those folk were very important parts of Ken's life and who he was. The students learned from Ken, but they in turn stimulated his intellectual thinking and also shared in many physical activities (such as building cabins, shearing sheep, or helping repair our fussy water system). It was the best of all worlds, and I'm grateful to all of them.

If you've read Ken's story, you know that it was written from the heart and that his adventures were rarely, if ever, done alone. He had a good rich life in both work and play, and took exceptional joy in family and friends, both young and old. It turned out to be true that he couldn't offer me lots of money, but he gave me riches that cannot be measured in dollars and are priceless in this wonderful world we live in. He was quite a guy!

Afterword 2
By Richard D. Norris

My father and I both wound up as university professors—he because he was fortunate to have grown up in a household where knowledge and curiosity about nature were valued and me because I grew up immersed in a tide of students, colleagues, and university politics that swept continuously through our various houses. My sisters and I did realize that we had a "different" kind of household from the rest of those in the neighborhood, but it was not until we were adults, looking back, that it became evident how outside the mainstream our family really was. We were the family with the local zoo, a menagerie of found animals, such as a tame bobcat, tortoises, opossums, an octopus that would snake out its arms to snag hermit crabs, a pair of placid alligators that liked nothing better than sunning themselves on the patio during beer parties, gar fish in the fishponds, and a long stream of more conventional dogs, cats, birds, lizards, and snakes. We spent, for a time, summers in Hawaii, helping out with experiments on dolphin echolocation or physiology, and went on long camping trips throughout the West in the days when seatbelts and air conditioners were still far in the future. My father was fond of telling stories that became fantastic so gradually that it was often difficult to decide where fact had changed to fiction. He was also given to dissecting dolphins in the backyard to psych out their sound-production system. No, we did not have a typical, suburban upbringing.

But then, neither did my father. He grew up in the San Fernando Valley of greater Los Angeles in the days when the valley was mostly orchards and chicken farms. His father took him on trips to the desert and the eastern Sierra Nevada and was, like his son, entranced by trout fishing, getting out in nature, and building things. His mother was an artist, making hooked rugs for the Hollywood stars. This could have been ordinary enough, but the Great Depression intervened, leading to family moves and a succession of houses, schools, and friends, and later, for Ken, a stint in the Navy, traveling around the world on a troop ship during World War II. Ken's transformation into a scientist began when he fell under the spell of a South African herpetologist at UCLA, Ray Cowles, who showed him that the animals under the rocks were more interesting than the rocks themselves, and it continued when he moved to Scripps Institution of Oceanography to work on fish behavior and physiology under Carl Hubbs. Ken's field notebooks from those days describe trips to Baja, Sonora, and the California deserts and are full of lists of species, observations, and drawings of the animals, as well as evidence of his well-formed ability to engage everyone in conversation and adventure.

Most of us who teach for any length of time develop a set of dictums that we keep returning to and that tend to summarize our way of looking at our subject and approach to life. One of Ken's dictums was: "The animal is the authority." He got this idea from his teacher, Ray Cowles, who took Ken into the field and taught him to see the interrelationships in nature. Ken learned how to cycle from close observation of nature to question formulation and then back to nature for more observations—a spin of the wheel of science. This process means, as an example, that one has to go beyond merely admiring a swallow twist and swerve as it matches the gyrations of a flying grasshopper to asking a series of questions such as, "Why is that bird's tail forked?" Then it means that one has to repeatedly return to observations of the bird to decide how the animal uses its anatomy and even delve into the genetics, physiology, and evolution of the species to really answer the initial query. Often the hardest part of this cycle of questions and observations is coming up with the first question—recognizing that there is something of interest in why a swallow's tail is forked and then carrying on with the discipline and excitement of following the chain of observations and the formulation of new questions.

Part of "going back to the authority" is not taking yourself too seriously and recognizing that our observations of nature are necessarily distracted and colored by everything from how we are feeling that day to our overall life experience. Science, Ken believed, is "a tool to keep us from lying to ourselves." He recognized the limitations on our ability to observe, but he also knew that if you cultivated that questioning stance, slowed down to "mountain time," and took some part of the world at its pace, you could develop an appreciation for how some corner of nature works. His process was not a drab affair of observations through a cold, gimlet eye behind a monocle, but a wonderful exploration in which we step outside our daily concerns to see something beyond ourselves.

Another aphorism that I inherited from Ken—to the amusement, and sometimes weariness, of my students—is: "We're off on the greatest adventure of our lives!" He really meant it, too, since part of his idea of "mountain time" was to delight in discovery, to revel in shared enthusiasm, and to see in others the glint in the eye that comes with having really "seen" nature. I think a key facet of the "greatest adventure" idea was sharing the joy of science with other people. Science can be done as a solitary pursuit, but it is much more fun to engage others in the scrum of ideas, controversy, arguments, and excitement of discovery. Ken, in particular, was a socially gifted man who loved to surround himself with people who loved a good time and were willing to mix it up in the marketplace of ideas and become caught up in new developments.

He was sufficiently self confident that he had no problem finding collaborators to develop discoveries, whether it was acoustics specialists to help analyze the signature whistles of whales or mathematicians to analyze the interactions of flocks of birds and schools of fish. His motto was, "If you have enough good ideas, you can afford to give some of them away." Accordingly, he was impatient with his fellow researchers who wanted to cling to "their contribution" and defend it against all comers, even when the evidence began to build against it. In his view, if you have lots of ideas—even if most of them are wrong—it is not necessary to always claim the credit or feel that any attack on your hypotheses is a personal affront. When life is a great adventure, you can invite lots of people to the party.

It doesn't hurt to be a bit of a prophet, too. Ken had a long history of dreaming up seemingly improbable schemes that I, being less prone to whimsy as a young man, was inclined to dismiss with a shake of my head. Some, like the aerial cable that was supposed to allow an observer ensconced in a suspended car to swing between the tops of redwood trees, were pretty dangerous, at least considering my father's engineering skills, but ultimately proved to be quite workable. The aerial cable idea, for example, has now been replicated in several canopy observatories in tropical and temperate forests. Others, like the gyrocopter—basically a chair and engine attached to a helicopter blade for observing marine mammals from the air—were just plain scary. The gyrocopter was flown only once, on a dry lakebed, by a willing graduate student. But many ideas developed a loyal following of relatives, students, and fellow researchers. One of these, the "semisubmersible seasick machine"—a jet-wing tank converted into an underwater-viewing vehicle for looking at the social behavior of spinner dolphins—was actually built and managed to stay afloat and functional.

Another notable manifestation of Ken's imagination—the Granite Mountain Bunny Club, the desert cabin built from found materials—still exists and continues to charm new students of nature. It never would have been built save for Ken's infectious enthusiasm (and his brother Bob's construction skills).

Indeed, although Ken did know how to build things—albeit with angles other than 90° and never to building codes—he was a master at convincing others of his vision. He did this repeatedly to seek foundation funding and private gifts for realizing one dream after another. Need money for a new marine lab? Go to Joseph Long—of the Long's Drug chain—to secure "a little running-around money" to see the project off. Need funds to start a grant competition to support undergraduates doing environmental research? Buttonhole donors to give you $40,000 a year to support a small grants program and show off the power of undergraduates to do novel research. Tired of having your research sites converted into strip malls? Convince the university to give you a jeep to survey the state of California for a new system of land reserves (now thirty-six in number) that preserve all manner of California native landscapes. Ken also exploited his motivational powers in more whimsical projects. After having been given a full-sized Nantucket whaleboat (a movie prop from *Mutiny on the Bounty*) at a Hollywood party, he convinced a crowd of somewhat skeptical but enthusiastic friends and relations to help raise it into the crown of a spreading California live oak and convert it into a tree house. As far as I know, the boat perches there still, overlooking Monterey Bay.

There is a redwood bench on the UC Santa Cruz campus that overlooks a little stream and is inscribed with another motto of Ken's: "Sure beats working." The place is quiet, and the bench, off the beaten path that leads from the UCSC Arboretum to College 8, is not visited as frequently as it deserves, given its contemplative setting. The motto is in some ways not all that fitting for Ken, who loved to work on all kinds of things and would often get up at 3AM in the black of night to write, but his saying does telegraph his overriding joy for life and his pleasure at finding out how things work. We would be down in the canyon up to our armpits in wet sand fixing the water system, and Ken would glance up and say, "Sure beats working" even before admiring the lofty redwoods on the stream bank. He convinced many students and friends to help him out on such projects, not in small part to hear him say those words. In this way, he could work nearly all the time and still remain as delighted and full of joy as he could be.

So what then was Mountain Time to Ken? It was partly about seeing the animal, the plant, or the ecosystem through a relatively unfiltered lens. It was also about bringing others along for the fun of it, encouraging them to love to learn and to find out for themselves how some corner of the world works. Most of all, a lot of Mountain Time was about sharing excitement—not just about science, but about everything—because there is really no point in studying something if you don't love what you are doing, and there is hardly enough excitement in making neat observations if you don't have someone around to tell all about it. The world may pass us by at different rates, we may struggle with trying to frame the right questions, and our first guesses may be wrong, but our basic humanity and love of what we do, as well as the joy of discovery with others, is an essential piece of Mountain Time.

The Norris clan at home in Bonny Doon, July 1997, with (back row, center) Ken and Phyllis Norris, and (to their left) their son Richard, surrounded by daughters, daughter-in-law, sons-in-law, and grandchildren.

Ken Norris in his Semisubmersible Seasick Machine (SSSM). The letters OI on the side of the SSSM stand for Oceanic Institute.

Notes

Chapter 1: The Granite Mountains

1 Munz, P. A. 1968. *A California Flora and Supplement.* Berkeley: University of California Press. This venerable text has since been largely displaced as the definitive flora of California by *The Jepson Manual: Higher Plants of California*, published in 1993.

Chapter 3: The Wind and the Sky

1 MacArthur, R., and E. O. Wilson. 1967. *The Theory of Island Biogeography.* Princeton University Press.

2 Garner, Chip. 1997. "A Glider Ride." *Soaring and Motor Gliding Magazine* 24–25. Journal of the Soaring Society of America. June 1997.

Chapter 5: The Canyon

1 Our discussions of Mountain Time at Big Creek barely hint at the intricate dynamics that take place among the various living and nonliving participants in such a canyon—the storage processes, the precarious equilibria, the catastrophes among them. Ecologists are only now sketching in how these dynamic processes proceed.

Chapter 6: The Two-legged Lizard

1 *Editors' note:* Three species of *Bipes* are now recognized. The third, *B. tridactylus*, occurs in a small area of coastal Guerrero, Mexico, not far from *B. canaliculatus*.

2 A discussion of this supposed Arizona *Bipes* can be found on page 432 of Smith, H. M. 1946. *Handbook of Lizards; Lizards of*

United States and Canada. Comstock Publishing Co., Ithaca, New York. I'm not convinced. The color Smith describes is wrong; the front legs are far too small. All in all, Smith's animal sounds like a skink when the observer forgot to note that it also had rear legs.

3 Simpson, G. G. 1947. *Tempo and Mode in Evolution.* Columbia University Press. 237 pp.

4 A detailed description of these Earth events is found in Sedlock, R., F. Ortega-Gutierrez, and R. Speed. 1993. *Technostratigraphic terranes and tectonic evolution of Mexico.* Special Paper 278. Geological Society of America. 153 pp.

Chapter 7: Adaptation

1 Dr. Warren P. Porter is now a much-respected biologist in the Department of Zoology at the University of Wisconsin-Madison and the author of an important body of work on the intertwining of the environment and animal life.

2 My master's thesis was on *Uma*: Norris, K. S. 1958. The evolution and systematics of the iguanid genus *Uma* and its relation to the evolution of other North American desert reptiles. *Bulletin of the American Museum of Natural History* 114 (3): 1–326.

3 This work is described in another scientific paper: Norris, K. S. 1965. Color adaptation in desert reptiles and its thermal relationships. A Symposium on Lizard Ecology. Edited by William Milstead. University of Missouri Press, Columbia, MO. Pp. 162–229.

Chapter 8: Desert Iguana

1 Both of these animals are now federal- and state-listed species, and under the threat of extinction.

2 I published my results in a paper: Norris, K. S. 1953. The ecology of the desert iguana, *Dipsosaurus dorsalis. Ecology* 34 (2): 265–

287. That temperature record wasn't to last for long; other workers recorded temperatures up to 118°F from similar lizards.

3 Alas, my concept of the partial animal, in this case, was later proven wrong. A study performed years after my ruminations about desert iguanas showed that, while most vertebrate enzymes are indeed destroyed by heat far below the temperatures the desert iguana tolerates, its digestive enzymes remain active at temperatures as high as 131°F (*see*: Karasov, W. 1983. *American Journal of Physiology* 249: G. 271–G. 283.). This work showed no decrease in glucose uptake (an indication of enzymatic action) at either 122°F or 131°F for the desert iguana. Back to the drawing board, I thought, when this study was pointed out to me. Another delicious theory for the scrap heap! Spin the wheel again! Fortunately, I knew that this is the way true science works; it is a bumpy road paved with little jogs of disappointment, of errors in perception, and, much more rarely, of new discovery.

Chapter 9: Girella

1 *Editor's Note:* This was the second of two sea-water temperature gradient chambers that Ken Norris built and used in experiments for his dissertation — an "Ichthyothermitaxitron." The first successful chamber was built at Scripps Institution of Oceanography and resulted from nine months of experimentation with different designs. The second successful chamber (shown here) was built at Marineland of the Pacific; it differed from the first essentially in being much larger. The large tanks at the top of the photo are primarily hot and cold water storage tanks. In the middle is the 24-chambered mixing tank from which water of a graded series of temperatures is led to water inlet valves on the gradient chamber. Thermometers, cloth hood, and viewing slit are not shown here.

2 My work with *Girella* is reported in a long paper that I think is about as good as this naturalist can make it: Norris, K. S. 1963. The functions of temperature in the ecology of the percoid fish, *Girella nigricans* (Ayres). *Ecological Monographs* 33: 23–62. At the time, I didn't write anything about the consciousness question; it was clearly too far-out to present to a doctoral committee.

3 With the bravery of an older scientist who feels he must have his say while there is still time, Donald Griffin, the soul of experimental scientific rigor, has published two books exploring the question of animal consciousness. We have, I think, reached the same general conclusion. In his books, Griffin has defined the debate far more completely than I do here. The books are: Griffin, D. R. 1981. *The Question of Animal Awareness, Evolutionary Continuity and Mental Experience*. Rockefeller University Press; and Griffin, D. R. 1984. *Animal Thinking*, Harvard University Press. Griffin has met with all the expectable resistances from those who have built a world around animals-as-mechanisms and has been immersed in debate ever since he had the temerity to raise his voice.

Chapter 11: Mabel, Myrtle, Frank, and Floyd

1 In a couple of years, Frank Brocato and Bill MacFarland solved the problem of catching local dolphins.

2 *Editor's Note:* John H. Prescott later (from 1972 to 1994) became the much-respected executive director of the New England Aquarium in Boston, which became the model for aquariums around the world and influenced the American Zoo and Aquarium Association to shift its focus from entertainment and attractions to conservation. On a national level, Prescott was chairman of the Marine Mammal Commission's Scientific Advisory Group and headed the National Humpback Whale Recovery Team. For five years, he served as member of the U.S. delegation to the International Whaling Commission and, from 1988 to 1993, was on the Marine Fisheries Advisory Committee of the National Oceanographic and Atmospheric Administration (NOAA).

3 Schevill, W., and B. Lawrence. 1956. Food-finding in a captive porpoise (*Tursiops truncates*). *Breviora* 53. Harvard University, Museum of Comparative Zoology. Pp. 1-15.

4 Evans, W., and B. Powell. 1967. Discrimination of different metallic plates by an echolocating delphinid. In: *Animal Sonar Systems, Biology and Bionics*. R-G Busnell, editor. N.A.T.O. Advanced Studies Institute, Lab. Physiol. Acoust. Jouy-en-Josas, France.

5 Pryor, K., R. Haag, and J. O'Reilly. 1969. The creative porpoise: Training for novel behavior. Jour. Exper. Anal. Behav., 12: 653-661.

6 Herman. Louis, ed. 1980. *Cetacean Behavior: Mechanisms and Functions*. John Wiley and Sons. 462 pp. In this book, Herman describes the remarkable series of discoveries that have emanated from his little laboratory-tank complex built alongside a boat harbor on a Honolulu beach.

Chapter 12: Dolphin Jazz

1 This curious behavior, we finally decided, represented certain school members marking out the dimensions of the school for the others, especially in the dark, so they could keep their vital school together. They could hear each other splash, or they could direct a burst of echolocation clicks toward the source of the splash and then pick up echoes from the swirl of bubbles the sinking dolphin made as it fell.

2 We have written three books about our open-ocean work with dolphins; two are popular accounts, and one our scientific findings. The first is Norris, K. S., 1974, *The Porpoise Watcher*, W.W. Norton, New York; the second, Norris, K. S., 1991, *Dolphin Days*, W.W. Norton, New York. The third, the comprehensive scientific work, is: Norris, K. S., B. Würsig, M. Würsig, and R. Wells, with individual contributions by S. Brownlee, C. Johnson, and J. Solow, 1994, *The Hawaiian Spinner Dolphin*, University of California Press, Berkeley, CA, 408 pp.

3 Committee on Reducing Porpoise Mortality from Tuna Fishing. 1992. Dolphins and the tuna industry. National Academy of

Sciences, Washington, D. C. 176 pp. Captain Harold Medina reported the false killer incident to me in conversation.

4 For a long time, I wondered about this sudden, unanimous exodus from the water, and then I remembered a recent discovery about leaping by dolphin schools. (Au, D. W., and D. Weihs. 1980. "At high speeds dolphins save energy by leaping." *Nature* 284[5756]: 548–550.) According to Au and Weihs, the school had simply speeded up until it exceeded the "crossover speed," the swimming speed at which it becomes more economical for a dolphin to leap rather than to swim totally underwater. For a spinner, this speed is about eight knots (9.5 miles per hour). That squared with our estimate of how fast our spinners were moving.

CHAPTER 13:
OF FIGHTER PILOTS, CHORUS LINES, AND SHARK ATTACKS

1 Bateson, G. 1966. *Whales, Dolphins and Porpoises.* Edited by K. S. Norris. University of California Press. Pp. 571-572.

2 Many observers in the century just past have considered the question of how open-space animal groups work to protect their members, and their ideas are nicely summarized in Pitcher, T., ed. 1986. *Behaviour of Teleost Fishes*, 2nd ed. Chapman and Hall, London. On and off during my time studying the lives of fishes, I pondered these same questions, and, somehow, the standard explanations never seemed quite enough.

3 Miller, G. 1956. The magic number seven, plus or minus two: Some limits on our capacity for processing information. *The Psychological Review* 63: 81-97.

4 Bridgeman, B. 1988. *The Biology of Behavior and Mind.* J. Wiley, New York. Pp. 178–184.

5 Landeau, L., and J. Terborgh. 1986. Oddity and the "confusion effect" in predation. *Animal Behaviour* 34:1372–1380.

6 Caldwell, M., and D. Caldwell. 1968. Vocalization of native captive dolphins in small groups. *Science* 159: 1121.

7 Potts, W. K. 1984. The chorus line hypothesis of maneuver coordination in avian flocks. *Nature* 309: 344–345.

8 Schiff, W. 1965. Perception of impending collision: A study of visually directed avoidant. *Psych. Mon.* 79(11): 1–26.

9 Norris, K. S., and C. R. Schilt. 1988. Cooperative societies in three-dimensional space: On the origins of aggregations, flocks, and schools, with special reference to dolphins and fish. *Ethology and Sociobiology* 9: 149–179.

10 An explanation for the evolutionist. Am I espousing group selection? No, I am not. What I am saying is that nearly all the examples of cooperation I have described here are clearly cooperative—the giver of cooperation receives as much as it gives. In fact, in schools absolute conformity is required of all members lest their cooperative system fail. Axelrod and Hamilton, using a game-theory model, showed that such cooperative systems can be developed by normal evolutionary process within interbreeding genetic populations (Axelrod, R., and W. D. Hamilton. 1981. The evolution of cooperation. *Science* 211:(4489) 1390-1396.). What is perhaps new in my conception is that I invoke the characteristic of conceptualization—Bateson's abstract thought—as an explanation for why even different species of animals may sometimes help each other (see chapter 11, "Mabel, Myrtle, Frank, and Floyd").

Chapter 14: Creation Myth

1 Norris, K. S. "Beluga: White Whale of the North." *National Geographic*. June 1994.

2 Miller, S. M., and L. E. Orgel. 1974. The Origins of Life on Earth. Prentice-Hall, Inc., Englewood Cliffs, New Jersey.

3 Schmidt-Nielsen, K. 1964. *Desert Animals: Physiological Problems of Heat and Water.* Clarendon Press, Oxford. xiv + 270 pp.

Chapter 15: Yin and Yang

1 Campbell, Joseph (with Bill Moyers). 1988. *Joseph Campbell: The Power of Myth.* Doubleday, New York, p. 181.

2 Fischer-Schreiber, et al. 1994. *The Encyclopedia of Eastern Philosophy and Religion*, vol. 1. Shambhala Press, Boston. See pp. 428–429.

3 Damasio, Antonio. 1994. *Descartes' Error: Emotion, Reason and the Human Brain.* Avon Books, New York.

4 Norris, Kathleen. 1996. *The Cloister Walk.* G. P. Putnam's Sons, New York. By the way, so far as I know she is no relation, but simply an admired other. I can't say that this situation makes me any happier.

Chapter 16: Uncharted Territory

1 The existence of Easy Cheese was brought to my attention by songwriter and instrument-maker extraordinaire Fred Carlson, the author of "The Easy Cheese Blues."

Chapter 17: The Salmon's Run

1 Arthur Hasler and his students performed the insightful experiments with salmon that form the basis for much of what we know about their migration and homing. See Hasler, A. D. 1966. *Underwater Guideposts: Homing of Salmon.* University of Wisconsin Press. 155 pp.

2 One thinker whom I respect has published musings about menopause, from a somewhat different viewpoint than mine: Jared Diamond. 1996. "Why women change." *Discover* 17 (7): 130–137.

3 *Editor's Note:* Dr. Norris alludes here to the "flying primates theory" that was current in the late 1980s. This theory, proposed by Australian neuroscientist Jack Pettigrew in 1986, advances that flying foxes (along with flying lemurs, formally known as colugos) are the evolutionary sisters of primates, having descended from the same group of early arboreal mammals. Evidence for this conjuncture came from analysis of brain and body characteristics shared by these various groups. More recent genetic studies comparing the DNA of bats to that of primates do not support the flying primates theory, while the flying lemurs have been judged to be neither lemurs nor primates.

4 I refer you here to an important, pioneering, even brave paper: Olshansky, S. J., B. A. Carnes, and D. Grahn. 1998. Confronting the boundaries of human longevity. *American Scientist*, 86: 52–61. In this paper, the authors very quietly confront not only the boundaries of human longevity, but also the establishment built around our aging population. They do this with all the delicacy of a knight confronting an alert, smoke-emitting dragon. The dragon is the research and political establishment built around the process of aging that, with all the zeal of the crusader, attempts to fight back this upper boundary of life. Anyway, this short paper, along with other work by the authors, blandly lays out the facts, pushing them quietly into the debate, where it is hoped they will be understood.

5 But it seems that I am the wrong guy to ask about all this. In the middle of the night not long ago, I woke my wife, Phylly, and said, "Lets go." I'd felt a pressure in my left shoulder and on my chest. A week later, I emerged from the hospital, where I had had bypass surgery done. While I was "out," they had "harvested" my left interior mammary vein for supplies. I didn't know I had one. It's that yin and yang thing again.

Chapter 18: A Natural History of Gods

1 Campbell, Joseph. *The Hero with a Thousand Faces.* MJF Books, New York. 1949. p. 391.

2 The Chemehuevi call themselves *Nüwüwü*; the name *Chemehuevi* is a label applied by the Mojave.

3 Laird, C. 1976. *The Chemehuevis*. Malki Museum Press, Morongo Indian Reservation, Banning, California.

Chapter 20: Embracing the Mountain

1 Miss Preen recommends this book highly (R. M. Norris and R. W. Webb. 1990. *Geology of California*, 2nd ed. John Wiley and Sons. 541 pp.) and not just because the author is my brother. In fact, it is not possible to influence Miss Preen on matters such as this. She said, brushing me off: "This is a very clearly written and comprehensive account of the geology of a most complex piece of the earth. Ideally suited for classes, it is filled with aids for students, such as geologic time scales, excellent photographs, and a good glossary of terms, which geologists in general seem to love beyond life itself."

Dr. Vandenburg Lives!

Index

Notes:
- Page numbers followed by (*2*) or (*3*) indicate two or three separate discussions on the page.
- Page numbers followed by *n* plus a number and *ch* plus a number in parentheses, as in 303*n1*(*ch8*), indicate numbered endnotes associated with given chapters.
- Page numbers followed by *q* indicate quotations.

A

aboriginal times: man–woman duality in, 215–216. *See also* hunter–gatherer societies
abstract thought. *See* thinking
acceptance: and fear (during adventures), 141; of old age, 243
adaptation, 109; by dolphins, 162. *See also* color adaptation
aerial cable idea (KN), 297
aerial or probability summation, 190–191
aestivation (summer hibernation), 117
aging. *See* old age
agriculture: development of, 255–256
ajolote. See *Bipes biporus*
alder trees, 264
Alexander the Great: life span, 240
Allanson, Al, 139, 150; KN's hiking adventure with, 139–145
altruism. *See* caring for others
amino acids: creation of, 200

amphibians: toads, red-spotted, 125–126, 127. *See also* frogs
amphisbaenid reptiles, 90, 97. See also *Bipes* ...
anchovies: larva mortality, 235–237
[The] animal is the authority, 295–296
animals: consciousness (*see* consciousness [awareness] [animal]); culture among, 225–226; male–female duality among, 218, 220; niche hunt (FQ), 75–76, 77–78, 78–79; Norris household pets, 292, 294–295; partial animal concept, 118–119, 303*n3*(*ch8*); Society for Informing Animals of Their Taxonomic Position, 293; specimen collection, 119; volitional animals, 135, 136. *See also* amphibians; birds; *under* fieldwork; fish; insects, mammals; reptiles; *and specific species*

Aristotle (owl), 292
arrowheads (Chemehuevi), 43, 252
art and science: synthesis (KN), xiii, 3, 80
Asadorian, Paul, 161
atmosphere: earth shadow on, 48; ionosphere, 49; pre-life atmosphere, 200–201; spiders and spores in, 49; as thin and fragile, 265, 267
Au, D. Whitlow, 162, 306*n*4(*ch12*)
[the] authority: Nature/the animal as, 97, 295–296
avarice of humans, 227–228
awareness. *See* consciousness
Axelrod, Dan, 8
Axelrod, R., 307*n*10(*ch13*)

B

bacteria: cyanobacteria, 206–207
Baja California: San Ignacio, 91–92; turtle, 92–93, 96; two-legged lizard. See *Bipes biporus*
balance of life, 288
baloney filter, 35
bands: intertidal band, 127, 202; of species along canyon/mountain slopes, 264, 278
Baptist church service, 247–248
Barry, Dave, 224
Batchelder Spring, 275
Bateson, Gregory, 163–164, 183*q*
beak-genital propulsion in spinner dolphins, 170
beat of life (metronome): chorus line effect, 190, 191; redwoods as, 74, 82; the tide as, 128–129. *See also* time-pulse
bedrock mortars (Chemehuevi), 252

beluga whales article (KN), 199, 307*n*1(*ch14*)
Bernoulli effect, 44–46
Big Creek, 72. *See also* the canyon
big-leaf maples, 264
biology: KN's switch to, 6
Bipes biporus (two-legged lizard), 89–96; locomotion, 95; myth attached to, 95–96; separation from *B. canaliculatus*, 89, 91, 96; specimens, 90–91
Bipes canaliculatus (two-legged lizard), 90
Bipes tridactylus (two-legged lizard), 301*n*1(*ch6*)
birds: as blown offshore, 49; culture among, 225; dove flight speed measurement, 4; geese over the Himalayas, 49; hummingbirds, 44, 83–84; kinglets, ruby-crowned, 38–39; owl (Aristotle), 292; raptors soaring, 51–52; raven and lizard encounter, 285; redwing blackbirds, 292–293; swifts, 44: black, 74, white-throated, 43–44; towhee, California, 40; vultures, 51–52; in the White Mountains, 278–279, 285
birth: origin, 204
Bishop Tuff (lava dam), 273–274, 283, 286
black sagebrush lizard: raven encounter, 285
black swifts, 74
black-headed snake, 36
blackbirds, redwing, 292–293
blame and innocence as not in Mountain Time, 85
blindfolds for dolphins, 159–160
boats: *Geronimo* (gillnetter), 150;

Maka Ala (underwater-viewing vessel), 168, 170, 174–175; *Nai'a* (cabin cruiser), 168, 171, 175, 176
body-environment awareness, 135–136
Boronda Camp, 81
Borrego Valley: hike to, 144–145
botete (pufferfish), 89
bottlenecks of mortality, 234–241
bottlenose dolphins, 195; blindfolds for, 159–160; brain, 154; gentility, 153; training of, 150–153, 159–161, 163–164. *See also* dolphins
boundary curve (yin-yang diagram), 212
bounding circle (yin-yang diagram), 211–212
[the] brain: collective (higher order) (*see* sensory integration systems of schools/flocks/herds); dolphin brain, 154, 183, 194; evolution of, 134(*2*); human brain consciousness centers, 134; relationship and, 183
Bridgeman, Bruce, 186, 188
bristlecone pines, 278–280, 286
brittlebush, 275
Brocato, Frank, 150, 304*n1*(*ch11*)
brother of KN. *See* Norris, R. M. (Bob)
Brownlee, Shannon, 175
Buffalo Boy, 76–77
Bunny Club. *See* Granite Cabin
bushes: brittlebush, 275; catclaw bush, 39, 47; creosote (*see* creosote bushes); *Dicoria*, 116, 117; flannel bush, 23; indigo bush, 275; Mormon tea bush, 47

bypass surgery of KN, 309*n4*(*ch17*)

C

cabin cruiser (*Nai'a*), 168, 171, 175, 176
cacomistle (ring-tailed cat), 26
Caldwell, Melba and David, 190
California Gull: Negit Island nesting grounds, 272–273
California nutmegs, 264
California towhee, 40
Cambrian seafloor worm-wrought volcano fossil, 283–284
Campbell, Joseph, 211*q*, 247*q*
Canada Goose decoy prize, 224
Canterbury bells, 35
[the] canyon (Big Creek), 71; Boronda Camp, 81; cotton-batting clouds, 73–74; discovery of the unknown in, 76; dynamic processes, 301*n1*(*ch5*); Field Quarter in, 72–85; Field Quarter participants as interlopers in, 81; flowers, 81; ignoring of, 228; life's beat candidates, 74, 82; Mountain Time crazy quilt, 76, 82; as the Mountain Time matrix, 72; niche hunt in, 75–76, 77–80; peace in, 85; Redwood Camp, 72, 74; survival strategies in, 82–84, 220–221
canyon's quilt (Mountain Time crazy quilt), 76, 82
canyons: bands of species along the slopes, 264; Lee Vining Canyon, 270–271; Painted Canyon retreat (KN), 281–285; submarine canyon (Monterey Bay), 21–22. *See also* the canyon (Big Creek)

cap of life, 241–244
car fixing story, 253–254
carbon as a constituent of life, 200
caressing behavior of spinner dolphins, 167, 170
caring: knowing and, 263–265
caring for others (helping behavior): by dolphins, 155–157; as driving evolution, 156–157, 248; as natural, 257
Carlson, Fred, 308*n1*(*ch16*)
Castro, Don Santos, 94–95
catclaw bush, 39, 47
caterpillar. *See* tent caterpillar's nest design
celibacy: purpose of, 219–220
cell origins, 204; multicellularity, 207
central question of our times, 208–209. *See also* first order of business
cetaceans, 149. *See also* dolphins, whales
challenging ignorance with irony, 223–225
change: jogs for KN to change ways, 276–277; as needed in religion, 258–259; social change cry, 277
Chemehuevi Indians, 251, 260–261; car fixing and spring sharing story, 253–254; chia gathering and sheep herding story, 261; cultivation scene, 255–256; KN and, 255; myths, 255; name for themselves, 309*n2*(*ch18*); signs/evidence of, 34, 43, 252; songs, 1, 253, 254
chemistry: KN's beginning with, 3
chia gathering story, 261
child's view of Nature, 35
chorus line effect, 190, 191

cities (the city), 71–72, 288; longing for the wholeness of Nature in, 287
city time, 71–72
Clear Dry Lake: hike to, 143–144
climate shift as the time-pulse of redwoods, 73–74
Cloister Walk, The (Kathleen Norris), 219–220
clouds: castles over the Mojave, 43; cotton-batting clouds of the canyon, 73–74; lenticular clouds, 52; mare's tails, 44
Coachella Valley: desert iguana, 113–120
collection of animal specimens, 119
collective leadership among spinner dolphins, 177–178
color adaptation: *Holbrookia maculata*, 108; *Uma scoparia*, 102–103, 105–107
columbine: and hummingbirds, 83–84
communication among dolphins, 183; caressing behavior, 167, 170; consensus decision-making, 177–178. *See also* vocalizations of dolphins
compassion: capacity for feeling, 250
competition for space. *See* fitting of lifestreams/numbers into the world
concealment circles of *Uma scoparia*, 102, 103
concept formation. *See* thinking
consciousness (awareness) (animal), 117, 136; body-environment awareness, 135–136; debate on, 133–135, 303–304*n2*(*ch9*); of dogs, 134–135; evolution of (beginnings), 134–135,

135–136; in the human brain, 134; mechanistic view, 133–134, 135; of opaleye perch, 132–133; volition and, 135–136. *See also* consensus decision-making; thinking
consensus decision-making: and the evolution of thinking, 249–250; among spinner dolphins, 177–178
continental transformations: and species distribution, 89, 97–98
controlling our numbers, 244
convincing/motivational powers of KN, 298
cooperation among/by dolphins, 159–160, 164, 179, 192, 193, 195, 307*n10*(*ch13*); helping behavior, 155–157
cottonwoods, 47–48
courtship displays, male, 218
Cove Spring, 47–48
Cowles, Ray, Dr.: field class, 4–6; and KN: career influence, 6–7, 295–296(*2*); rattlesnake-catching-and-handling demonstration, 4–5; wildland concerns, 121
coyness: origin of, 218
crabs in mudflats, 67
creation myth, 199–208
creosote bushes, 35, 43; desert iguana in, 113–114; life span, 280; sand dunes among, 113
cruise prize, 224
cultivation scene (Chemehuevi), 255–256
culture: abstract thought and, 250; as a biological attribute of humans, 225, 226–227; foundation of, 225–226; human excesses (*see* humans and the environmental crisis); language power, 226–227; and natural selection, 226. *See also* religion
cyanobacteria, 206–207

D

daily personal journals (Field Quarter), 20; Observation Series entries, 21; reading of by KN, 40–41
Damasio, Antonio: on consciousness, 134, 135–136
dealing with humans and what they do, 223
death (mortality): cap of life, 241–244; defeating, 243–244; first bottleneck, 234–239; infant mortality, 234, 238; origin, 204; as a presence in life, 241; reproduction and, 232, 239; second bottleneck, 239–241; selective stages (bottlenecks and cap), 234–244; significance, 206; as a testing/weeding out process (*see* fitting of lifestreams/numbers into the world)
decayed or worn-down teeth, 240
defeating the cap of life/death itself, 242–243, 243–244
dehydrated librarian. *See* Miss Preen
desert flowers, 23
desert iguana, 113–120; behavior, 113–114, 115–116, 117(*2*), 118–119; habitat (prime), 113–114, 116; heat tolerance, 114, 116–117, 118–119, 303*n2*, 3(*ch8*); ingestion and digestion, 116, 118, 119; KN's paper on, 303*n2*(*ch8*); study plot, 114–115, 119–120

desert life as dependent on water, 207–208
desert life research (KN), ix, 3–10; *Bipes* expedition, 89–96; desert iguana study, 113–120; evolution detection tests, 8–10; frog observations, 145–147; red-spotted toad experiments, 125–126, 127; *Uma* study, 101–108
desert moss, 208
desert night lizard (*Xantusia vigilis*), 23–24
desert plants: survival strategy, 83. *See also specific species*
desert scaly lizard shooting, 141
desert turtle, 92–93, 96
deuterolearning by dolphins, 163–164
the devil, 260
Devil's Creek, 72
Diamond, Jared, 309*n*2(*ch17*)
Dicoria bushes: desert iguana in, 116, 117
diet. *See* ingestion
digestion: in desert iguana, 116, 118, 119; in opaleye perch, 131
dimorphism: male–female duality, 216–217
Diposaurus dorsalis. *See* desert iguana
diseases of old age: defeating, 242–243
distress concept, 156–157
DNA: appearance of, 203, 205
Dobzhansky, Theodosius, 8; field class with, 8–9
doctoral thesis of KN, 303*n1*(*ch9*)
doctrine (dogma): vs. myths, 256–257
dogs: consciousness, 134–135; guilt as felt by, 157–158
Dohl, Tom, 168

dolphin society, 153, 154–155, 173, 177, 195–196. *See also* dolphins: schools; social behavior of dolphins
dolphins: adaptation by, 162; blindfolds for, 159–160; brain, 154, 183, 194; communication (*see* communication among dolphins); cooperation (*see* cooperation among/by dolphins); ecolocation capability, 159–162; ecolocation clicks, 161, 162, 185; eyes, 194; gentility, 153, 154, 179; helping behavior, 155–157; hierarchy among, 177–178, 189–190; KN's writings on, 305*n2*(*ch12*), 307*n9*(*ch13*); land ancestors, 154; leadership among (spinners), 177–178; learning by: conceptual, 163–164, observational, 153; life patterns, 155, 169; as mammals, 149, 154–155; mentality (*see* mentality of dolphins); mimicry, 164–165; schools, 179: bottlenoses, 195, spinners, 176–177, 179–180, 194–195 (*see also* school processes among dolphins); shark attacks on (*see* shark attacks on dolphins); sleeping/resting behavior, 173, 175, 193–194; social behavior (*see* social behavior of dolphins); society (*see* dolphin society); studies of, 10–11, 189–190, 193–194: bottlenoses, 150–157, 159–165, spinners, 164–165, 167–180; training

Index

of (bottlenoses), 150–153, 159–161, 163–164; vocalizations (*see* vocalizations of dolphins); vulnerability to sickness or accidents, 155. *See also* bottlenose dolphins; rough-tooth dolphins; spinner dolphins; white-sided dolphins
Doudoroff, Peter: opaleye perch experiments, 127–128
dove flight speed measurement, 4
Dr. Vandenburg, 55–56, 270, 289
drowning of bees, 35–36
duality: of humans, 257; of leadership, 248; ramifications, 219; of survival, 238–239; in thermostat functionality, 212–213; in the yin-yang diagram, 211–212(*3*), 215, 239. *See also* male-female duality
dugongs, 149
dust devils, 45
dwarf spider, 78–79
Dyson, Freeman, 203, 205

E

eagles, 52; and gliders, 51
earless lizard: color adaptation, 108
[the] earth/Earth, 212; commands, 261; continental transformations and species distribution, 89, 97–98; formation of, 200; fragility, 267; horizon: unbroken view of, 266–267; intertidal band, 127, 202; invasion of the land, 207; limits on life, 238–239; the new understanding of, 286–287; oldest living things on, 280; primordial sea on, 201–202; process, 265; as the rule-giver, 259–260, 260–261, 284–285; shadow on the atmosphere, 48; surrender to the imperatives of (KN), 284; wrathful as well as loving side, 259, 261. *See also* atmosphere; Nature; ocean
earthquakes: and magic curves, 59
Easy Cheese prize, 224
echelon formation, 190, 191
ecolocation capability of dolphins, 159–162
ecolocation clicks, 161, 162, 185
elders: Field Quarter as a society of, 17
emotion: vs. rationality, 258; and science, 285; and thinking, 250–251
encapsulation of life. *See* cell origins
energy release vs. storage in rivers, 61–63
energy-compensation system of rivers, 66
environment: body-environment awareness, 135–136; *umwelt*, 109, 132, 135–136
environmental crisis. *See* humans and the environmental crisis
environmental insensitivity essay contest prizes, 223–225
epimeletic behavior. *See* caring for others
Epling, Carl, 7; field classes with, 8–10
essay contest on environmental insensitivity prizes, 223–225
ethics: advances in, 276; coercive approach to, 257; the new ethic, 260, command for, 287; the source of, 208–209, 257. *See also* rules for living
Evans, Bill, 161

evolution, 109–110; of the brain, 134(2); of consciousness (beginnings), 134–135, 135–136; debate on, 7–8; detection tests, 8–10; driving forces, 156–157, 248; of God (as a concept), 259–260(2); stored up variation and, 9; of thinking, 157, 249–251. *See also* natural selection

eyes: of dolphins, 194; of prey school members under attack, 186; of vertebrates: and hue discrimination, 106, 107, 108. *See also* vision

eyes of one's own: open-eyed times as priceless, 37; trusting, 38

F

faith systems. *See* religion

false killer whales, 174

false sense of superiority among humans, 265–266

fatalism of mothers, 238

father of KN, 2–3

fear: of aging, 243; innocent acceptance and (during adventures), 141

[the] feminine (yin), 215, 216. *See also* male–female duality

field classes: with Cowles, 4–6; with Dobzhansky and Epling, 8–10; with KN (*see* Field Quarter)

Field Quarter, ix, 11–12; in the canyon (Big Creek), 72–85; flight log, 26–27; gathering, 17–18; in the Granite Mountains, 17–30, 33–41, 43–49; journals (*see* daily personal journals); leader–student dynamics (*see* leader–student dynamics during Field Quarter); leaders (*see* leaders of Field Quarter); librarian, dehydrated (*see* Miss Preen); library (Parnassus), 17, 74; marriage rituals during, 12; on the Mattole River, 55–68; niche hunt, 75–76, 77–80; oral presentations, 20; participants as interlopers, 81; parting words of KN, 282, 283, 285–288; resource persons (invited visitors), 19, 269; seeing in Nature class, 33–40, niche hunt, 75–76, 77–80; as a society, 17; student–leader dynamics (*see* leader–student dynamics during Field Quarter); students (*see* students in Field Quarter); triad routine, 19; in the White Mountains, 269–289

fieldwork: *Bipes* expedition, 89–96; desert iguana study, 113–120; focal follows, 114–115; frog observations, 145–147; niche hunt (FQ), 75–76, 77–80; opaleye perch studies, 127–133; seeing in Nature class (FQ), 33–40, niche hunt, 75–76, 77–80; spinner dolphin studies, 164–165, 167–180; *Uma* study, 101–108

fingerlings (salmon), 231

finite limit of sound, 162

fires. *See* wild fires

first bottleneck of mortality, 234–239

first order of business, 223. *See also* central question of our times

Index

fish: anchovy larva mortality, 235–237; KN's writings on, 303*n1*(*ch9*), 307*n9*(*ch13*); pickerel and prey fish, 189; pufferfish, 89; pupfish rescue, 274; steelhead trout, 80–81; sunfish, giant ocean, 218; tidepool (*see* opaleye perch). *See also* salmon; sharks
fish studies (KN), 120; opaleye perch, 127–133
fishing snake, 77–78
fitness of a species, 109
fitting of lifestreams/numbers into the world, 146–147, 234, 237, 238–239; and reproductive force, 147; stages of mortality (bottlenecks and cap), 234–244
flannel bush, 23
flat-tailed horned lizard, 114, 303*n1*(*ch8*)
flatworms, 136, 209
flexibility of opaleye perch, 132
flight log, 26–27
flight response to predator looming, 192–193
Flodin, Mary, 19
flowers: canyon flowers, 81; desert flowers, 23; intermittent stream flowers, 34–35; iris drawings, 79–80; in the White Mountains, 275, 277–278
fly, 135
flying in formation, 191–192
focal follows (fieldwork), 114–115
fog as caught by redwoods, 73–74, 264
Ford, Larry: as Field Quarter leader, 17, 18, 24, 56, 64, 65, 74; and *Mountain Time*, xiv
forest species bands along canyon/mountain slopes, 264, 278
forgoing self-centeredness, 260
formation-flying, 191–192
Frank (FQ leader). *See* Murphy, Frank
freedom of desert iguana at high temperature, 114, 116, 119
freedom to take part in Field Quarter, 29–30
Fremont cottonwoods, 47–48
fringe-toed lizard. See *Uma scoparia*
frogs: of Hidden Spring, 145–147; tree frog male–female duality, 218
fruit fly evolution detection test, 8–9
fusion-fission/pickup society (dolphins), 173, 177

G

Gaines, David, 272
Garb, Yaakov, 269, 271
garter snake, western aquatic, 77–78
geese over the Himalayas, 49
gel. *See* syncytial gel
genetic hard-wiring of humans, 227–228
gentility of dolphins, 153, 154, 179
geology: continental transformations and species distribution, 89, 97–98; KN's flight to, 3–4
Geology of California (R. M. Norris and R. W. Webb), 273–274*q*, 310*n1*(*ch20*)
Geronimo (gillnetter), 150
giant ocean sunfish male–female duality, 218
gillnetter (*Geronimo*), 150
Girella nigricans. *See* opaleye perch
gliding with Jim Norris, 50–53

Gliessman, Steve: as Buffalo Boy, 76–77; as Field Quarter leader, 17, 18, 33, 65, 72, 74, 77(*2*), 271–272, on identifying plants, 23, refuge, 19, salute to students, 281, [on] wind and water, 46–48; and *Mountain Time*, xiv

God (as a concept): evolution of, 259–260(*2*); wrathful as well as loving side, 248

Grandview Camp, 278

Granite Cabin (the cabin) (Bunny Club), 24–26, 291, 298; landscape around, 252–253; spring behind, 253, 254; star-watching on the deck, 33

Granite Mountains: Field Quarter in, 17–30, 33–41, 43–49; journal entry on, 40–41; reserve for teaching and research, 26

gratitude and love, 261

gray whales: killer whale attack on, 84–85

great blue whale: KN's encounter with, 10

Great Britain: decline, 244

"greatest adventure" idea (KN), 291, 296–297

Greenland: Nuuk's rocks, 199

Griffin, Donald, 303–304*n2*(*ch9*)

grinding stones (Chemehuevi), 252

ground squirrel, round-tailed, 114, 303*n1*(*ch8*)

group distance in schools/flocks/herds, 186

groups: mammals wandering in, 249–250, 256. *See also* schools/flocks/herds

guilt: capacity for feeling, 250; as felt by dogs, 157–158

Gulf of California: fish study, 120

gyrocopter idea (KN), 297

H

Hamilton, W. D., 307*n10*(*ch13*)

hana nai'a, 167, 170

Hana Nai'a (project), 168, 172

hard-wiring of humans, 227–228

Hart, David: and *Mountain Time*, xiv

Hasler, Arthur, 308*n1*(*ch17*)

hatchling mullet, 235

Hawaii: marine life research (KN), ix–x, 10–11; Oceanic Institute (Sea Life Park), 162–163

Hawkeye. *See* Dr. Vandenburg, 55-56

hawks, 52; red-tails and gliders, 51

hearing: in sensory integration systems, 193

heat tolerance of desert iguana, 114, 116–117, 118–119, 303*nn2*, 3(*ch8*)

helping behavior. *See* caring for others

helping concept, 156–157, 307*n10*(*ch13*)

Herman, Louis, 164–165, 305*n6*(*ch11*)

herpetothermometry, 116

Hidden Spring, 142; frogs, 145–147; hike to, 141–143

Hideaway Bar, 64

hierarchy among dolphins, 177–178, 189–190

high-altitude winds, 49

hiking adventure with Al Allanson (KN), 139–145

Holbrookia maculata (earless lizard): color adaptation, 108

homeland of KN north of Santa Cruz, 263–265; view of the ocean from beneath, 265–267

Index

hope in reverence for the wild, 228
horizon: unbroken view of, 266–267
horned lizard, flat-tailed, 114, 303n1(ch8)
Hubbs, Carl, 125, 295
hue discrimination: vertebrate eyes and, 106, 107, 108
human individuals: importance in shaping the world, 274, 286–287; insignificance and kinship with all life, 254–255, 284; need to see beyond our limits, 249
human society: Field Quarter as a society, 17; hunter–gatherers, 241, 251; nomadic societies, 215–216; of pilots, 192. *See also* culture
humans: avarice, 227–228; brain consciousness centers, 134; controlling our numbers, 244; culture as a biological attribute of, 225, 226–227; dealing with humans and what they do, 223; death in the history of, 241; duality, 257; and the environmental crisis (*see* humans and the environmental crisis); false sense of superiority, 265–266; as genetically hard-wired, 227–228; ignorance: challenging with irony, 223–225, turning of our backs on Mountain Time, 228, 256–258, 287–288; as individuals (*see* human individuals); kinship with all life (*see* kinship with all life); language power, 226–227; longing for the wholeness of Nature, 287; man as the mystery, 247*q;* need to see beyond our individual limits, 249; numbers of (*see* numbers of humans); parasites, 241; as privileged, 284; reach toward the ineffable, 249–250; rules of Nature for (*see* rules for living); self-centeredness, 228, 265–266 (*see also* ignorance, *above*); selfishness, 223, 227–228; smallness–impact paradox, 283; understanding ourselves/who we are, 208–209, 225; viewpoint, 265–266. *See also* man–woman duality
humans and the environmental crisis, 223, 225, 226–228, 258; challenging ignorance with irony, 223–225; smallness–impact paradox, 283
hummingbirds, 44; columbine and, 83–84
hunter–gatherer societies: keeping up in, 241; religion in, 251. *See also* wandering in groups
Hutsipamamau'u, 254–255
hydrogen: as a constituent of life, 200

I

ichthyothermitaxitron, 128
identifying plants, 23
ignorance: challenging with irony, 223–225; turning of our backs on Mountain Time, 228, 256–258, 287–288. *See also* self-centeredness
imbrication of rocks, 60–61
incubation of life, 201–202, 202–204

Indian mano, 34
Indian paintbrush, 35
Indians. *See* Chemehuevi Indians
indigo bush, 275
individuals: salmon as, 234;
    spinner dolphins as, 179.
    See also human individuals
[the] ineffable: human reach
    toward, 249–250
infant mortality, 234, 238
ingestion: in desert iguana, 113–114,
    116; in opaleye perch, 131
innocence and blame as not in
    Mountain Time, 85
innocent acceptance: and fear
    (during adventures), 141
inquiry. *See* seeing; spinning the
    wheel
insects: as blown offshore, 48;
    fly, 135; fruit fly evolution
    detection test, 8–9; mosquito
    larvae, 34; moth and Joshua
    tree, 5–6; semelparous
    species, 233. *See also* spiders
insignificance of individuals and
    kin-ship with all life, 254–
    255, 284
interlopers: Field Quarter
    participants as, 81
intermittent stream flowers, 34–35
internal waves: sea slicks, 129
intertidal band, 127, 202
invasion of the land, 207
inventions of KN, 293, 297
ionosphere, 49
iris drawings, 79–80
iron deposits, 207
irony: challenging ignorance with,
    223–225
island effect (ocean currents), 172
isostasy, 4

J

jazz tempos of spinner dolphins,
    178–179, 180
jogs for KN to change ways,
    276–277
Johnson, Chris, 169, 170, 174–175
Jordan, Joe, 19, 49
Joshua trees, 22–23; fallen tree duff
    residents, 23–24; moth and, 5–6
journals. *See* daily personal journals
joy of KN: in family and friends,
    294; in science and discovery
    with others, 296–297, 298–299

K

Kathy (bottlenose dolphin), 159–161
Kealake'akua Bay: spinner dolphin
    rest cove, 167–168
keeping up in hunter–gatherer
    societies, 241
Kelso Sand Dunes, 101; piling up
    of, 44–46
Kenneth S. Norris Endowment
    Fund for the California
    Environment, x
Kerr, Clark, 122
killer whales: attack on gray
    whales, 84–85; false killer
    whales, 174; pygmy killer
    whales, 174
kinetic energy, 62
King Range: formation of, 60
kinglets, ruby-crowned, 38–39
kinship with all life, 209, 284;
    individual insignificance and,
    254–255, 284
knowing. *See* understanding

L

Lake Crowley, 273
land: invasion of, 207. *See also* the
    earth/Earth

land ancestors of dolphins, 154
Landau, Laurie, 189
language power, 226–227
Larry (FQ leader). *See* Ford, Larry
Lasker, Reuben: anchovy studies, 235–237
lava dam (Long Valley Caldera). *See* Bishop Tuff
leader–student dynamics during Field Quarter, 17, 20, 21, 277; discord over rattlesnake-catching-and-handling demonstration, 276, 277; sexuality, 27–29
leaders of Field Quarter, 17, 18, 20; as interlopers in the canyon, 81; roles, 27–28, 29; social defenses, 18–19; and students (*see* leader–student dynamics during Field Quarter). *See also* Ford, Larry; Gliessman, Steve; Murphy, Frank; Norris, Ken; Usner, Don (Santiago)
leadership: duality, 248; among spinner dolphins, 177–178
leaf-blower prize, 224
leaping of spinner dolphins, 168–169, 176–177, 305*n1*(*ch12*), 306*n4*(*ch12*)
learning: by dolphins: conceptual, 163–164, observational, 153; and culture, 225–226
learning the story/stories of life, 208–209, 288. *See also* seeing; seeing in Nature
Lee Vining Canyon, 270–271
lekking behavior (sage grouse), 218
lenticular clouds: soaring, 52
Lewis, Harlan, 8
librarian, dehydrated. *See* Miss Preen

library of Field Quarter (Parnassus), 17, 74
lichens: survival strategy, 84
life: balance, 288; beat of (*see* beat of life); cap of life, 241–244; cell origins, 204, multicellularity, 207; constituents, 199, 200–202; creation myth, 199–208; death as a presence in, 241; as dependent on water, 207–208; earth limits on, 238–239; incubation of, 201–202, 202–204; kinship with all (*see* kinship with all life); learning the story/stories of, 208–209, 288 (*see also* seeing; seeing in Nature); magic curve for all life, 288; oldest living things on earth, 280; origin story, 199–208; in the wild (*see* Mountain Time)
lifestreams, 82, 204. *See also* fitting of lifestreams/numbers into the world
lightning: as a constituent of life, 200–201
lightning tubes, 200
Linanthus parryi evolution detection test, 9
Lindberg, Bob, 4
list memory of dolphins, 164
Little Kids Day (Field Quarter), 75
liverworts, 34
"lives linked" survival strategy, 83–84
"lives locked" survival strategy, 84
Liza (dog), 134–135
lizards: desert iguana (*see* desert iguana); desert night lizard (*Xantusia vigilis*), 23–24; desert scaly lizard shooting,

141; earless lizard, 108; flat-tailed horned lizard, 114, 303*n1*(*ch8*); fringe-toed lizard (see *Uma scoparia*); raven and lizard encounter, 285; side-blotched lizard (*Uta*), 83, 84; two-legged lizard: distribution, 89, 91, 96 (see also *Bipes* ...)
locust cycles, 220
Logan, Dick, 253–254
Long Valley Caldera, 273; lava dam (*see* Bishop Tuff); magma body beneath, 273, 274, 286
longing for the wholeness of Nature, 287
looming (of predators): flight response to, 192–193
love (loving): capacity for feeling, 250; gratitude and, 261; lovers in the thrall of, 213–214; reverence for the wild, 228; surrender to the Earth and, 284; understanding and, 263–265
Lowe, Arlene, 89, 94
Lowe, Charlie, 6, 7, 89, 90, 94, 108
Lucy (dog), 158

M

Mac the campus cop, 126
MacFarland, Bill, 304*n1*(*ch11*)
MacKinnon, C. S., 93–94
magic curve(s): for all life, 288; of mountains and rivers, 58–59; restoration of, 59, 63–64
magma body beneath Long Valley Caldera, 273, 274, 286
main question. *See* central question of our times
Maka Ala (underwater-viewing vessel), 168, 170, 174–175
male courtship displays, 218
male–female duality, 217–219, 220–221; dimorphism, 216–217; man–woman duality, 213–214(*2*), 215–216, 217. *See also* yin and yang
Malia (rough-tooth dolphin), 163–164
mammals: cetaceans, 149 (*see also* dolphins; whales); concept formation in (*see* thinking); ground squirrel, round-tailed, 114, 303*n1*(*ch8*); male–female duality among, 219; mouse courtship and mating, 38; ring-tailed cat, 26; wandering in groups, 249–250, 256. *See also* dogs; dolphins; humans; whales
man: as the mystery, 247*q*. *See also* humans
man-in-the-ground (wild cucumber), 78, 82
man–woman duality, 213–214(*2*), 215–216, 217
manatees, 149
mano, Indian, 34
manzanita, 82
map sense: in opaleye perch, 130, 132
mare's tails, 44
marine life research (KN), ix–x, 10–11; dolphin studies, 10–11: bottlenoses, 150–157, 159–161, spinners, 164–165, 167–180; opaleye perch studies, 127–133
Marineland of the Pacific: KN at, 10–11, 149–150, 291–292
marriage rituals during Field Quarter, 12
[the] masculine (yang), 215–216(*2*). *See also* male–female duality

Index

master's thesis of KN, 302*n2*(*ch7*)
Mathias, Mildred, 8, 123
Mattole River: Field Quarter on, 55–68; running, 56–57, 65, 66
Mayhew, Bill, 8, 123
Medina, Harold, 305–306*n3*(*ch12*)
Melville, Herman: on spinners, 168–169
memory of dolphins, 164
men: cap of life, 242. *See also* man–woman duality
menopause, 239, 240–241
mentality of dolphins, 153, 154–155, 164–165. *See also under* caring for others (helping behavior); ecolocation capability of dolphins; *under* learning; social behavior of dolphins
metabolism in syncytial gel, 203–204
metaphysics: vs. natural history, 110
Methuselah, 280
metronome. *See* beat of life
migration: opaleye perch, 130–132
Miller, George Armitage, 186–187
Miller, Loye, 141
Miller, S. M., 201
mimicry by dolphins, 164–165
Mimulus guttatus (water monkeyflower), 35
minerals: iron deposits, 207; in the primordial sea, 202
Miss Preen (dehydrated librarian), 18, 74, 289, 310*n1*(*ch20*)
Moby Dick: on spinners, 168–169
Mojave Desert: cloud-castles over, 43; east-sloping margin, 23
Mojave Green rattlesnake, 4–5
Mono Lake, 271; Negit Island, 272–273
Mono Lake Committee, 272–273

Monterey Bay: submarine canyon, 21–22
Monterey Bay Aquarium Research Institute, 21–22
Mormon tea bush, 47
mortality. *See* death
mosquito larvae, 34
moss, desert, 208
moth and Joshua tree, 5–6
mother of KN, 2
mothers: fatalism, 238
motivational powers (KN), 298
Mountain Sheep Song, 253, 254
Mountain Time, 14, 66; beginnings, 206, 207; the canyon as the matrix of, 72; competition for space in (*see* fitting of lifestreams/numbers into the world); continental transformations and, 97–98; essence to Ken, 299; fitness equation, 109; intertidal band versions, 127; as passionless/elemental, 85; persistence of, 264; sexuality in, 220–221; turning of our backs on, 228, 256–258, 287–288. *See also* the canyon
Mountain Time (KN): biographical selectivity, xviii; chapter selection/organization, xvi–xvii, 13–14; didactic power, xi; editing of the manu-script, xiv–xix; imagery, xv; introduction, xiv–xv, xvii, 1–14; resurrection and reassembling of the manuscript, xiv; sections, xvii; title, 14; writing of the manuscript, xiii–xiv
Mountain Time crazy quilt (canyon's quilt), 76, 82

mountains: bands of species along the slopes, 278; formation of, 57–60, 66; King Range, 60; life in (see Mountain Time); Table Mountain, 43, 44; White Mountain, 275, 284; Woods Mountain observations, 43–44; worship of the mountain, 228. See also Granite Mountains, magic curve(s), White Mountains
mouse courtship and mating, 38
Mud Festival, 67–68
mudflats: formation of, 67
mudflows, 65
mullet hatchling, 235
multicellularity, 207; and death, 232
Murphy, Frank: as Field Quarter leader, 270, 271–272, 280–281
muscular mobilization among spinner dolphins, 190
mushrooms: mycorrhizae, 84
music: jazz tempos of spinner dolphins, 178–179, 180. See also songs
myths: Chemehuevi myths, 255; vs. doctrine, 256–257

N

Nai'a (cabin cruiser), 168, 171, 175, 176
Nantucket whaleboat as a tree house, 298
National Institutes of Health: dolphin brain investigation, 154
natural history: vs. metaphysics, 110
natural history studies (KN), 11. See also Field Quarter
Natural Reserve System. See UC Natural Reserve System (NRS)

natural selection (selective process): beginnings, 206, 207; and color adaptation in *Uma scoparia*, 107; culture and, 226; near the edges of possibility, 113
Naturalistic Ethic, The (KN), 7
Nature, 14; as the authority, 97, 295–296; balance of life, 288; child's view of, 35; longing for the wholeness of, 287; rules (see rules of Nature); seeing in Nature class (FQ), 33–40, niche hunt, 75–76, 77–80. See also the earth/Earth
negentropy: life as, 203
Negit Island (Mono Lake), 272–273
"new" concept as learned by a dolphin, 163–164
[the] new ethic, 260; command for, 287
[the] new understanding of the earth, 286–287
niche hunt (Field Quarter), 75–76, 77–80
nitrogen: as a constituent of life, 200
nomadic societies: man–woman duality in, 215. See also wandering in groups
Norris, Jim (nephew of KN): KN's gliding with, 50–53
Norris, Kathleen, 219–220, 308n4(ch15)
Norris, Ken: career (life work), ix–xi; collaborators, 292, 297, 298; convincing/motivational powers, 298; Cowles' influence, 6–7, 295–296(2); at Marineland of the Pacific, 10–11, 149–150,

291–292; natural history studies, 11; at Scripps Institution of Oceanography, 10, 120, 125, 149; search for, 3–6; sharing of ideas/excitement, 293, 297, 299; synthesis of science and art, xiii, 3, 80; UC Natural Reserve System founding, x, 121–123; at UCLA, ix, 3–10, 121, 295. *See also* desert life research; marine life research; writings
and the Chemehuevi, 255
childhood, 295
and children, 291–292
curiosity, patience, and wonder, 292–293
family: adventures, 291, 295; brother (*see* Norris, R. M. [Bob]); parents, 2–3, 295; resurrection of the *Mountain Time* manuscript, xiv; son's afterword, 294–299; students and colleagues as, 293–294; wife's afterword, 291–294
as Field Quarter leader, 18, 271–272, 277, 285–286; jogs to change ways, 276–277; niche hunt, 75–76, 77–80; Painted Canyon retreat, 281–285; parting words, 282, 283, 285–288; rattlesnake-catching-and-handling demonstration, 276, 277; seeing in Nature class, 33–40; social defenses, 18–19. *See also* leader–student dynamics during Field Quarter
gliding with Jim Norris, 50–53
hiking adventure with Al Allanson, 139–145
homeland north of Santa Cruz, 263–265; view of the ocean from beneath, 265–267
household pets, 292, 294–295
inventions, 293, 297
joy: in family and friends, 294; in science and discovery with others, 296–297, 298–299
kinship with all life, 209; individual insignificance and, 284
marriage: engagement, 291
old age: bypass surgery, 309n4(*ch17*)
sayings (dictums/aphorisms/mottos), 295–296, 296–297, 298–299
stories and tall tales, 293, 295
surrender to the Earth's imperatives, 284
writing of *Mountain Time*, xiii–xiv, 1
writings. *See* writings
youth: attraction to a young woman, 213–214
Norris, Phyllis (wife of KN): afterword, 291–294
Norris, R. M. (Bob) (brother of KN), 3, 298; *Geology of California*, 273–274q, 310n1(*ch20*)
Norris, Richard (Dick) (son of KN): afterword, 294–299; and *Mountain Time*, xiv

Norris, Tom (son of KN): and *Mountain Time*, xiv
NRS. *See* UC Natural Reserve System (NRS)
numbers: prey number required for predator attack failure, 189; river rock numbers, 60; sensory information limit, 187–188
numbers of a species: fitting into Mountain Time. *See* fitting of lifestreams/numbers into the world
numbers of humans: controlling, 244; development of agriculture and, 256
nutmegs, California, 264
Nuuk, Greenland: rocks, 199

O

oak trees: of California, 22; life span, 280; tanoaks, 264
observation process. *See* seeing
Observation Series entries (daily personal journals), 21
observational learning by dolphins, 153
ocean: primordial sea, 201–202; sea slicks, 129; as thin and fragile, 265; trash lines in, 174; view of from beneath KN's homeland north of Santa Cruz, 265–267
ocean currents: island effect, 172
Ocean Woman (Chemehuevi), 254–255
Oceanic Institute (Sea Life Park), 163
ocolote. See *Bipes biporus*
old age (aging): acceptance of, 243; bypass surgery of KN, 309$n4$(*ch17*); the cap of life, 241–244; debate on, 309$n3$(*ch17*); fear of, 243; of salmon, 232
oldest living things on earth, 280
ollas (Chemehuevi), 252
opaleye perch (tidepool fish), 127–133; consciousness, 132–133; ingestion and digestion, 131; KN's doctoral thesis on, 303$n1$(*ch9*); map sense, 130, 132; migration, 130–132; temperature selection experiments, 127–128; wariness and flexibility, 129, 132
open eyes: as priceless, 37
opposites. *See* duality
optic brain of dolphins, 194
oral presentations (Field Quarter), 20
origin of life story, 199–209
owl: Aristotle, 292
oxygen: production of, 206–207

P

Pacific white-sided dolphins. *See* white-sided dolphins
Painted Canyon retreat (KN), 281–285
Panamint rattlesnake, 275–276
papers of KN. *See* writings
Paramecia, 136
parasites of humans, 241
parents of KN, 2–3
Parnassus (Field Quarter library), 17, 74
partial animal concept, 118–119, 303$n3$(*ch8*)
peace in the canyon, 85
Perkins, Paul, 161
photosynthesis, 206
phraetophytes, 47–48

pickerel and prey fish, 189
pictographs (Chemehuevi), 252
pilot whales, 174; individual as assisted by dolphins, 156
pilots: formation-flying, 191–192; society, 192
pines: ponderosa, 82. *See also* bristlecone pines
Pister, Phil, 274
plants: identifying, 23; niche hunt (FQ), 75–76, 78, 79–80; semelparous species, 233; sexual circumvention among, 220; sexual differentiation among, 218, 220; wind and water and, 46–48. *See also* bushes; flowers; trees; *and specific species*
poetry: as like/unlike science, 37, 38
Poleta Formation, 282–283
polynucleotides: DNA and RNA, 203, 205
ponderosa pine, 82
Pono (rough-tooth dolphin), 291
Porter, Warren, 101–108, 302*n1*(*ch7*)
potential energy, 62
pots (ollas) (Chemehuevi), 252
Potts, W. K., 190
Powell, Bill, 161
power of language, 226–227
predators: looming: flight response to, 192–193; prey number required for attack failure, 189; prey track prediction, 188; of spinner dolphins, 173–174. *See also specific species*
Preen, Miss. *See* Miss Preen
pregnancy: survival advantages, 219
Prescott, John, 159, 304*n2*(*ch11*)

prey: flight response to predator looming, 192–193; number required for predator attack failure, 189; track prediction by predators, 188. *See also* schools/flocks/herds; *and specific species*
primates: thinking by, 251. *See also* humans
primordial sea, 201–202
Prince's plume, 275
prizes for environmental insensitivity essay contest, 223–225
probability summation, 190–191
Project Hana Nai'a, 168, 172
protective school member number, 189
Pryor, Karen, 163–164
pseudomatching of body and surrounding colors: in *Holbrookia maculata*, 108; in *Uma scoparia*, 105–106, 107
pufferfish, 89
pupfish rescue, 274
pygmy killer whales, 174

Q

question of our times. *See* central question of our times

R

racial barrier disappearance among pilots, 192
railroad ties, 25
raptors, 52; and gliders, 51
rationality vs. emotion, 258
rattlesnakes: catching and handling demonstrations, 4–5, 276, 277; Mojave Green, 4–5; Panamint, 275–276; sidewinder, 114, 116

raven and lizard encounter, 285
recording of dolphin vocalizations, 175–176, 189–190
recording reflectance spectrophotometer, 103–105
red-spotted toads, 125–126, 127
red-tailed hawks: and gliders, 51
redbud, 23
reduced iron deposits, 207
redwing blackbirds, 292–293
Redwood Camp, 72, 74
redwoods (coastal): as the beat of life, 74, 82; fog as caught by, 73–74, 264; second-growth trees, 264; southern limit, 73; survival strategy, 82–83; time-pulse, 73; wild fire history in, 72–73
reflectivity analysis: lizard against sand, 105–106, 107
refrigerator plant, 47
relationship: and the brain, 183; group distance in schools/flocks/herds, 186; hierarchy among dolphins, 177–178, 189–190; between yin and yang, 211q
religion (faith systems), 248–249; Baptist church service, 247–248; change as needed in, 258–259; as coercive, 257–258; genesis/birth, 249–251; in hunter–gatherer societies, 251; rigidity, 256–257; and rules for living, 249, 257, 258, 284–285; suffering caused by, 257–258; as vital, 249, 258
reproduction: of bristlecone pines, 279; and death, 232, 239; force (*see* sexuality); semelparity, 233
reptiles: amphisbaenids, 90, 97 (see also *Bipes* ...); turtle of Baja California, 92–93, 96. *See also* lizards; snakes
research areas. *See* reserves for teaching and research; study plots
reserves for teaching and research: Granite Mountains, 26. *See also* UC Natural Reserve System
resource persons (invited visitors) for Field Quarter, 19, 269
rest coves of spinner dolphins, 172, 173; Kealake'akua Bay, 167–168; white sand in, 174–175
resting behavior of dolphins, 173, 175, 193–194
reverence for the wild, 228
rhubarb, wild, 47
rhyolite, 43, 252
rhythm: chorus line effect, 190, 191; zigzag behavior of spinner dolphins, 172, 176–177, 178: as compositions, 178–179, 180. *See also* beat of life (metronome); time-pulse
ridges of air: soaring, 52
right and wrong as not in Mountain Time, 85
ring-tailed cat, 26
rivers: energy release vs. storage, 61–63; energy-compensation system, 66; formation of, 57–59, 66; mudflats at the mouths of, 67; obstacle removal, 59, 63–64; rock arrangement and numbers, 60–61; rules, 60–64, 68; storms and, 61, 66; tributaries, 63, 64. *See also* magic curve(s); Mattole River

Index

RNA: appearance of, 205
rocks: Nuuk's rocks, 199; Poleta Formation, 282–283; river rock arrangement and numbers, 60–61
rough-tooth dolphins, 163–164, 291
round-tailed ground squirrel, 114, 303n1(ch8)
ruby-crowned kinglets, 38–39
rule-giver: the Earth as, 259–260, 260–261, 284–285
rules for living: natural vs. imagined, 6–7; religion and, 249, 257, 258, 284–285. *See also* ethics
rules of Nature, 6; for humans (*see* rules for living); for rivers, 60–64, 68; for wind: Bernoulli effect, 44–46
Rumsey, Susan Gee: and *Mountain Time*, xiv
running the Mattole, 56–57, 65, 66

S

sage grouse: lekking behavior, 218
salmon: aging of, 232; fingerlings, 231; as individuals, 234; schools, 233; semelparity, 233(2); spawning run, 231–232
Salmon Creek, 73
salt pills, 118
salts in the primordial sea, 202
salute to students by Steve, 281
Samuelson, J. Roger, 123
San Andreas Fault, 22
San Ignacio (Baja California), 91–92
sand: reflectivity analysis, 105; in spinner dolphin rest coves, 174–175
sand dunes: among creosote bushes, 113. *See also* Kelso Sand Dunes

Santa Ana winds, 48–49
Santa Cruz: homeland of KN north of, 263–265: view of the ocean from beneath, 265–267. *See also* UC Santa Cruz
Santa Cruz Island trip, 28
Santa Rosa Mountain hike, 139–145
Santiago (FQ leader). *See* Usner, Don
sayings (dictums/aphorisms/mottos) of KN, 295–296, 296–297, 298–299
Schevill, Bill and Barbara, 161
Schilt, Carl, 185–186, 188–193
school processes among dolphins, 176–177, 180, 189–191; zigzag behavior, 172, 176–177, 178: as compositions, 178–179, 180. *See also* social behavior of dolphins
school processes among dolphins during shark attacks, 185–194; collective leadership, 177–178; flight response to predator looming, 192–193; melting away, 185, 186, 189, 192–193; muscular mobilization, 190; sensation summation, 190–191; tightening, 185–186
schools/flocks/herds: of dolphins, 179: bottlenoses, 195, spinners, 176–177, 179–180, 194–195 (*see also* school processes among dolphins); echelon formation, 190, 191; group distance in, 186; KN's paper on, 307n9(ch13); protection question, 306n2(ch13); protective member number, 189; of salmon, 233; sensory integration systems, 193

Schulman Grove hike, 278–279
Schultheis thermometer, 116
science: and art: synthesis (KN), xiii, 3, 80; emotion and, 285; imperatives, 105; joy of KN in science and discovery with others, 296–297, 298–299; as like/unlike poetry, 37, 38; as not enough, 258
Scripps Institution of Oceanography: KN at, 10, 120, 125, 149
sea. *See* ocean
Sea Life Park Oceanarium, 162–163
sea lions, 149
sea slicks, 129
seafloor worm-wrought volcano fossil, 283–284
seals, 149
second bottleneck of mortality, 239–241
"second harvest" of desert iguana, 116
seeing: process of observation, 296; scientific imperatives, 105; trusting one's own eyes, 38
seeing in Nature (Field Quarter class), 33–40; niche hunt, 75–76, 77–80. *See also* spinning the wheel
selective process. *See* natural selection
self-centeredness, 228, 265–266; forgoing, 260. *See also* ignorance; selfishness
selfing plants, 220
selfishness: as driving evolution, 156–157, 248; of humans, 223, 227–228
semelparity, 233
semisubmersible seasick machine idea (KN), 297

sensation summation among spinner dolphins, 190–191
sensory information limit, 187–188
sensory integration systems of schools/flocks/herds, 193
seven: as a sensory information limit, 187–188; prey number required for predator attack failure, 189
sexuality (reproductive force): celibacy, 219–220; circumvention among plants, 220; cycles in spinner dolphins, 170; differentiation (*see* male–female duality); fitting of numbers and, 147; lovers enthralled, 213–214; in leader–student dynamics during FQ, 27–29; in Mountain Time, 220–221
shark attacks on dolphins, 174, 177, 183–185; prey track prediction, 188; school processes during (*see* school processes among dolphins during shark attacks); sensory information limit, 187–188
sharks, 174; visual system, 188. *See also* shark attacks on dolphins
sheep herding story, 261
shootings: animal specimen collection, 119; desert scaly lizard, 141
shore: intertidal band, 127, 202; metronome along, 128–129
sick dolphin and helpmate story, 155–156
side-blotched lizard (*Uta*), 83, 84
sidewinder rattlesnake, 114, 116
Sierra Nevada: crossing, 270–271
Simpson, George Gaylord, 97
singing: during Field Quarter,

76–77. *See also* songs
SISs (sensory integration systems): schools/flocks/herds as, 193
skinny dipping episode (during Field Quarter), 28
sleeping behavior of dolphins, 173, 175, 193–194
Slevin, Joseph, 90–91
Smith, H. M., 302*n2*(*ch6*)
snakes: black-headed snake, 36; western aquatic garter snake, 77–78. *See also* rattlesnakes
soaring, 52
social behavior of dolphins, 154–155(*2*); caressing, 167, 170; communication (*see* communication among dolphins); cooperation (*see* cooperation among/by dolphins); gentility, 153, 154, 179; helping, 155–157. *See also* school processes among dolphins
social change cry, 277
society. *See* dolphin society; human society
Society for Informing Animals of Their Taxonomic Position, 293
songs: around the campfire, 76–77, 280–281; Chemehuevi songs, 1, 253, 254
sound: ecolocation clicks, 161, 162, 185; finite limit, 162
Spam march and songs, 280–281
species: fitness, 109; as lifestreams, 82, 204; testing/weeding out process (*see* fitting of lifestreams/numbers into the world)
species distribution: bands along canyon/mountain slopes, 264, 278; continental transformations and, 89, 97–98; two-legged lizard, 89, 91, 96
species studies. *See* fieldwork
spectrophotometer, recording reflectance, 103–105
spiders: in the atmosphere, 49; dwarf spider, 78–79
spinner dolphins, 167–180, 195–196; association among, 173; caressing behavior, 167, 170; consensus decision-making, 177–178; daily activity, 172–173; feeding behavior, 172; as individuals, 179; leadership among, 177–178; leaping, 168–169, 176–177, 305*n1*(*ch12*), 306*n4*(*ch12*); life span, 173; movement toward and from the open sea, 171–172, 175–177 (*see also* zigzag behavior *below*); physical characteristics, 168; predators, 173–174; range, 171; reproduction cycles, 170; rest coves, 172, 173: Kealake'akua Bay, 167–168; resting behavior, 173, 175; rhythmic compositions, 178–179, 180; schools, 176–177, 179–180, 194–195 (*see also* school processes among dolphins); shark attacks on, 177, 183–185 (*see also* shark attacks on dolphins); vocalizations (*see* vocalizations of dolphins); zigzag behavior, 172, 176–177, 178: as compositions, 178–179, 180. *See also* dolphins
spinning the wheel, 36–37, 39–40, 75, 295–296; dog

guilt, 157–158; dolphin sleep inquiry, 193–194; *Girella* investigations, 127–132; partial animal theory, 303*n*3(*ch8*); river vision, 66; spinner dolphin behavior, 164–165, 168. *See also* seeing in Nature

spiritual sensibility: preconditions for, 249–250. *See also* religion

spores in the atmosphere, 49

spring behind the Granite Cabin, 253, 254

spring sharing story, 253–254

star-watching on the Granite Cabin deck, 33

starfish dance, 38

steelhead trout, 80–81

Steve (FQ leader). *See* Gliessman, Steve

stones. *See* rocks

stored up variation: and evolution, 9

stories: car fixing and spring sharing story, 253–254; check dam story, 62–63; chia gathering and sheep herding story, 261; KN's stories and tall tales, 293, 295; learning the story/stories of life, 208–209, 288 (*see also* seeing; seeing in Nature); origin of life story, 199–208

storms: and mountains, 59; and rivers, 61, 66

streams: clarity of, 84; of life (*see* lifestreams). *See also* rivers

student–leader dynamics. *See* leader–student dynamics during Field Quarter

students in Field Quarter: finding their own way/place, 27, 40, 269; freedom to take part, 29–30; leaders and (*see* leader–student dynamics during Field Quarter); salute to by Steve, 281; women students and KN, 28–29

study plots: desert iguana study, 114–115, 119–120; disappearance of, 119–120, 121

submarine canyon (Monterey Bay), 21–22

suffering caused by faith systems, 257–258

summer hibernation, 117

sunfish, giant ocean, male–female duality, 218

superiority, false sense of, among humans, 265–266

"Sure beats working," 298–299

surrender to the Earth's imperatives, 284

survival: duality of, 238–239

survival strategies in the canyon, 82–84, 220–221

swifts, 44; black, 74; white-throated, 43–44

symbol use by dolphins, 164

syncytial gel and the incubation of life, 202–204

synthesis of science and art (KN), xiii, 3, 80

systems of faith. *See* religion

T

Table Mountain, 43, 44

tanoak trees, 264

Tantilla hobartsmithi (black-headed snake), 36

teachers. *See* leaders of Field Quarter

teaching: and culture, 225–226

teeth: decayed or worn-down, 240

tent caterpillar's nest design, 36–37

Terborgh, John, 189

testing/weeding out process. *See* fitting of lifestreams/numbers into the world
theodolite station (spinner studies), 169
thermals, 45, 51
thermometer, Schultheis, 116
thermostat: functional duality, 212–213
thinking (concept formation/abstract thought): distress concept, 156–157; emotion and, 250–251; evolution of, 157, 249–251; guilt as felt by dogs, 157–158; helping concept, 156–157, 307*n10(ch13)*; "new" as learned by a dolphin, 163–164. *See also* consciousness
[the] tide: as the metronome, 128–129
tidepools of the primeval sea, 202; syncytial gel in, 202–204
tidepool fish. *See* opaleye perch
time-pulse: of redwoods, 73. *See also* beat of life
time-worlds, 38; city time, 71–72; river time, 59. *See also* Mountain Time
timing: chorus line effect, 190, 191; of dolphin vocalizations, 189–190
Tioga Pass road, 271
toads, red-spotted, 125–126, 127
torpor of desert iguana at high temperature, 118–119
towhee, California, 40
training of dolphins (bottlenose), 150–153, 159–161, 163–164
trash lines in the ocean, 174
tree frog male–female duality, 218
tree house: Nantucket whaleboat as, 298

trees: bands of species along canyon/mountain slopes, 264, 278; cottonwoods, 47–48; ponderosa pine, 82; in the Sierra, 270. *See also* bristlecone pines; Joshua trees; oak trees; redwoods
triad routine, 19
tributaries of rivers, 63, 64
trilling experiments (red-spotted toads), 125–126, 127
trout, steelhead, 80–81
trust in the Field Quarter group, 29–30
trusting one's own eyes, 38
turtle of Baja California, 92–93, 96
two-legged lizards: distribution, 89, 91, 96. See also *Bipes* ...

U

UC Natural Reserve System (NRS): founding of, x, 121–123
UC Santa Cruz: natural history class (*see* Field Quarter); natural history studies (KN), 11; redwood bench motto, 298–299
UCLA: KN at, ix, 3–10, 121, 295
Uma scoparia (fringe-toed lizard), 101–108; color adaptation, 102–103, 105–107; concealment circles, 102, 103; KN's master thesis on, 302*n2(ch7)*; physical characteristics, 102; reflectivity analysis, 105–106, 107
umwelt, 109, 132, 135–136
understanding (knowing): and caring, 263–265; and loving, 263–265; the new understanding of the earth, 286–287

understanding ourselves/who we are, 208–209, 225
underwater-viewing vessel (*Maka Ala*), 168, 170, 174–175
Usner, Don (Santiago): as Field Quarter leader, 74, 77(2)
Uta (side-blotched lizard), 83, 84

V

Valenzuela, Ray, 151–152
Van Denburgh, John, 56, 93
Vandenburg, Dr. *See* Dr. Vandenburg
variation, stored up: and evolution, 9
vertebrate eyes: and hue discrimination, 106, 107, 108
vertebrates: invasion of land, 127; male–female duality among, 218
viewpoint of humans, 265–266
vision: in echelon formation, 190, 191; in sensory integration systems, 193; shark visual system, 188. *See also* eyes; seeing
vocalizations of dolphins, 176, 178; mimicry, 164–165; recording of, 175–176, 189–190; timing, 189–190
volition and consciousness, 135–136
volitional animals, 135, 136
vultures: smelling ability, 51–52

W

"waiting it out" survival strategy, 82–83
Walker, Boyd, 120, 121
wandering in groups (mammals): the end of, 256; and the evolution of thinking, 249–250
war planes flying in formation, 191–192
wariness of opaleye perch, 129, 132
watching the stars at the Granite Cabin, 33
water: as a constituent of life, 200; and the incubation of life, 201–202; life as dependent on, 207–208. *See also* ocean; rivers
water monkeyflower, 35
waves, internal: sea slicks, 129
"We're off on the greatest adventure of our lives," 296–297
Webb, R. W.: *Geology of California*, 273–274*q*, 310*n1(ch20)*
wedding song, 76–77
weeding out process. *See* fitting of lifestreams/numbers into the world
Weihs, D., 306*n4(ch12)*
Wells, Randy, 169, 170
western aquatic garter snake, 77–78
whaleboat as a tree house, 298
whales: great blue whale encounter (KN), 10. *See also* killer whales; pilot whales
"What a lousy bird," 40
White Mountain, 275, 284
White Mountains: birds, 278–279, 285; Field Quarter in, 269–289; flowers, 275, 277–278; Grandview Camp, 278
white pelicans, 52; and gliders, 51
white-sided dolphins, Pacific, 10; pilot whale as assisted by, 156; sleeping behavior, 193–194
white-throated swifts, 43–44
[the] wild: life in (*see* Mountain Time); reverence for, 228
wild canyon. *See* the canyon (Big Creek)

Index

wild cucumber (man-in-the-ground), 78, 82
wild fires: history in redwoods, 72–73; and wild cucumber, 78
wild heliotrope, 46–47
wild rhubarb, 47
wild world gestalt, 35
wildlife as embattled, 120–121
wind: birds as blown offshore, 49; high-altitude winds, 49; insects as blown offshore, 48; rules: Bernoulli effect, 44–46; Santa Ana winds, 48–49
wind and water: and plants, 46–48
women: menopause, 239, 240–241. *See also* man–woman duality
women students and KN (during Field Quarter), 28–29
Woods Mountain: observations on, 43–44
words: choosing with care, 38
worms: flatworms, 136, 209
worship of the mountain, 228
wrathful as well as loving side: of the Earth, 259, 261; of God (as a concept), 248
writings (KN): on beluga whales, 199, 307*n1*(*ch14*); on *Diposaurus*, 303*n2*(*ch8*); on dolphins, 305*n2*(*ch12*), 307*n9*(*ch13*); on fish, 303*n1*(*ch9*), 307*n9*(*ch13*); on *Girella* (doctoral thesis), 303*n1*(*ch9*); *The Naturalistic Ethic*, 7; on *Uma* (master's thesis), 302*n2*(*ch7*). See also *Mountain Time*
wrong and right as not in Mountain Time, 85
Würsig, Bernd and Mel, 169

X

Xantusia vigilis (desert night lizard), 23–24

Y

yang, 215–216; as the masculine, 215
yin, 216; as the feminine, 215
yin and yang, 211–221; in functional terms, 215; genetics, 239; relationship between, 211*q*. *See also* duality; male–female duality
yin–yang diagram, 211–212(*3*), 215, 239
yucca, 24; semelparity, 233

Z

zigzag behavior of spinner dolphins, 172, 176–177, 178: as compositions, 178–179, 180
Zweifel, Dick, 6, 55, 108

Made in the USA
Las Vegas, NV
08 June 2022